The Turnpike Rivalry

The Turnpike Rivalry

The Pittsburgh Steelers and the Cleveland Browns

RICHARD PETERSON AND STEPHEN PETERSON

Black Squirrel Books® 🐿️®

an imprint of The Kent State University Press
Kent, Ohio 44242   www.KentStateUniversityPress.com

ISBN 978-1-60635-413-1
Manufactured in the United States of America

BLACK SQUIRREL BOOKS® 🐿®
Frisky, industrious black squirrels are a familiar sight on the Kent State University campus and
the inspiration for Black Squirrel Books®, a trade imprint of The Kent State University Press.
www.KentStateUniversityPress.com

Cataloging information for this title is available at the Library of Congress.

24 23 22 21 20   5 4 3 2 1

To all the sons who watched their first Steelers-Browns

game with their fathers.

CONTENTS

ACKNOWLEDGMENTS

Since the Pittsburgh Steelers and the Cleveland Browns began playing each other in 1950, many voices have contributed to the narrative of what has become one of the greatest rivalries in American sports. We are grateful to those on each side of the rivalry who contributed to our narrative, ranging from fans, sportswriters, and broadcasters to players, coaches, and team officials. We are particularly grateful for the sons who told the story of going to their first Steelers-Browns game with their fathers.

We are also grateful to the organizations that were helpful in providing material for our book, but we'd like to single out the Heinz History Center, for its generous support. Especially helpful were Anne Madaraz, Director of the Western Pennsylvania Sports Museum, Matthew Strauss, Chief Curator, and Craig Britcher, Project Coordinator and Assistant Curator.

We like to express our gratitude and debt to the editors of Kent State University who provided so much help and support until our book crossed the goal line. Will Underwood, former Acquiring Editor, was there from the beginning with his encouragement; Susan Wadsworth-Booth, Director, moved the project forward; and Mary Young, Managing Editor, skillfully turned a work-in-progress into a publishable manuscript.

Finally, we'd like to acknowledge that our book was a family affair. It began when a son suggested to his father that they collaborate on a book about the Steelers-Browns rivalry. Along the way, our wives, Anita and Anna, were there for us with their patience and help with our research. And we couldn't have put together the artwork for the book without Dean Marshall, who married into the family and, despite being surrounded by the Steelers, remains faithful to the Chicago Bears.

While we admittedly are die-hard Pittsburgh Steelers fans, we know that the passion that we have for our Steelers is equaled by the passion that Cleveland Browns fans have for their Browns. We hope that out book reflects that passion on both sides of a rivalry that began 70 years ago and remains as strong as ever.

PROLOGUE

The Voices

THE VIEW FROM CLEVELAND

"A six-pack drive along the Turnpike [for Steelers and Browns fans]."
—Hal Lebovitz, Cleveland *Plain Dealer* sports editor

"Pittsburgh and Cleveland are almost clones. From an ethnic, from a historical, and from a traditional stand point—with the tremendous diversity and the people who follow those teams for years. They're very, very much alike."
—Sam Rutigliano, Browns head coach (1978–1984)

"When I came to Cleveland, I heard the Pittsburgh game was a matter of life or death. But I soon found out it was more than that."
—Bill Belichick, Browns head coach (1991–1995)

"The toughest part of the game [in Pittsburgh] was getting there and living."
—Art Modell, Browns owner (1961–1995)

"The Browns-Steelers rivalry has always been considered one of the greatest rivalries despite the fact that RARELY have the two teams been good at the same time. Usually one team has been good and the other bad going all the way back to the 1950s."
—Roger Gordon, author of *Cleveland Browns: A–Z*

"I remember as a player with Cleveland we used to make fun of Pittsburgh. They'd wear different colored helmets sometimes."
    —Chuck Noll, Browns offensive lineman and linebacker (1953–1959)

"I was as big as the linemen I ran against, so I didn't worry about them. And once I ran over a back twice, I didn't have to run over him a third time."
    —Marion Motley, Browns running back (1946–1953)

"And when Pittsburgh came to town, Marion had a big day. After the game Motley joked that he played well because 'It was easier to run downhill.'"
    —Mike Brown, Cincinnati Bengals owner (1991–)

"Paul Brown is a football coach who highly prizes that elusive quality known as 'desire' and he found it in quantity at Forbes Field. However, the major portion belonged to the seething squad of Pittsburgh Steelers who proceeded to hand the once almost unbeatable Browns a 55–27 trouncing to the delight of 33,262 unbelieving partisans. . . . The first Pittsburgh victory over Cleveland in nine games."
    —Chuck Heaton, Cleveland *Plain Dealer* sportswriter

"There are too many people in this league who would like to see Johnson carried off on a stretcher. This uncharitable attitude stems from hard-blocking John Henry's tendency to break things. Like jaws and cheek bones. Noses and teeth."
    —Jim Brown, Browns running back (1957–1965)

"One of my biggest thrills was to go into Pittsburgh one time and see a big bed sheet on the wall that said, Thanks Bill Austin for Bill Nelsen."
    —Bill Nelsen, Steelers quarterback (1963–1967) and
            Browns quarterback (1968–1972)

"I remember people telling me, 'We don't care if you don't win another game all year.' That was the mentality. They hated the Steelers."
    —Cody Risien, Browns offensive tackle (1979–1983, 1985–1989)

"You were indoctrinated as a young player to hate Pittsburgh."
    —Dick Ambrose, Browns linebacker (1975–1983)

"I had a lot of friends that played on the Pittsburgh team. But for some reason. . . . Man, we hated Pittsburgh. For those four hours I hated my friends."
—Greg Pruitt, Browns running back (1976–1984)

"Jack Lambert would have kicked my grandmother's cane out. . . . Joe Greene got fined like $500 (for kicking Bob McKay in the groin). Deleone got fined like $100 (for punching Greene). And Bob McKay got fined for getting kicked in the groin."
—Doug Dieken. Browns offensive tackle (1971–1984)

"To me, Jack Lambert was the Pittsburgh Steelers. The Steelers have lost a lot of great players . . . but what hurt them the most was losing Jack Lambert. In all my years in professional football, I never played against a guy, in any position, who was more of a dominating force."
—Sam Rutigliano, Browns coach (1978–1984)

"I was at the 18–16 victory in 1976 during which Joe 'Turkey' Jones threw Bradshaw on his head and invented the 'in-the-grasp' rule. That was the first game where I noticed the edge of violence in the stands. There weren't a lot of fights—in fact, I saw more fighting at other games—but the fans exuded a hair-trigger fierceness."
—Scott Huler, author of *On Being Brown: What It Means to Be a Cleveland Browns Fan*

"When you have people who share similar passions such as drinking beer and being crazy, and you put that in a football stadium, it's combustible. I always said that I was so glad I was playing because I wouldn't want to be in the stands. That was the worst place to be in that game."
—Thom Darden, Browns defensive back (1972–1974, 1976–1981)

"All the drunks from Cleveland and Pittsburgh are here, but our drunks at least made it off the bus."
—Lt. William Stilnack, Cleveland police

"I've seen tough, big, grown men reduced to tears in the Pound during Steelers games. A couple of years ago we had a huge bonfire using stuff we ripped off [Steelers] fans. We were burning them to keep warm and roast wienies."
—John "Big Dawg" Thompson, rabid Browns fan and leader of the Dawg Pound

"The Browns and Steelers are like twin brothers who never get along, always trying to knock each other down to show mom and dad who's tougher."
—Jonathan Knight, *Kardiac Kids: The Story of the 1980 Cleveland Browns*

"Marty [Schottenheimer] loved Bill [Cowher]. Marty loved his competitiveness and willingness to get things done."
—Ernie Accorsi, Browns executive vice president (1984–1991)

"I ain't going to lie. I hate Pittsburgh. I really hate Pittsburgh. Anything yellow and black, I hit it. That's how I was brought up."
—Orlando Brown, Browns offensive lineman (1994–1995, 1999)

"Roethlisberger has tormented the Browns ever since they passed on him in the 2004 draft."
—Terry Pluto, Cleveland *Plain Dealer* sportswriter

"'Dad, I just signed with the Steelers.' Dad's response: 'How am I going to tell your mother? How am I going to tell my friends? How am I going to work the next day?'"
—John Banaszak, Cleveland native and Steelers defensive end (1975–1981)

THE VIEW FROM PITTSBURGH

"Due to the ferocity of the competition, the Browns are always the team that the medical staff double-checks on medical supplies, stretchers, and EMS supplies."
                    —Joseph Maroon, Steelers team neurosurgeon

"It's been like that right from the start. People really got into the rivalry. The closer you are the more nasty it gets."
                    —Pat Livingston, *Pittsburgh Press*

"You have two steel towns. . . . There are more fights in the stands than there are on the field."
                    —Ed Bouchette, *Pittsburgh Post-Gazette*

"My only sense of this 'rivalry' is that I always wished the Browns were better, not so much for the team, but for the city, and especially for the writers. How many different ways can you cobble together that Browns lost again column."
                    —Gene Collier, *Pittsburgh Post-Gazettte*

"I first started playing and coaching there. It's a city a lot like Pittsburgh. There's a lot of passion and pride in the football teams. This is a rivalry that has stood the test of time."
                    —Bill Cowher, Steelers coach (1992–2006)

"When I first got here, I didn't think anything of the rivalry. Then I saw the way the coaches reacted to the Browns game. Usually you can make mistakes on Friday, and they'd be tolerated. But when we were playing Cleveland, mistakes [were corrected] on Wednesday, or else."
                    —John Stallworth, Steelers wide receiver (1974–1987)

"It's the players who make the great coaches. . . . Look at Otto Graham. He'd throw the ball behind Lavelli or Speedie, and a defensive guy would have perfect coverage on them. You'd see those receivers reach back with their left hand and just roll the ball in. They were comparable to the receivers Bradshaw had when he won all those Super Bowls. These are the types of players who create championships."
                    —Dale Dodrill, Steelers middle guard (1951–1959)

"Well, if you think [Paul] Brown has anything on [Buddy] Parker, just look at the record and see who won the most games when they played each other. And look at what Paul Brown has to work with. He has the league best power [back] in Jimmy Brown. He has the league's best breakaway back in Bobby Mitchell. . . . Give Buddy two running backs who can run like that. . . . This team would be so far ahead of the pack, the race would be over."
                    —Ernie Stautner, Steelers defensive lineman (1950–1963)

"People ask me, 'Who was the greatest running back you ever played against?' Unquestionably Jim Brown. One thing about Brown, he could run over you or he could make you miss. He could do both. . . . Every time I thought he was going to run over me, he made me miss. And every time I thought he was going to make me miss, he ran over me."
                    —Andy Russell, Steelers linebacker (1963, 1966–1976)

"My rookie year I remember we went to Cleveland Municipal Stadium. Just the feeling that I was on the same field as Jim Brown. Electricity in the air. We loved playing the Cleveland Browns . . . It was the Turnpike Bowl. Fans could go to the games. That was a big part of it."
                    —Franco Harris, Steelers running back (1972–1981)

"They were always up for us. Always a great game. It was fun for us, fun for the fans. . . . Never that far apart."
                    —Mel Blount, Steelers defensive back (1970–1981)

"It was a beautiful blue-collar rivalry. Trash-talking chatter. It was loud. We didn't have to worry about the fans because we were protected by security, but the wives didn't go to Cleveland."
                    —Terry Hanratty, Steelers quarterback (1969–1975)

"Mostly Red drinks beer, but like a good Browns fan, he will improvise when necessary. 'If you can pour it, I can drink it, he boasts.' Red's biggest bag is the Browns and yesterday he was numbered among the 4,500 or so Cleveland fans who came to town to watch the Steelers calmly absorb another measure of humility. Between sips, Red admitted that the 12 cases of beer that traveled with him and 39 buddies had not held out as well as expected. 'We let it all hang out when we come to Pittsburgh, it's really a one-day blast.'"
                    —Phil Musick, *Pittsburgh Press*

"Browns fans would roll Browns fans down the aisle because they were dead drunk. Then they would prop them up in their seats."
—Myron Cope, Steelers broadcaster and sportswriter

"Turkey Jones slipped by Mullins and grabbed me around the waist. . . . I continued to struggle to get free. So he simply picked me up, drove me backward about six yards, turned me upside down, and drilled for oil with my head."
—Terry Bradshaw, Steelers quarterback (1970–1983)

"We thought Bradshaw was dead."
—Ed Bouchette, *Pittsburgh Post-Gazette*

"Brain [Sipe] had a chance to get out of bounds, but he decided not to. He knows I'm going to hit him. End of story. . . . Maybe it would be a good idea to put dresses on them. That might help a little bit."
—Jack Lambert, Steelers linebacker (1974–1984)

"I didn't know what he [Cleveland fan] was going to do. So I waited until he turned his back on me. Then I thought I could safely take him down and hold him until the authorities got there."
—James Harrison, Steelers linebacker (2002, 2004–2012, 2014–2017)

"I'm sick about [the Browns' move to Baltimore]. This is the best rivalry in sports. To go up there to play in Cleveland on that grass field on a gray day—I don't want to get dramatic, but it really is something. It's the essence of football."
—Dan Rooney, Steelers president (1975–2003)

"This is still a huge rivalry for me personally. It is Ohio. It is the Browns. I thought I was going to the Browns. I am kind of over that, but for me this is AFC North football. Like I said, it is the Browns. This is a huge rivalry for us."
—Ben Roethlisberger, Steelers quarterback (2004–)

"Anything that has to do with beating up on Cleveland and making their life miserable for one day, the city of Pittsburgh loves that."
—Hines Ward, Steelers wide receiver (1998–2012)

"I hated the Browns when I was around 10 to 12 years old. I mean I hated them. Good healthy sports hate, but I hated them. I hated Cleveland because they were right up the road."
                    —Colin Dunlap, *Pittsburgh Post-Gazette*

"I'm glad the Steelers-Browns rivalry is back. I don't hate anyone in Baltimore."
                    —Bill Hillgrove, Steelers broadcaster

"We don't like them. They don't like us. It's a rivalry."
                    —Pat Haden, Browns cornerback (2010–2016) and
                    Steelers cornerback (2017–).

"I grew up a Browns fan, and you can't like the Steelers and the Browns at the same time. It just can't happen. You're either in or you're out."
                    —Deondre Layne, father of Steelers defensive back
                    Justin Layne (2019–)

INTRODUCTION

A VIEW FROM THE 1950s
Richard Peterson

I was an 11-year-old, die-hard Pittsburgh Steelers fan when they played their first game against the Cleveland Browns on October 7, 1950. In their fourth game of the 1950 season, played at Forbes Field, the Steelers outran and outpassed the Browns, but they also committed six turnovers, including five lost fumbles, and bumbled their way to a 30–17 loss.

Three weeks later, they played the Browns in Cleveland and suffered their most humiliating defeat of the season. With the Browns rushing for 338 yards, including 188 for Marion Motley, who had a 69-yard touchdown run, the Browns so completely dominated the Steelers that Otto Graham threw only nine passes, including two for touchdowns. The Browns didn't need any help in winning the game, but the Steelers turned the ball over a season high eight times on six interceptions and two fumbles in what ended in a 45–7 shellacking.

Nearly a decade earlier, after watching his team go through eight straight losing seasons, owner Art Rooney ran a contest that led to his team changing its name from the Pirates to the Steelers. Watching his team at its 1941 training camp, he made the mistake of saying that, despite the change in name, they looked like "the same, old" team to him. By the time the Steelers played the Browns for first time in NFL history, that tag, the "Same Old Steelers," had become so commonplace among Pittsburgh fans that if you asked someone what the Steelers had done that Sunday and the reply was "SOS," you knew the Steelers had lost.

The Steelers that I grew up watching in the 1950s were a ragtag, misfit team plagued by Rooney's cronyism and mismanagement, but they were actually the perfect misfits for a hardfisted, hard-drinking steel-mill town. They were fun to watch, even when they were losing, because their defense was mean and tough and routinely beat up other teams. Hall of Fame defensive tackle Ernie Stautner, the meanest and the toughest of the Same Old Steelers, wore makeshift casts on his hands even though they weren't broken, so he could pound offensive linemen, like the Browns' Chuck Noll, into submission.

The Steelers games against cross-state rival, the Philadelphia Eagles, were like barroom brawls, where more players made it into the emergency room than the end zone. NFL Commissioner Bert Bell, who once was co-owner of the Steelers, had to warn the two teams against using their "forearms, elbows, or knees" to maim each other, a warning that was ignored at game time.

While the Steelers-Eagles brawls seem suited to Pittsburgh's working-class character, the Steelers-Browns rivalry was another matter. Unlike the misfit Steelers, the Browns were all smugness and precision. They had a football genius in Paul Brown for a coach, while we had a succession of Rooney's cronies. They had a flawless quarterback in Otto Graham and a bulldozing fullback in Marion Motley, while we had tailbacks who prepared for games by drinking at local nightclubs and beer joints. The Browns were smug, precise, and we hated them.

The Browns made my life miserable in the 1950s by winning the first eight games against the Steelers and winning 16 out of their first 18 meetings before quarterback Bobby Layne led the Steelers to two wins over the Browns in 1959. Thanks to Hall of Fame running backs Jim Brown and Leroy Kelly, things remained the same for Steelers fans in the 1960s, when the Browns nearly matched their 1950s record against the Steelers by winning 15 of their 20 meetings. Unfortunately, two moves that I made during the decade made the misery of the Browns-Steelers rivalry closer and more painful for me.

In the early 1960s, I attended Edinboro State College in Pennsylvania and was stuck with the Browns appearing on Erie television instead of the Steelers. When I went to graduate school at Kent State University in Ohio, I was only a football throw from Cleveland and much too close to Tony Adamle, an All-Pro Browns linebacker who played against the Steelers in the early 1950s and was the team doctor for Kent State sports teams. When I came to bat in a softball game, Adamle, the other team's catcher, took out his dentures to distract me. My only hope, as I tried to ignore him, was that some Steelers player had knocked out Adamle's teeth.

It took a few seasons, but the Steelers finally turned their rivalry around in the 1970s. On December 3, 1972, after the Browns had defeated the Steelers two weeks earlier on a last-second field goal, the Steelers and the Browns, tied at 8–3 for the Eastern Division lead, met at Three Rivers Stadium in a game that would decide the division championship. The Steelers dominated the Browns 30–0 and went on to win their division, the first championship of any kind in franchise history. The Browns also made the playoffs as a wild card team but lost to Miami. A week later, the Dolphins defeated the Steelers on their way to an undefeated season and a Super Bowl championship. Had the Browns defeated the Dolphins, they would have played the Steelers for the AFC Championship and a trip to the Super Bowl.

The 1972 season, highlighted by Franco Harris's "Immaculate Reception," was the beginning of the Steelers dominance of the NFL after decades of frustration and ineptness. Led by Terry Bradshaw, Franco Harris, and the "Steel Curtain," they would go on to win four Super Bowls and finally end the curse of the Same Old Steelers. During their Super Bowl runs from 1974 through 1979, to the delight of long-suffering Steelers fans, they would win 11 of 12 games against the Browns.

Going into the 1980s, there seemed no reason why the Steelers wouldn't continue their championship ways. To help them, they also had a new die-hard fan, my nine-year-old son, Stephen, who was born on November 23, 1971, just two weeks after the Steelers defeated the Cleveland Browns.

A VIEW FROM THE 1980s
Stephen Peterson

In 1972, Franco Harris caught a deflected pass from Terry Bradshaw for a last-second winning touchdown against the Oakland Raiders in a play that would become known in NFL history as the Immaculate Reception. That miraculous play heralded the beginning of the Steelers' NFL dominance in the 1970s. Unfortunately, I was too young to remember any of it.

I was born in 1971, and, even though my dad had me baptized as a Steelers fan, I probably wasn't even in front of a television set when the Immaculate Reception happened. The play that brought joy to my life as a Steelers fan took place in 1988 when I was 16 years old and the Steelers weren't even playing.

The date was January 17 and much to my unhappiness, the hated Cleveland Browns were in the AFC championship game. As the Browns drove down the field against the Denver Broncos for a game-tying touchdown with a little more than a minute left in the game, running back Ernest Byner fumbled away the ball at the 3-yard line. The fumble ended the game and the Browns' chance to defeat the Broncos in overtime and send Cleveland to their first Super Bowl. The Browns would never come that close again.

Just as the Immaculate Reception is remembered as the play that began the Steelers' dynasty, "the Fumble" is remembered as the moment that sent the Browns into decades of futility. The eventual loss of the team to Baltimore, the struggles of the expansion Browns, including a 1–31 record over a two-year stretch from 2016 to 2017, and all that misery for Cleveland fans goes back to the Fumble. It was a devastating moment for Browns fans, but it was a wonderful moment for my generation of Steelers fans. It was our sour grapes version of the Immaculate Reception.

I was too young to experience the joy of the Steelers' four Super Bowls in the 1970s, but I do remember being taught to root for the Steelers and hate the Cleveland Browns. But I was never told why. All I know is that the only thing more loathsome than Darth Vader for me was a player dressed in a Browns uniform.

I could understand, after the Steelers' Super Bowl victories, why Cleveland fans, after watching their Browns struggle during the same period, hated the Steelers, but I never really got Pittsburgh fans' hatred for the Browns, including their dumb orange-and-brown uniforms and their stupid Dawg Pound masks. It would take me years before I realized that bitter rivalries have little to do with logic and more to do with the passion of the fans. And there are no more passionate fans than those who root for the Steelers and the Browns.

By the early 1980s, most of the great Steelers were gone. My memories of those four Super Bowl wins were fuzzy, but I was raised to believe that the Steelers were soon going to win "one for the thumb." I felt there were more Super Bowls on the way, but, though the Steelers made the playoffs in 1983 and 1984, they weren't the same. Mark Malone led the Steelers to the 1984 AFC championship game, but he was no Terry Bradshaw. The 1980s Steelers simply were not the dominant team of the 1970s.

What made matters worse in the 1980s was the resurgence of the Browns. After a decade of frustration, Cleveland fans watched Brian Sipe usher in the 1980s with an MVP season, much to the chagrin of Steelers fans. The Browns suffered unbearably painful playoff losses, but they also made the playoffs for five straight years from 1985 to 1989. During the same period, the Steelers made the playoffs once, in 1989, and that was in an odd season that began with an opening blowout 51–0 loss to the Browns.

It was during the 1980s that my hatred for the Browns intensified, much like an earlier generation of Cleveland fans' hatred for the Steelers grew in the 1970s. Even when the Steelers played their way out of the mediocrity of the 1980s, my distain for the Browns never diminished. I never felt sympathy for Cleveland fans when the Browns' fortunes took a turn for the worse in the 1990s and they eventually lost their team.

When Art Modell moved the franchise to Baltimore, I didn't miss the Browns; I just directed my hatred at the Ravens. When the Browns returned as an expansion team for the 1999 season, I rooted against the new Browns, but I still hated the Ravens because they were the old Browns. I have to admit, however, that I'll always be grateful to the new Browns for giving the Steelers a wonderful gift that led to two more Super Bowl victories when they passed on Ohio native Ben Roethlisberger in the first round of the 2004 draft.

It's been hard to sustain a deep hatred for the Browns during their recent plunge into the NFL abyss, but, every once in a while, they do something that arouses the passion of Steelers fans. After a surprisingly easy win over the Steelers in a 2014 game, Cleveland quarterback Brian Hoyer said that he was bored by the end of the game. That statement was enough to remind Pittsburgh that nothing is more important than beating and humiliating the Browns. In 2019, the Steelers experienced another reminder when Browns defensive end Myles Garrett attacked Steelers quarterback Mason Rudolph with his Rudolph's own helmet.

After the Steelers pretty much had their way with the Browns in the 20 years since Cleveland returned to the NFL, the football scales seem to be shifting. But knowing that the Steelers are in turmoil and transition after losing All-Pros Antonio Brown and Le'Veon Bell, two of their "Killer Bees," and that the Browns hope they may have finally found a franchise quarterback in Baker Mayfield makes me want the Steelers to dominant the Browns more than ever. But that's what happens with rivalries. They can change shape or direction, become dormant or intensify, but they are never ending.

CHAPTER ONE

The 1940s

The Same Old Steelers

At their Hershey, Pennsylvania, training camp in 1941, owner Art Rooney was watching his team prepare for the upcoming season. Since 1933, when Pittsburgh became a member of the National Football League, his team had never had a winning season. After Pittsburgh finished a dismal 2–7–1 in 1940, Rooney, who critics claimed was more interested in local politics and horse racing than his football team, decided that it was time to make some changes.

The biggest change came as a shock to Pittsburgh when Rooney, who grew up on the city's north side, sold his struggling pro football franchise to Boston playboy Alexis Thompson, who operated out of New York. While Rooney was condemned by Pittsburgh newspapers, the deal was really the beginning of an ownership swap.

After selling his franchise to Thompson, Rooney bought a major interest in the Philadelphia Eagles with half of the money he made in selling his Pittsburgh franchise and became co-owners of the Eagles with future NFL Commissioner De Benneville "Bert" Bell. Art Rooney and Bert Bell then proposed a swap to Thompson, who would take over the Philadelphia franchise while Rooney and Bell would run the Pittsburgh franchise. Once Thompson, who wanted a team closer to New York, agreed to the proposal, a relieved Rooney convinced Bell to take over as Pittsburgh's coach.

After the swap, Rooney thought that his newly acquired Pittsburgh franchise needed a new team name for the 1941 season. In 1933, when Rooney paid the $2,500 fee out of his racetrack winnings to become the owner of an NFL franchise, he decided to call his team the Pirates—after Pittsburgh's baseball franchise and in gratitude to its owner, Bernhard "Barney" Dreyfuss, for allowing his team to play its home games at Forbes Field.

After watching his team play like a laughing stock for nearly a decade, Rooney decided that a new name would help the team improve its image with its frustrated fans. He sponsored a contest that was won, rather suspiciously, by the club's ticket manager's wife. She thought "Steelers" would be a great team name because it reflected the tough, steel-driving image of Rooney's hometown.

As Art Rooney looked out at his Steelers at their 1941 training camp, one of his cronies asked him, "Art, now that you've seen them, what do you think about your new Steelers?" Remembering that his team hadn't had a winning season in its eight years of existence and watching his "new Steelers" botch plays on the practice field, he replied, "It's a new team all right—new uniforms, a new coach, and a new name. But they look like the same old Pirates to me."

Beginning with the 1941 season, that comment would hang around Art Rooney's neck like a deflated football. After a disastrous preseason that ended with a lopsided loss to the Chicago Bears, the Steelers opened the season with losses to the Cleveland Rams and, ironically, to the Philadelphia Eagles. After the loss to the Eagles and talking things over with Rooney, Bert Bell announced at a press conference that he was stepping down as Steelers coach: "I believe it to be for the best interest of Pittsburgh fans that I resign and continue my duties to the business end of the corporation. . . . I realize if our club is to get any place in this high-pressure league, there would have to be a change."

In one of the oddest decisions in a franchise plagued by odd decisions, Rooney offered the Steelers coaching job to Aldo "Buff" Donelli, the successful head football coach of Duquesne University, located on a bluff just east of downtown Pittsburgh. Donelli agreed to coach the Steelers, but only if he could continue coaching at Duquesne. Donelli proposed spending his mornings coaching the Steelers, then his afternoons coaching the college football Dukes.

The arrangement worked out perfectly for Donelli's Dukes. They would go undefeated, at 8–0, and earn the No. 8 ranking in the Associated Press college football poll. The arrangement also worked out perfectly for the Steelers, but it turned into a perfect disaster when the Steelers lost their first five games under Donelli. Faced with the choice of staying with the Steelers or going with the Dukes on a West Coast trip, Donelli turned in his resignation as Steelers coach and left town with the Dukes.

With four games left to play and his Same Old Steelers at 0–7, Rooney turned to Walt Kiesling to finish out the season. A powerful guard with the Duluth Eskimos in the early days of the NFL and future Hall of Famer, Kiesling had been an assistant coach with the Steelers under the notorious "Johnny Blood" McNally, once described by pro football historian Ray Didinger as "part-myth, part-man." Kiesling had finished out the 1940 season as head coach when McNally, who loved the nightlife, was fired. Under Kiesling's performance in 1941 as interim head coach, the Steelers managed a tie and a win, but they lost their last two games to finish at 1–9–1.

For the 1942 season, Rooney and Bell decided to keep Kiesling on as head coach. It proved to be a rare smart decision, but it was another decision, this time in the NFL draft, that would give the Steelers their first winning season in 10 years. The Steelers had a way of botching the NFL draft by making bad selections or trading away their picks for mediocre talent. Going into the 1939 season, for example, they had the second pick in the draft but traded it away to the Chicago Bears. With the pick, Chicago Bears coach George Halas selected All-American quarterback Sidney Luckman. The future Hall of Famer went on to win four NFL championships for the Bears in the 1940s.

With their first pick in the draft going into the 1942 season, the Steelers selected "Bullet Bill" Dudley, a triple threat from the University of Virginia. The selection was a risk for the Steelers because Dudley, despite his nickname, didn't have great size or speed and threw passes that often resembled wounded ducks. But Dudley had great football instincts and proved that in his first game with the Steelers, played at Forbes Field against the Eagles. In the Steelers' first offensive series, Dudley thrilled Pittsburgh fans by bursting through the offensive line on a 44-yard touchdown run. In his next game, in Washington, he returned the second-half kickoff 86 yards for a touchdown.

The Steelers lost their first two games; however, led by the sensational play of their rookie, they won seven of their next eight games and finished with a 7–4 record, their first winning season in the Steelers' 10-year history in the NFL. Dudley led the league in rushing with 696 yards, scored six touchdowns, and passed for three more. He also intercepted three passes and played outstanding defense. He was an All-Pro selection, but, more importantly, he brought an excitement to Steelers football that had been missing since the team's inception.

That excitement from the 1942 season, however, was undercut by the impact of World War II on the NFL, beginning with the 1943 season. The Steelers lost so many players to military service, including Dudley, that they didn't have enough players to fill their 25-man roster. Desperate, Art Rooney and Bert Bell contacted Eagles owner Alexis Thompson, who was facing the same shortage of players. The Steelers and the Eagles decided to combine their roster and form the Phi-Pitts, a team that became known as the Steagles. Coached by the Steelers' Walt Kiesling and the Eagles' Alfred Earle "Greasy" Neale, the Steagles, despite the predictable dissension on a team with divided loyalties, managed to finish with a 5–4–1 record.

The Steelers found themselves in the same predicament going into the 1944 season, but this time Rooney and Bell agreed, with serious misgivings, to merge their franchise with Charles Bidwell's Chicago Cardinals—as long as half of the home games were played in Pittsburgh. The merger would produce arguably the worst team in Steelers history. The woeful Cardinals had gone 0–10 in 1943 after losing their last eight games in 1942 and seemed headed for another winless season in 1944.

The Car-Pitts, coached by Walt Kiesling and the Cardinals' Phil Handler, were so bad in 1944 that the press dubbed them "the Carpets." On their way to a 0–10 season, they scored more than seven points in just three games and finished with just 108 points for the season. The opposition scored 328 points, including 34–7 and 49–7 drubbings by the Chicago Bears. But perhaps the most bitter loss came on opening day when the Steelers lost to the Cleveland Rams, coached by Buff Donelli, who had lost every game as a Steelers coach.

In 1945, with World War II coming to an end, the Steelers managed to avoid a third merger, though the team struggled through another miserable season. Under new coach and former Kiesling assistant Jim Leonard, the Steelers managed to score only 79 points on their way to a 2–8 record. However, there was a glimmer of hope for Steelers fans when Bill Dudley returned from military service and scored five touchdowns in the team's final five games. With attendance down to 1,500 per game, the Steelers were desperate for a major change in fortune just as pro football, with so many players returning from military service, was about to enter a golden age.

Before the NFL could take advantage of America's postwar boom, it would have to wage its own war with a rival league. In the 1930s, Arch Ward, the sports editor of the *Chicago Tribune,* had come up with two brilliant ideas to showcase baseball and football during the Great Depression. In 1933, Ward proposed that Chicago host a baseball all-star game during its World Fair. The game was so successful that, when Chicago mayor Edward J. Kelly extended the World Fair for another year, he asked Ward to propose another game for 1934. After consulting with Chicago Bears coach George Halas, Ward came up with the idea of a game between the country's best college players and the NFL champions. The game became known as the College All-Star Football Classic.

Arch Ward's latest idea was to organize a new postwar professional football league. While the new league, called the All-American Football Conference, would last only four years, it had an enduring impact on the NFL. It brought several new franchises into professional football, forced pro football to expand to the West Coast, and opened the door for integration. It also had an immediate effect on the Pittsburgh Steelers. Needing an experienced leader to face the challenge of a new rival, the NFL named Steelers co-owner Bert Bell its new commissioner. Rooney bought out Bell's interest in the Steelers, and Bell went on to become NFL commissioner for the next 14 years. He eventually brought about a merger between the two leagues, then guided the NFL into an age of prosperity that was prompted by the growing popularity of television.

Facing the loss of Bert Bell and the threat of his players signing with the new league, Art Rooney was determined nevertheless to turn his Same Old Steelers into winners. To accomplish that, he reached out to a Pittsburgh coaching legend. During his brilliant 15-year career as the University of Pittsburgh's head football coach, John "Jock" Sutherland had led Pitt to four NCAA championships and four Rose Bowl appearances. When Sutherland left Pitt after the 1938 season because of a dispute with school administrators, Rooney tried but failed to sign Sutherland, who eventually took the head coaching job with the NFL Brooklyn Dodgers. This time around, Rooney managed to convince Sutherland to coach the Steelers, starting with the 1946 season.

With a Pitt legend signed as the Steelers' head coach and Bill Dudley back from military service, Steelers fans were thrilled at the prospects of their perennial losers going into the 1946 season. On opening day, a rare capacity crowd watched the Steelers defeat the Chicago Cardinals 14–7. After tying the Washington Redskins on the road, the Steelers moved into a tie for first place by winning four of their next seven games, only to lose their final two games and finish the season at 5–5–1.

While it wasn't a winning season, it was a major improvement over the past two years and preserved Jock Sutherland's record of never having a losing season since he began coaching in 1922, including his two seasons with the NFL Dodgers. Sutherland brought to the Steelers a disciplined approach to the game that stressed a hard-hitting, smothering defense and a powerful single-wing running game. Once a defensive doormat, the Steelers gave up only seven points in six of its games in 1946 and didn't allow any team to score more than two touchdowns.

While the Steelers' defense was dominant and reflected Pittsburgh's steel-town toughness, it was Bill Dudley's offensive brilliance in 1946 that thrilled fans and brought capacity crowds to Forbes Field. Playing tailback in the Steelers' single wing, Dudley led the NFL in rushing with 604 yards. He also passed for another 452 yards and had 109 yards in receptions. He scored three touchdowns rushing, threw two touchdowns passes, and caught a touchdown pass. He did the team's punting, led the NFL in punt return yardage, and kicked extra points and fields goals. To top off his sensational year, he led the NFL with 10 interceptions.

On the field, it looked like Rooney's team, thanks to Sutherland and Dudley, had shattered their Same Old Steelers image and was well on their way to an NFL championship. But off the field, the Steelers had a serious problem: Rooney's legendary coach and his triple-threat star couldn't stand each other. Sutherland demanded discipline and conformity from his players, but the inventive Dudley often took over the team once the game began and made up his own plays. Sutherland was so enraged by Dudley's independence that he constantly criticized his star player and even accused him of faking injuries.

At the end of the 1946 season, Bill Dudley informed Rooney that he could no longer play on a team coached by Jock Sutherland. Faced with the choice of losing his legendary coach or his top player, Rooney reluctantly traded Dudley to the Detroit Lions. It was a painful decision for Rooney, who regarded Dudley as his all-time favorite Steelers player. He later admitted that trading Dudley was "like losing one of my own sons."

Despite the loss of Dudley, the Steelers still looked like contenders going into the 1947 season. They opened at Forbes Field with a victory over the Detroit Lions but then lost their next two games against the Los Angeles Rams and the Washington Redskins. The 49–7 loss to the Rams and their quarterback Bob Waterfield was an embarrassment to the defensive-minded Sutherland. But the 27–26 loss to the Redskins—when Joe Glamp's field goal attempt, with time expiring, hit the left upright and bounced away—may well have cost the Steelers an NFL championship. Sutherland drove his team to six straight wins after the heart-breaking Redskins loss and, at 7–2, put the Steelers on top of the Eastern Division with three games left to play. But they lost their next two games and, after defeating the Boston Yanks, finished in a tie with the Philadelphia Eagles at 8–4.

Had Joe Glamp made that field goal in the 27–26 loss to the Redskins, the Steelers would have clinched a division championship for the first time in the team's history and played against the Chicago Cardinals in the 1947 NFL title game. Instead, the Steelers first had to defeat the Eagles in a playoff game during a cold, wintry day at Forbes Field. Before the game, Art Rooney was delighted. He claimed that he was so used to being a loser that he found it strange to be a winner: "It's a great feeling not having to duck down the side streets anymore." However, the Steelers brought back that same old feeling to Rooney when they were shut out by the Eagles 21–0 while playing with injured and struggling star tailback Johnny "Mr. Zero" Clement (Bill Dudley's replacement).

After the game, Rooney told Sutherland that, despite the playoff loss, he was thrilled with the Steelers' season and looked forward to next year. Sutherland was disappointed, but he felt that the Steelers would be even stronger in 1948. In early spring, he left Pittsburgh by car for a working vacation in the South. He planned on visiting some old coaching friends and doing a little scouting along the way.

Shortly after Sutherland left Pittsburgh, Kentucky state troopers discovered an abandoned car with its motor still running on the side of the road. Wandering near the car was a dazed and confused individual whom they eventually identified as Steelers coach Jock Sutherland. He was taken to a Cairo, Illinois, hospital where he was initially diagnosed as suffering from nervous exhaustion. When his condition worsened, he was rushed to a Pittsburgh hospital where doctors discovered that Sutherland had a brain tumor. He died on April 11, two days after a second surgery was performed to remove the malignant tumor.

Steelers fans were shocked at the news of Sutherland's death, but Art Rooney was devastated. He had idolized Sutherland and regarded him as family, He now had to find a replacement for someone he regarded as irreplaceable. Rooney decided that the best and only choice was Sutherland's 32-year-old assistant coach, John Michelosen. A star quarterback for Sutherland's 1937 Rose Bowl championship team, Michelosen became an assistant coach under Sutherland at 21 after graduating from the University of Pittsburgh. He eventually became Sutherland's top assistant and stayed with him when Sutherland left Pitt and went on to coach in the NFL. Sutherland once said that "as long as I'm coaching there will always be a place on my staff for a man with the capabilities of John Michelosen."

As a disciple of Jock Sutherland, Michelosen seemed the obvious choice to coach the Steelers and continue the team's recent success after nearly two decades of futility. But he faced some serious problems beyond dealing with the emotional impact of Sutherland's death. Michelosen had an absolute faith in Sutherland's strategy of dominating opponents with power football. To prove himself worthy as Sutherland's successor, he drove his players in practice even harder than Sutherland. Steelers defensive tackle and future Hall of Famer Ernie Stautner claimed that "it was as if John knew people talked about Jock being tough so he had to prove he could be tougher."

Facing player discontent and dissension on the practice field, Michelosen also had to deal with a major change taking place in the game itself. While the Steelers still ran a single-wing, run-oriented offense that Pittsburgh fans mockingly called "three yards and a cloud of soot," pro football teams were changing over to a T formation that featured the passing game. Instead of relying on tailbacks who ran more than they passed, pro football teams now had great passers—like future Hall of Famers Sid Luckman, Sammy Baugh, Bob Waterfield, and Otto Graham—leading their teams.

Before his death, there was some talk that Jock Sutherland was interested in changing his offense for the 1948 season, but the rumor faded when he traded away his first-round pick, the third overall in the NFL draft, when the obvious choice, University of Texas quarterback Bobby Layne, told the Steelers he didn't want to play in the single wing. Sutherland did select an excellent passer, Notre Dame quarterback Joe Gasparella, with his third-round pick, but Michelosen, determined to stay with Sutherland's single wing, decided Gasparella wasn't an effective runner and instead used him as a defensive back. A year later, Michelson drafted another excellent passer, Jim Finks, from the University of Tulsa but decided to use him primarily as a defensive back. The decision nearly cost Finks his career when he broke his back making a tackle.

Just before the 1948 season began, tragedy would strike the Steelers again when their best defensive player, ex-marine Ralph Calcagni, complained of severe stomach pain after playing in a preseason game. He was taken to the hospital and had an appendectomy. Calcagni seemed to be recovering from the operation, but hours after Michelosen and some teammates visited him, he passed away. An autopsy revealed that Calcagni died from a gangrenous blood clot.

Despite all the turmoil and tragedy, the Steelers won two of their first three games in 1948, but they soon began to play like the Same Old Steelers rather than Sutherland's Steelers. Struggling with an inconsistent offense and a vulnerable defense, they lost six of their next seven games and finished with a 4–8 record after going 8–4 under Sutherland in 1947. Benefiting from a strong performance from University of Georgia rookie tailback Joe Geri and the trial use of a new NFL free-substitution rule that enabled Michelosen to use outstanding players like Bill McPeak and Howard Hartley strictly on defense, the Steelers bounced back in 1949, though they had to win their final game of the season to finish at 6–5–1. It was Michelosen's first and, as it turned out, only winning season as Steelers coach.

The program for a September 14, 1949, exhibition game between the Pittsburgh Steelers and the Chicago Cardinals included a brief history of the Steelers written by publicity director Ed Kiely. At the conclusion of the essay, after summarizing all of the Steelers' misfortunes over the years, Kiely wrote: "One of these years, Rooney is bound to get lucky in a football way." There were also all those beer and whiskey advertisements, reminders that Pittsburgh was both a hard-working and hard-drinking town. Standing out among the beer advertisements was an "all-star lineup" of bottles of Duquesne pilsner arranged fittingly in a single-wing formation.

The advertisement was a graphic reminder that, a year away from the 1950s, the Steelers were driving their fans to drink by still using the single wing after every other pro football team had abandoned it. For nearly two decades, the Steelers had validated Murphy's Law that if it can go wrong, it will go wrong. For that to change, for Rooney's teams finally to experience the luck of the Irish, they would have to leave behind their outdated approach to the game and catch up with the rest of the league.

The need to change was to become even more compelling in 1950, when the AAFC and the NFL, after four years of warring against each other, finally worked out a merger. The immediate impact on the Steelers was the placement of the most powerful AAFC team, the Cleveland Browns, in the Steelers' division. It would mark the beginning of one the greatest rivalries in NFL history; however, early on, their games were more mismatches than football classics.

CHAPTER TWO

The Birth of the Browns

The 1950 Cleveland Browns were not the first NFL team to play in Cleveland, and they were not the first to win an NFL championship.

In 1920, the Cleveland Tigers—owned by local sports promoter Jimmy O'Donnell and a part of the Ohio League with the Canton Bulldogs, the Akron Pros, and the Dayton Triangles—became a member of the newly formed American Professional Football League. After two years of operation and at the recommendation of Chicago Bears owner George Halas, the APFL rechristened itself the National Football League.

Coached by Stan Cofall, Notre Dame All-American, and Al Pierotti, who pitched for the Boston Braves and became a professional wrestler, the Tigers struggled to score touchdowns and ended the 1920 season with a losing record. In 1921, the Tigers signed Jim Thorpe, who had been the league's commissioner, to a contract as player-coach. They renamed the team the Cleveland Indians to take advantage of Thorpe's notoriety and the recent success of the baseball Indians, who had defeated the Brooklyn Dodgers in the 1920 World Series. But the aging Thorpe couldn't do much on the field to help the football-playing Indians. They ended the season with another losing record and folded at season's end.

In 1923, Cleveland jeweler Samuel Deutsch bought the defunct Indians franchise. The team went on to finish fifth that season in a league that had expanded to 20 teams. Going into the 1924 season, Deutsch purchased the Canton Bulldogs for $1,500 and suspended the team's operations. He moved the best players to his Cleveland franchise and renamed it the Cleveland

Bulldogs. While the scheduling and record keeping were erratic, league officials declared the Bulldogs, with their recognized record of 7–1–1, NFL champions for 1924.

However, any hope that the Cleveland Bulldogs would become one of the NFL's stable franchises ended when Deutsch sold his control of the Canton franchise for $3,000 and Cleveland's best players headed back to Canton. After finishing with a losing record in 1925, Cleveland suspended operations. They returned to the NFL in 1927, but despite the team's fourth-place finish, behind only the New York Giants, the Green Bay Packers, and the Chicago Bears, the Cleveland franchise was sold to Detroit, where it eventually became the Lions.

In the early 1930s, as America plunged into the Great Depression, the NFL lost a number of teams. When the Orange Newark Tornados folded at the end of the 1930 season, league officials decided to move the franchise to Cleveland because of the recent construction of the 78,189-seat Cleveland Municipal Stadium. They assigned the team to Art "Bunny" Corcoran, who played on the 1921 NFL Indians team. Coached by former Canton Bulldogs players Al Cornsweet and Harry "Hoge" Workman (who pitched briefly for the Boston Red Sox), the team struggled to break a losing record and failed to attract fans. Only 2,000 showed up for its home opener. At the end of the season, the franchise was sold to George Preston Marshall, who moved the team to Boston and called them the Redskins.

Whether Tigers, Bulldogs, or Indians, no NFL franchise in Cleveland lasted more than a season or two. Cleveland did have that Bulldogs NFL championship team in 1924, but the title was granted by declaration rather than earned in a playoff game. Nevertheless, the NFL remained open to the city of Cleveland as a potential site for a stable and successful franchise—if it had the proper financial backing.

In 1937, even through the country was deep into the Great Depression, a group of businessmen headed by attorney Homer Marshman approached the NFL about buying a franchise for its Cleveland Rams team, which had played in the loosely organized American Football League for the 1936 season. Marshman and his associates purchased an NFL franchise for $15,000 and had another $55,000 in operating capital. Named after a powerful Fordham Rams college football team that had Vince Lombardi among their fabled "Seven Blocks of Granite" linemen, the Rams began in the NFL in 1937 and would remain in Cleveland for the next several years. They would also give the city its first legitimate NFL championship.

The Cleveland Rams' first significant move as an NFL franchise was to hire Hugo Bezdek as head coach. Bezdek was a highly successful college football coach and had led Oregon and Penn State to the Rose Bowl. He had also managed the baseball Pittsburgh Pirates from 1917 to1920. The players who Bezdek managed during his Pirates tenure included Honus Wagner and Casey Stengel. When he accepted the Cleveland Rams' head-coaching job, Bezdek became the first and only individual in sports history to both coach an NFL team and manage a Major League Baseball team.

Unfortunately for Bezdek, the Cleveland Rams—the first expansion team in the NFL since 1933—had problems filling their roster with established players. Operating with mostly rookies and a handful of defectors from the American Football League, the team scored the fewest points in the NFL and allowed the most points. After winning their second game of the season against the Philadelphia Eagles, the Rams lost their next nine games and finished the 1937 season with a dismal 1–10–0 record, by far the worst in the NFL.

When the Rams lost three of their first four games of the 1938 season, a frustrated Hugo Bezdek resigned as head coach and was replaced by assistant coach Art Lewis. With the Rams scheduled to face the Chicago Bears in their next two games, Lewis, with an inexperienced team that had only two players over 25, accomplished the seemingly impossible by upsetting the Bears in both games. Though they lost their next four games, the Rams defeated the Pittsburgh Steelers in the last game of the season to finish with a record of 4–7.

Instead of bringing Lewis back for the 1939 season, the Rams once again made a big-time hire by signing Earl "Dutch" Clark, a six-time All-Pro tailback for the Detroit Lions, to a two-year contract as their new head coach. Clark, who as a player led the Lions to the 1935 NFL championship, was highly regarded for his understanding of the game. His coach at Detroit, George "Potsy" Clark, called him "the most intelligent man to ever play football."

Clark had ended his playing career and turned to coaching the Lions because of mounting injuries and advancing age, but when he signed a contract to coach the Cleveland Rams he decided to play again. Unfortunately for Clark and the Rams, the NFL ruled that the player rights to Clark still belonged to the Detroit Lions. Unable to work out a trade with the Lions, the Rams—with Clark restricted to the sideline—struggled in the first half of the 1939 season but bounced back with four wins and a tie to finish with a 5–5–1 record. In their upset win over the Lions, 25,000 fans turned out for the game, setting a Cleveland attendance record for an NFL game.

With rookie tailback Parker Hall (under the tutelage of Dutch Clark) leading the NFL in passing and earning MVP honors in 1939, the Rams were expected to contend for the NFL title in 1940. However, after opening the season on the road with a victory over the Eagles, the Rams lost their home opener to the Lions, then lost their next two games to the Bears and the Packers. With attendance dwindling, the Rams struggled through the rest of the 1940 season and ended up with a losing 4–6–1 record.

When a disappointed ownership decided to sell the Cleveland Rams, they attracted the attention of Dan Reeves, a New York sports entrepreneur and son of a grocery store chain magnate. Reeves dreamed of owning an NFL team, so when the Rams became available, he and business partner Robert Levy purchased the franchise for $135,000.

Reeves and Levy didn't know what to expect from a franchise that was struggling on and off the field, but they were thrilled when they watched Dante Magnani return the opening kickoff for 95 yards and a touchdown against the Pittsburgh Steelers. When the Rams, under returning coach Dutch Clark, won their home opener against the Steelers and their next game against the Chicago Cardinals, Reeves and Levy were delighted and thought they had bought into a championship franchise. Unfortunately, the Rams, struggling with a lack of depth on offense and defense, lost their next nine games and finished the 1941 season with a 2–9 record.

The Rams improved in 1942, but that had much to do with the impact of World War II on the NFL. With the draft draining several NFL teams of their best players, the Rams were able to beat the most depleted teams—like the Philadelphia Eagles, the Brooklyn Dodgers, and the Detroit Lions—and move up to third place in their division with a 5–6 record. Their losses at home and away to the Chicago Bears and the Green Bay Packers, two teams not hurt as yet by the draft, however, showed that their improvement was more a matter of attrition than talent.

With their co-owners drafted into the military, the Rams successfully petitioned the NFL for a suspension of play for the 1943 season, while other teams tried to survive by merging franchises. The Cleveland Rams returned to NFL play in 1944 with a new head coach, Buff Donelli. The Rams, under Donelli, opened the 1944 season with a victory over the Chi-Pitts, dubbed the Carpets by critics. It was Donelli's first NFL victory after his brief, winless stint with the Steelers. The Rams went on to wins against the Bears and the Lions, but their loss to the eventual NFL championship Packers sent them reeling for the rest of the season. Their only win in their last seven games came against the Chi-Pitts. They would finish with a record of 4–6 and send Buff Donelli back to coaching college football.

For the 1945 season, the Cleveland Rams looked to college football for a new head coach and hired Adam Walsh, who had been an assistant coach at Yale, Harvard, and Notre Dame and the head coach at Santa Clara and Bowdoin. Walsh was an All-American center on Knute Rockne's 1924 undefeated team that featured the fabled "Four Horsemen." As a coach, he was as innovative as Rockne and brought the T formation to the Rams at the perfect moment in NFL and Cleveland Rams history.

In the fifth round of the draft going into the 1945 season, the Rams selected quarterback Bob Waterfield. A triple threat at UCLA, he had led the Bruins into the 1943 Rose Bowl and, later in the year, added to his reputation as a glamour boy by marrying actress Jane Russell, who would go on to star with Marilyn Monroe in *Gentlemen Prefer Blondes*. He seemed the perfect hero for Hollywood, but not so much for Cleveland and its working-class, shot-and-a-beer fans.

Cleveland's hard-nosed football fans, however, quickly took to Waterfield when he led the Rams to victories in their first four games. After a loss to the Eagles, the Rams won their last five games, including a West Division title-clinching 28–21 victory over the Lions in which Waterfield, playing with torn rib muscles, passed for 329 yards, threw two touchdown passes, and ran for a third.

At the end of the season, Waterfield led the league in total yards (1,627), touchdown passes (14), and yards per completed pass (18.1). He also rushed for five touchdowns, did the team's punting and placekicking, returned punts, and intercepted six passes. Though only a rookie, Waterfield was awarded the Joe F. Carr Trophy as the NFL's Most Valuable Player over the Washington Redskins' Sammy Baugh, who had led the Redskins to an 8–2 record and an East Division championship.

The Rams and the Redskins met for the 1945 NFL title on December 16 in Cleveland on a bitterly cold, windy day that made passing the ball a challenge for the two best quarterbacks in the league. The only score in the first quarter came when Sammy Baugh dropped back into his own end zone and threw a pass that a gust of wind carried into the goalpost. The football bounced back into the end zone and was ruled a safety under the NFL rule at the time.

After Baugh left the game in the second quarter with bruised ribs, his substitute Frankie Filchock threw for a touchdown to give the Redskins a 7–2 lead, but Waterfield brought the Rams back with a touchdown pass. His extra-point try hit the goalpost but bounced through to gave the Rams a 9–7 lead at halftime. Waterfield threw another touchdown pass in the third quarter, but when he missed the extra point, the score remained at 15–7.

After Filchock matched Waterfield with his second touchdown pass, the Redskins converted the extra point to make the score 15–14. When neither team scored in the fourth quarter, the Cleveland Rams became NFL champions in a freakish game decided by two footballs that hit the goalpost and bounced luckily in the Rams' favor. It was a bizarre but happy ending to the Rams' season.

The Cleveland Rams made history in 1945 by giving the city its first legitimate NFL championship. Twenty years earlier, NFL officials had awarded the championship to the Cleveland Bulldogs after sorting through the league's uneven scheduling, but this time the NFL title was earned in a thrilling playoff victory. Unfortunately for Cleveland fans, their joy was short lived. The Rams were about to make another kind of history by becoming the first NFL team to move to another city after winning the league championship.

While the Rams had a successful season on the field in 1945, they still had trouble attracting fans. The 1945 title game against the Redskins drew only 32,178 paying customers. Dan Reeves, the Rams' controlling owner, decided, after losing money in every season since purchasing the team in 1941, that it was time to move the franchise to another city. Just a few months after the Cleveland Rams won the NFL championship, he announced that the Rams were heading to Los Angeles.

Besides declining attendance and the attraction of becoming the first NFL team to play in a potentially lucrative market on the West Coast, Reeves had another reason for leaving Cleveland. Anticipating a postwar boom in America's interest in sports, Arch Ward, sports editor of the *Chicago Tribune,* came up with the idea of a new professional league to challenge the NFL's monopoly. He found wealthy owners to finance teams—ranging from New York and Miami to Los Angeles and San Francisco—and formed the All-American Football Conference. Dan Reeves was well aware that the AAFC would also include a franchise in Cleveland.

Ward's AAFC would last only four years, but it would have a major impact on the NFL by eventually bringing teams in Baltimore, San Francisco, and Cleveland into the league. When Arch Ward was looking for an owner for a Cleveland franchise, he found his man in Arthur "Mickey" McBride, who had made his fortune in the taxi business and in real estate and was rumored to have mob connections. Willing to spend money on his new franchise, McBride thought about trying to hire legendary Notre Dame coach Frank Leahy but finally settled on Paul Brown. Brown was a highly innovative coach who had become a legend in his own right at Massillon Washington High School in Massillon, Ohio, where his team lost only 10 games in 11 seasons. He went on to Ohio State, where his team became college football's national champions in 1942.

When McBride offered Brown, who was coaching the football team at the Great Lakes Naval Training Station, a $17,500 contract (the highest at that point for a pro football coach) and a $250 monthly stipend until he was released from military service, all Brown could say was, "Where do I sign?" But Brown balked when McBride wanted to name the team after his new coach. Only when fans voted in a poll for the Panthers, the name of a losing professional team from Cleveland's past, did Brown reluctantly agree to the Cleveland Browns. He was happier when McBride worked out a plan to hire some extra players as taxi drivers, so Brown could have a reserve beyond his roster. The players never drove a cab, but they did become a part of pro football's first taxi squad (i.e., a practice squad).

Paul Brown told the press at his first news conference that "I want to be what the New York Yankees are in baseball and Ben Hogan is in golf," but his first task was fielding a team. He would rely heavily on signing players that he had coached at Ohio State and the Great Lakes NTS, including future Hall of Famers Lou Groza, Dante Lavelli, Bill Willis, and Marion Motley. The signing of Willis and Motley was an important moment in sports history because it was the beginning of the modern integration of pro football along with the signings of Kenny Washington and Woody Strode by Dan Reeves of the Los Angeles Rams. Reeves was told that the Rams could use the Los Angeles Memorial Coliseum, but only if he signed minority players.

While Brown was building the foundation of his team with his former Ohio State players, his first and most important signing was Otto Graham, a player who had made Brown's life miserable in the past. Graham, an All-American at Northwestern, twice defeated Browns' Ohio State teams while setting the Big Ten passing record. Once fierce opponents, Paul Brown and Otto Graham were perfect for each other. Brown demanded discipline and close attention to details from his players; Graham, who was dubbed "Automatic Otto," ran Brown's team with intelligence and precision.

Playing in the AAFC West Division with the San Francisco 49ers, the Los Angeles Dons, and the Chicago Rockets, the Browns opened the season in front of 60,000 Cleveland fans with a 44–0 trouncing of the Miami Seahawks. Sensing something great was happening, fans turned out at Municipal Stadium for a record average attendance of 57,000 as the Browns won their first six games and, after a midseason stumble against San Francisco and Los Angeles, won their last six games to finish with a 12–2 record and a West Division title. The Browns went on to defeat the East Division championship New York Yankees 14–9 in a hard-fought contest that was decided by an Otto Graham touchdown pass to Dante Lavelli with less than 4 minutes left in the game. The Yankees' effort at a last-minute victory ended when Graham intercepted a pass deep in Cleveland territory.

The Cleveland victory over the Yankees in the 1946 AAFC title game was the beginning of one of the most remarkable runs of consecutive pro football championships, a run that would span two professional football leagues. In 1947, the Browns finished the season with a 12–1–1 record and earned their second East Division title and a rematch in the AAFC championship game against the New York Yankees.

The Browns' most impressive performance during the 1947 regular season was their late-season tie against the Yankees. Trailing 28–0, the Browns, behind the passing of Graham, who set an AAFC single game record of 325 yards, and the running of Motley, who scored two touchdowns, fought back with four unanswered touchdowns. A few weeks after the dramatic 28–28 tie, the Browns, with Motley running for over 100 yards and Graham and Edgar "Special Delivery" Jones rushing for touchdowns, defeated the Yankees 14–3 in front of more than 60,000 Cleveland fans for their second AAFC title.

While their second championship victory over the Yankees had sportswriters beginning to wonder how the Browns would fare in the established NFL, the Browns' performance in 1948 was a compelling argument that they could compete with even the NFL's best. The Browns finished the 1948 regular season with an undefeated and untied 14–0 record, including two dramatic wins against their chief rival, the San Francisco 49ers. During the season, in front of more than 82,000 Cleveland fans, the Browns defeated the 49ers 14–7 in a defensive struggle before traveling to San Francisco and winning a come-from-behind 31–28 victory with a brilliant performance by Otto Graham. Playing with an injured knee, Graham threw four touchdown passes. After the game, Paul Brown said that "Under the circumstances, it was Otto's greatest performance."

After their dramatic wins against the 49ers, the Browns went on to gain their third consecutive AAFC title by trouncing the East Division champion Buffalo 49–7 in a dominating performance by Marion Motley, who ran for 133 yards and three touchdowns. The Browns would be seeking a remarkable fourth AAFC championship in 1949, but the biggest sports story was talk of a merger between the AAFC and the NFL. With AAFC owners losing money and the league down to a single division of four teams for the 1949 season, the NFL agreed to add three AAFC teams (the Cleveland Browns, the San Francisco 49ers, and the Baltimore Colts) for the 1950 season and distribute players from other AAFC teams among NFL rosters.

In the AAFC's last season, the league arranged a playoff series between its remaining four teams. After the Browns defeated Buffalo 33–21 and San Francisco beat New York 17–7, the Browns went on to win their fourth consecutive AAFC championship in an easy 21–7 victory over the 49ers.

As the 1950 season approached, the sports world eagerly waited to see if the AAFC powerhouse Browns could compete in the NFL. Among the skeptics was George Preston Marshall, president of the Washington Redskins. He declared that "the worst team in our league could defeat the best in theirs." Marshall, whose Redskins once played in Cleveland, would soon have to eat his words.

CHAPTER THREE

The 1950s

Running Downhill

Over the decades, the games between the Cleveland Browns and the Pittsburgh Steelers became known as the "Turnpike Rivalry" because of their similar working-class character, the proximity of the two cities and the easy access by car and bus. But in 1950, when the two teams met for the first time in their NFL history, there was no turnpike connection between the two cities.

Started in 1940, the Pennsylvania Turnpike wouldn't complete its section from the Irwin exit near Pittsburgh to the Ohio border until 1951. The Ohio Turnpike wouldn't be completed until 1955. Fans could still drive on bumpy roads and narrow highways, but there was little incentive to travel the distance between the two cities to watch a football game because the games between the Browns and the Steelers were rarely competitive in the 1950s.

In *On Being Brown,* Scott Huler wrote about his father's love of the Cleveland Browns: "He was there from the beginning." His father remembered buying "a general admission-type seat for a buck, maybe two bucks and by the middle of the first quarter you'd be sitting on the fifty-yard line." He loved his Browns and watching games at the cavernous and, in those days, rarely-filled-to-capacity Cleveland Municipal Stadium, but, more than anything else, he revered Otto Graham: "He'd just stand back there and nickel and dime you to death. He was smart and he had a beautiful pass."

Huler's father also had high praise for Paul Brown for turning the Browns into the class act of the league both on and off the field: "It wasn't just us loving the team. It was the team respecting us too." He also admired Brown for bringing so many innovations to pro football, but the one that he remembered the most was the invention of the first face mask: "My dad was at the game the day Paul Brown invented the face mask because Otto Graham was bashed in the face in the first half. In the second half Graham came out with a plastic shield over his face protecting the wound. My dad was there. He saw that."

That memorable game for Scott Huler's father was played on November 13, 1953, at Municipal Stadium.

Prominent Pittsburgh photographer Jack Wolf remembers going to Steelers home games with his father. At Forbes Field, he had to sit closer to his father when the Steelers played the Browns because "it was like a combat zone" because of all the "beer" and "fat, strong men." His father was also among the first Steelers fans to make the trip to Cleveland: "After Friday night high school football, Dad would be gone Saturday morning, off to Cleveland with his pals by train. God knows how drunk they were when arriving. God knows what they did Saturday night in the name of Otto Graham."

Young die-hard Steelers fans whose working-class families couldn't afford a ticket to Steelers games, let alone allow them to travel to Cleveland, had a way to get into Steelers home games, and it didn't cost a dime. Richard "Pete" Peterson remembers as a teenager how, on Sunday mornings of a Steelers game, he and his buddies would head out to a decaying Forbes Field, find a bench in adjacent Schenley Park, carry it to the outer wall next to the iron gate, and prop the bench upside down against the wall. All they had to do was climb up the bench, avoid the barbwire, tightrope walk along the ledge, and take a football leap of faith into the grandstand.

They'd have to hide from ushers and policemen, but once the gates opened, they could join the paying customers and get ready for another Steelers loss—especially if the Steelers were playing the Cleveland Browns. The only consolation when they played the Browns was watching Otto Graham scream at his offensive linemen, including Chuck Noll, because they were roughing him up when he went back to pass. If the Steelers weren't going to beat Cleveland, at least they could give a measure of pride to the working-class fans by inflicting pain on the Browns' hated leader.

At a reunion of the 1950s Steelers, defensive back and Hall of Famer Jack Butler said that "the Steelers have always been a physical team. We didn't make a lot of money, but we loved the game. Other teams may have beaten us, but we gave them a battle." Wide receiver Ray Mathews, who would become the hero of the first Steelers win against the Browns after eight straight losses, pointed out that it was a different atmosphere back then: "The game was rough but it was fun. . . . You have to hit someone. You have to draw blood. You have to think about getting that elbow up. That's the name of the game. . . . That's football."

Redskins owner George Preston Marshall might have been cynical about the Cleveland Browns, but the NFL decided to open the season with a matchup between the four-time AAFC championship Browns and the NFL defending championship (as well as the Steelers' cross-state rival) Philadelphia Eagles in a Saturday night game in Philadelphia. The game was advertised as the World Series of pro football, even though the Browns were the clear underdogs and dismissed by the press as a pass-happy lightweight.

The Browns were so eager to prove themselves in their NFL showcase opener that Otto Graham said, "we were so fired up for this, we would have played them anytime, anywhere—for a keg of beer or a chocolate milk shake. It didn't matter." Paul Brown told his Browns, "Remember, the worst thing that you can do to an opponent is to defeat him. Nothing stings as bad as losing."

The heavily favored Eagles were to feel the sting of defeat that night when Otto Graham threw for two touchdowns and ran for a third in a lopsided 35–10 Browns victory. Eagles defensive tackle and future Hall of Famer Bucko Kilroy admitted that "they didn't upset us. Man for man, they were just the better team." Impressed, NFL commissioner Bert Bell told the press, "Cleveland is the best football team I have ever seen."

The Browns went on to a 10–2 record and a tie with the New York Giants for the American Conference title. They defeated the Giants 8–3, in a bitterly fought playoff game in a frigid Cleveland Municipal Stadium after losing twice to the New York in the regular season. In a thrilling NFL championship game played on Christmas Eve in Cleveland on a snow-ringed field, the Browns played the team that had deserted the city after winning the NFL title in 1945. Trailing the Los Angeles Rams 28–20, Graham rallied the Browns in the fourth quarter to a 30–28 victory on a Lou Groza field goal with 28 seconds left in the game.

Writing in the Cleveland *Plain Dealer,* Harold Sauerbrei declared that "this was a story that the people in Hollywood would reject as preposterous if submitted for a movie. And if you believe in Santa Claus this Christmas morning, you can believe the story that unfolded." In his second edition of *Classic Browns: The 50 Greatest Games in Cleveland Browns History,* Jonathan

Knight ranked the playoff game against the Giants at #9, the season opener against the Eagles at #4, and the championship game against the Rams as the greatest in Browns history.

While the Cleveland Browns were electrifying their fans, Pittsburgh fans were watching their Same Old Steelers struggle through another mediocre season. The only team still using the outdated single wing, the Steelers scored only 180 points in 1950, the lowest in the NFL. Only a tough, aggressive defense, led by rookie and future Hall of Famer Ernie Stautner, kept them in football games. They ended the season with an 6–6 record that included two losses to the Cleveland Browns.

The Browns and the Steelers met for the first time in Pittsburgh on Saturday night, October 7, 1950, at Forbes Field in their fourth game of the season. That first meeting was a perfect reflection of the nature of the two teams going into the1950s. While the Browns' offense played the game with discipline and precision, the Steelers were sloppy and careless with the ball. The Steelers led 3–0 and actually outgained Cleveland in the game, but they set up easy touchdowns for the Browns by committing six turnovers, including five fumbles. Instead of trying to overcome a rugged Steelers defense, the Browns simply allowed the Steelers to beat themselves. Leading comfortably 21–3 at halftime, Cleveland went on to an easy 30–17 win.

One game hardly makes a rivalry, but the attendance for the first game between the Browns and the Steelers in Pittsburgh indicated that fans would soon be making the 130-mile drive between Cleveland and Pittsburgh. While only 24,699 fans attended the Steelers' home opener against the Giants, a sellout and overflowing crowd of 35,590 showed up for the Browns-Steelers game. Only the Steelers' long-standing intrastate rivalry with the Eagles drew more fans to Forbes Field in 1950—but just barely—at 35,662. It was the appearance of often rowdy Cleveland fans at Browns-Steelers games in Pittsburgh that was to become an early source of irritation for disgruntled Steelers fans, who would watch the Browns defeat the Steelers season after season in the early 1950s.

The second meeting between the Browns and the Steelers in their eighth game of the 1950 season would add another measure of aggravation for Pittsburgh fans. In the first game, played at Forbes Field, the Steelers played the generous hosts by turning the ball over six times to the Browns. In Cleveland, they were even more generous as visitors. They committed eight turnovers, including six interceptions, in the Browns' 45–7 romp over Pittsburgh.

Otto Graham suffered a broken nose in the first half and threw only one pass in the game. The Browns, accused of being solely a passing team, turned the ball over to fullback Marion Motley, who had his greatest game as a Browns player. He rushed for 188 yards, including a 69-yard touchdown run in which he seemed to run through or bounce off several Steelers on his way to the end zone. Motley ended up setting an NFL record by averaging an incredible 17 yards per carry.

Motley later said that he had no trouble running against the Steelers' tough defense because at 235 pounds, he was as big, if not bigger, than the Steelers' linemen—including Ernie Stautner, who weighed only 215 pounds as a rookie. However, it was a remark Motley allegedly made to Pittsburgh sportswriter Pat Livingston that seemed more insult than boast to Steelers fans. Livingston wrote that Motley claimed that "running against the Steelers was like running downhill." While Motley later denied that he had made the remark, the Livingston quote or misquote would convince long-suffering Steelers fans that the Browns were bullies.

The Browns opened the 1951 season with a 24–10 road loss to its old AAFC rival, the San Francisco 49ers. Any hope by the rest of the NFL teams that the Browns' dominance was coming to end, however, was dashed when the Browns went on to win their next 11 games, including two victories over their major conference rival New York Giants, and to finish the season at 11–1. Their 14–13 and 10–0 wins against a Giants team that finished the season at 9–2–1 were the only Browns games decided by 10 points or less.

Seeking their sixth championship in a row and their second in the NFL, the Browns met the Los Angeles Rams team they had defeated in the 1950 championship game, but this time the Browns fell short of another title. Late in the fourth quarter, with the score tied at 17–17, Rams quarterback Norm Van Brocklin threw a 75-yard touchdown pass to Tom Fears to give the Rams a 24–17 victory. It was the end of a remarkable run of championships for the Browns and the beginning of a frustrating run of losses in NFL championship games.

While the Browns were chasing another championship, the Steelers continued their struggle to win in the 1950s with their 1930s offense. Led by All-Pros Ernie Stautner, Jack Butler, and Dale Dodrill, the Steelers' defense was one of the best in the NFL. But the only time the Steelers, handicapped by their outdated single-wing offense, won a game on their way to a 4–7–1 season was when the defense held the opposing team to 10 points or less. In their two games with the Browns, they failed to score in 17–0 and 28–0 losses.

In their last game of the 1951 season, while the Browns prepared to face the Rams for the NFL title, Steelers coach John Michelosen finally used defensive back Jim Finks, who was an outstanding passer at the University of Tulsa, at tailback. With the Steelers trailing 10–0 at halftime, Finks entered the game and threw three touchdown passes to give the Steelers a 20–10 victory against the Redskins. It was a great performance by Finks, but it wasn't enough to save Michelosen's job.

During the dismal 1951 season, Steelers owner Art Rooney had urged John Michelosen to do something with his offense to generate excitement among disgruntled fans. Chicago Bears coach George Halas had told the Steelers owner, "I know we take a physical beating when we play you, but the opposition is still getting the points and beating you. The other team takes that beating once. Your team takes it every week. In the long run your team is the team that suffers most from the single wing." Rooney hated cutting a player or firing a coach, especially if he had ties to the Pittsburgh area, but faced with declining attendance, he decided to fire Michelosen.

At a press conference, held on December 19, 1951, Rooney introduced his new coach, Joe Bach, who, in a way, didn't need an introduction because he had coached the Steelers in the past. Bach played college football at Notre Dame under coach Knute Rockne. He was an offensive lineman, one of the "Seven Mules" who blocked for the legendary "Four Horsemen" on their way to a Rose Bowl victory and the 1924 college championship. When the Steelers—still the Pirates in those days—finished the 1934 season, only their second in the NFL, with a dismal 2–10 record, Rooney convinced Bach, who had gone into college coaching and was coming off a successful season as head coach at local Duquesne University, to take the head-coaching job with his Pirates. After a disappointing 4–8 finish in 1935, Bach's Pirates improved to 6–6 in 1936, but Bach, unhappy with the stress of coaching pro football, decided to return to coaching college football at the end of the season.

When Rooney announced that he was bringing Joe Bach back to coach the Steelers, Steelers fans might have wondered if Rooney had, once again, hired one of his old cronies and nothing was going to change with the Same Old Steelers. But Bach said exactly what fans were waiting to hear at his press conference. He told reporters, "I am convinced that pro fans want an exciting open style of offense." When asked if he had a quarterback to run the Steelers' new T formation attack, he responded, "I know Jimmy Finks is a great passer." Steelers fans hoped that the days when bleeding and broken bones were substitutes for winning were over.

While Steelers fans had reason to be optimistic about the 1952 season, Browns fans had reason to feel apprehensive after their team's loss to the Rams in the 1951 title game. For the first time in the team's six-year history, the Browns were not entering a new season as defending champions. Cleveland fans certainly were relieved after the Browns opened the season at home with an impressive 37–7 victory over the defending championship Rams, but, after an unexpected yet surprisingly close 21–20 win on the road against the Steelers, the Browns struggled the rest of the way, losing two games to the Giants and one to the Eagles. They finished with an 8–4 record, their worst season in franchise history.

The Browns were fortunate, however, that the Giants and the Eagles failed to take advantage of the Browns' struggles and finished in a tie for second at 7–5. The Browns went on to their third NFL title game and faced a new nemesis in the Detroit Lions, coached by eccentric Raymond "Buddy" Parker and led by brash quarterback Bobby Layne. A model of consistency in past title games, the Browns uncharacteristically made critical mistakes in the NFL title game and lost to the Lions 17–7. It was the beginning of an animosity that would eventually become a part of the Steelers-Browns rivalry.

The Browns-Steelers games in 1952 were a reflection of the Browns' surprisingly erratic play and the Steelers' new offensive prowess, but the results were the same. In their first matchup, played in Pittsburgh, Finks passed for two touchdowns and ran for a third to give the Steelers a 20–7 lead in the third quarter, but Otto Graham, despite throwing four interceptions in the game, rallied the Browns with two touchdown passes for a 21–20 win. The difference in the game was a missed extra point after the Steelers' first touchdown.

In their second encounter, played in Cleveland, Finks threw four touchdown passes in the second half, but the Browns held on for a 29–28 win. This time the difference in the game came when Finks was tackled in the end zone for a safety. Only a missed extra point and a safety in their games against the Browns prevented the Steelers, who finished with a 5–7 record, from having a winning season at 6–5–1 and the Browns, who finished a game ahead of the Eagles and the Giants at 8–4, from finishing in third place in the conference with a 7–4–1 record.

. . .

In the summer before the 1953 season, controversial owner Mickey McBride sold the Browns for $600,000 to a group that included Homer Marshman, founding owner of the Cleveland Rams, and Ellis Ryan, former principal owner of the Cleveland Indians baseball team. McBride, whose wire service provided bookmakers with the results from horse races, was thought to have ties with organized crime and had appeared before the Kefauver Committee, which investigated organized crime in interstate commerce, in 1951. The former owner told reporters that "he had his fling" with pro football and, while he hadn't made money, he "came out clean."

While Browns fans hoped for a rebound from their team in 1953, they hardly noticed a decision made in the NFL draft that would have far-reaching implications for NFL history as well as an eventual impact on the Browns-Steelers rivalry. Paul Brown used a messenger guard system to bring plays in to Otto Graham, so when veteran guard Lin Houston retired, Brown placed an emphasis on drafting his replacement. After already drafting three guards, the Browns selected yet another guard, Chuck Noll from the University of Dayton, in the 20th round.

Not expecting to be picked in the NFL draft, Noll first thought the Browns' phone call was from the Selective Service draft. So much a perfectionist that his Dayton coach called him "the Pope," he was ideal for Paul Brown's system. Brown's only question when he met Noll was whether he was brave enough. Years later, Noll would prove he had courage when he took the head-coaching job with the woeful Pittsburgh Steelers.

The undersized Noll seemed to have little chance of making the squad, but he was intelligent and disciplined, the type of player that Paul Brown admired and the type of player that someday would make a successful coach. With Noll as part of a tandem of guards bringing in plays, Otto Graham had a great season in 1953, despite the loss of reliable receiver and future Hall of Famer Mac Speedie to Canadian football and an aging and injured Marion Motley. Graham led the Browns to 11 straight wins before they lost a meaningless last game of the season to the Philadelphia Eagles after already clinching their fourth straight NFL conference title.

However, Graham played poorly in an NFL title rematch with Bobby Layne and the Detroit Lions. He completed only two passes out of 15 attempts, and his fumble and interception in the first half gave the Lions a 10–3 lead. The Browns managed to take a 16–10 lead in the fourth quarter, but Bobby Layne drove the Lions down the field and, with 2 minutes left in the game, hit Bobby Doran with a 33-yard touchdown pass that gave the Lions a stunning 17–16 victory.

While Browns fans were hoping for a rebound after disappointing loss in the 1952 NFL championship game, Steelers fans were looking for a continuation of the team's offensive surge in 1952 and the possibility that the Steelers would move up from being competitive to becoming a contender. Despite the team's 5–7 finish in 1952, the Steelers had demolished the New York Giants 63–7 in their last home game of the season and had fans so excited that for the first time in team history they tore down the goalposts. The 1952 Steelers scored a team record 310 points, second in the NFL only to the Browns, while Finks set individual Steelers records in 10 categories, including 2,307 in total yardage and 20 touchdown passes.

When the Steelers and the Browns met for the first time in 1953 in Cleveland, the Browns were 6–0 on the season, while the Steelers were a respectable 3–3. The Steelers jumped off to a 9–0 lead in the first quarter, but the Browns bounced back to go ahead, 17–9. In the second half, the Browns' defense shut out the Steelers, and the Browns coasted to a 34–16 victory.

Two weeks later, the undefeated Browns, at 8–0, traveled to Pittsburgh to face a Steelers team that had won its last game against the Giants and stood at 4–4. The Steelers held a 9–7 lead going into the second quarter, but a Graham touchdown pass gave the Browns a 17–9 lead at halftime. The Steelers did score a touchdown late in the fourth quarter, but the Browns held on for a 20–16 victory, their ninth in a row in the 1953 season and their eighth straight over the Steelers since the Browns entered the NFL in 1950. The Steelers finished the season at a 6–6 and avoided another losing season, but it was only a one-game improvement over their 5–7 record in 1952.

Going into the 1954 season, no one could blame Browns or Steelers fans if they believed their teams were in a state of crisis. The Browns had won their fourth straight conference title since joining the NFL but had now lost their third straight championship game. There were rumors that Otto Graham—who, after an MVP season in 1953, had played so poorly in the title game against the Lions—was going to retire. There were also complaints from Cleveland sportswriters and fans that the NFL had caught up to Paul Brown, that he had become too rigid and conservative in a league that had become more dynamic with its wide-open offenses.

Steelers fans were disappointed by a team that, after setting passing records in 1952, struggled offensively in 1953 and had to win its last two games to finish at 6–6 and avoid another losing season. They also had to deal with another coaching change when Joe Bach stepped down after two years because of poor health.

To make matters worse, owner Art Rooney decided to promote assistant coach Walt Kiesling to take over from Bach. This would be the third time that Rooney, who prized loyalty and was criticized for cronyism, turned to Kiesling to coach his Steelers—in tenures that at that time ranged from the 1930s to the 1950s and included the World War II Steagles. For Steelers players, it was the return of a coach who valued toughness. Defensive back Jack Butler said that, under Kiesling, "if there wasn't a bunch of guys bleeding and fighting during practice, we were loafing."

The good news for Cleveland fans was that Graham decided to return to the Browns because he wanted to give the city one last championship. But the fans weren't sure that Graham had made the right decision when the Browns lost their opener 26–10 to the Eagles on the road. However, after their home opener against the Lions was canceled and then rescheduled because of a conflict with the Indians-Giants World Series, a Browns 21–7 home win against the Cardinals had them cheering.

Worried that Kiesling was out of touch with the current game, Steelers fans were both relieved and excited when they opened with a road 21–20 win over the Packers, the first over Green Bay in team history, and easily defeated the Washington Redskins 27–7 in their home opener. Even a 22–20 loss in Philadelphia to the Eagles in their third game didn't dampen their fans' excitement because the Steelers had played well and lost the game on a controversial call, when a referee denied Steelers rookie running back John Lattner's forward progress on a fourth down play that would have clinched a Steelers victory.

When the Steelers and the Browns met for the first time in 1954, the Steelers stood at 2–1, while the Browns, with the cancellation of their second game of the season against the defending championship Lions because of a conflict with the World Series, were at 1–1. Played in Pittsburgh, the game took on a familiar pattern when the Browns scored first on former University of Pittsburgh All-American Billy Reynolds's short touchdown run. Finks tied the game with a touchdown pass, but a Graham touchdown pass gave the Browns a 14–7 lead going into the second quarter. The second quarter, however, was the beginning of an incredible Steelers rout of the Browns after Pittsburgh had suffered so many lopsided losses. It was also the end of a streak of eight straight losses to the Browns ever since the teams first played each other in 1950.

After the Steelers had tied the game at 14–14, the turning point came when Butler intercepted a Graham pass and returned it 41 yards for a touchdown that gave the Steelers a 20–14 lead. After an exchange of touchdowns, Finks hit Ray Mathews with a 78-yard touchdown pass that gave the Steelers a 34–20 halftime lead.

Any fears among Steelers fans that the Browns, as they had in the past, would overcome the Steelers' lead ended in the third quarter when Mathews scored on an 8-yard pass from Finks and a 3-yard run, giving the Steelers player, who took pride in keeping his elbows up and drawing blood, four touchdowns on the day and the Steelers a commanding 48–20 lead. It was the greatest game of Mathews's career.

In the fourth quarter, Russ Craft's 81-yard touchdown return of an interception gave the Steelers a stunning 55–27 victory over a Browns team that, playing like the Same Old Steelers, committed eight turnovers, including six interceptions. Craft's interception was particularly gratifying, because the former Eagles player had been humiliated by the Browns' receivers in Cleveland's stunning win over Philadelphia to open the 1950 season. As for the Steelers' offense, defensive-minded head coach Walt Kiesling told reporters, "In all my football years, I've never seen a better offensive team in action."

When asked about the lopsided loss to the Steelers, Paul Brown thought that the Steelers were so furious about losing to the Eagles on a bad call that they took it out on the Browns. Otto Graham agreed: "This has been a tough game every year, but it looks like the Steelers saved everything up for today." Chuck Heaton wrote in the *Plain Dealer* that he thought the Browns had simply and inexplicably collapsed in the second half: "The Browns seemed almost bewildered by the surprising turn of events." A philosophical Brown concluded, "I knew there would be days like this. No team goes on winning forever.'

The stunning victory over the Browns put the Steelers at 3–1 and a game behind the 4–0 Eagles, with a return match coming up in Pittsburgh. With Jim Finks wearing a catcher's mask to protect a broken jaw that he had suffered earlier in the season, the Steelers defeated the Eagles 17–7 in one of the most thrilling wins in Steelers history. The victory put the Steelers in a first-place tie with the Eagles, but so many Steelers players were injured in the brutally played game that the team never recovered. The Steelers lost six of the next seven games and finished the season with a losing record at 5–7.

After suffering a humiliating defeat in Pittsburgh, the 1–2 Browns went on a tear, winning their next eight games before losing a meaningless game against the Lions that had been canceled earlier in the season and was played during the off week before the NFL title game that matched the Browns and the Lions for the third straight time. In the final meeting between the Steelers and the Browns, played in Cleveland, the Browns avenged their humiliating loss in Pittsburgh and clinched the Eastern Conference with an easy 42–7 victory.

A few weeks later, the Browns finally defeated the Lions for the NFL championship in a 56–10 romp in which Otto Graham threw three touchdown passes and ran for three more, while Bobby Layne, in the worst game of his career, threw six interceptions. Before the game, Paul Brown, responding to critics who reminded him of his team's two earlier title game losses to the Lions, quipped, "they're going to let us play the game aren't they?"

After the game, the usually stoic Brown praised the "emotional outburst" of his players and told the press that this was the finest team effort he ever seen from one of his Browns teams. As for a relieved Graham—who had never thrown a touchdown pass before against Buddy Parker's Lions in exhibition, regular-season, or playoff games—he told reporters, "Haven't changed my mind about retiring."

Otto Graham's brilliant performance in the 1954 NFL championship game was the perfect ending to his Hall of Fame career, but when the Browns were faltering in the 1955 preseason, Graham agreed to return for one more season at Paul Brown's urging. They also improved their running game by trading an aging Marion Motley to the Steelers for Pittsburgh's former No. 1 draft pick, fullback Ed Modzelewski. After the Browns lost their home opening to the Washington Redskins, they won their next six games on their way to their tenth straight conference title and sixth in the NFL. They went on to easily defeat the Los Angeles Rams 38–14 in the NFL title game in which Graham ended his brilliant career with two rushing and two passing touchdowns.

The Steelers' trade of Ed Modzelewski to the Browns for Marion Motley was an awful decision and rankled Steelers fans. Modzelewski rushed for 619 yards and scored six touchdowns for the Browns, while Motley, with his bad knees, played in only three games at linebacker with the Steelers. But the trade was not the worst decision that the Steelers made going into the 1955 season. In the ninth round of the NFL draft, they selected Johnny Unitas, a local kid who played college football at the University of Louisville. In training camp, Steelers coach Walt Kiesling thought Unitas was too slow and dumb to play pro football, so the Steelers cut him before the start of the season. Unitas spent 1955 playing quarterback for a local semipro team, the Bloomfield Rams, where he was spotted and signed by the Baltimore Colts.

The Steelers matched their great start in 1954 by winning four of their first five games, but again they struggled, losing their last seven games of the season and finishing with a 4–8 record. They didn't play the Browns until their ninth and eleventh games of the season, and any hope that the Steelers could compete with the Browns, after their stunning victory last season, was dashed when the Browns easily won both games, extending their overall record against the Steelers to 11–1. At regular season's end, the Cleveland Browns were headed to the NFL championship game, while Pittsburgh, once more, was looking like the Same Old Steelers.

After the Browns defeated the Rams for the 1955 NFL championship, Otto Graham announced his retirement, but this time he would not return to football as a player. Since becoming the Browns' quarterback, he had led the team to 10 straight conference titles and seven league titles. His win-loss record with the Browns over a span of 10 years was 114–20–4, including a 11–1 record against the Steelers. Regarded as a coach on the field for Paul Brown, after a year away from football Graham took up coaching as assistant in the College All-Star Game. He eventually went on to coach at the US Coast Guard Academy and with the Washington Redskins.

The Steelers also lost their starting quarterback to retirement, but for entirely different reasons. Jim Finks joined the Steelers in 1949. Though an outstanding quarterback at the University of Tulsa, he was first used as a defensive back because Steelers coach John Michelosen thought Finks was too small at 5'10" and 175 pounds to play tailback. When Joe Bach took over from Michelosen in 1952, he converted the Steelers' offense to the T formation and inserted Jim Finks at quarterback, where he became an All-Pro and in four years broke every Steelers passing record. Finks, however, couldn't get along with Bach's replacement, Walt Kiesling, and going into the 1956 season decided to retire and take an assistant coaching job at Notre Dame.

Walt Kiesling's problem with the Steelers was his old-school attitude toward football players. A lineman in his career, he had little patience with his offensive starters but was devoted to hard-nosed players, like fullback Fran Rogel. The Steelers opened their first offense series so often with a Rogel run that fans chanted, "Hi diddle, diddle, Rogel up the middle" when the team broke huddle. He had cut Johnny Unitas in 1955, and entering the 1956 season, the defensive-minded Kiesling, with the bonus pick in the

NFL draft, had passed over talented Penn State running back Lenny Moore and selected Gary Glick, an obscure defensive back and placekicker from Colorado A&M.

The Steelers and the Browns met for the first time in their second game of the 1956 season. While the Browns were coming off a disappointing 9–7 opening loss to the Chicago Cardinals, the Steelers had opened at home with an impressive 30–17 win over the Washington Redskins. With Otto Graham's backup, George Ratterman, now the starting quarterback, the Browns struggled to score points, as they had in their opener. However, trailing 10–7 late in the fourth quarter, the Browns won the game when former Steelers player Ed Modzelewski, much to the chagrin of frustrated Steelers fans, ran 13 yards for a touchdown and a 14–10 victory.

Three weeks later, the Browns and the Steelers met in Cleveland. The Browns, at 1–3, hadn't won since they defeated the Steelers in Pittsburgh and were hoping for another win over a Steelers team who had dominated in the past. The Steelers, also at 1–3, hadn't won since their opening game and looked to salvage their season as they headed to Cleveland. With Vito "Babe" Parilli replacing an injured Ratterman at quarterback, the Browns surged to a 13–0 lead, but Steelers quarterback Ted Marchibroda led the Steelers to three touchdowns. Leading 21–13 at halftime, the Steelers held on to a 24–16 victory, only their second against the Browns in team history.

After the win over the Browns, the Steelers lost their next two games and ended the season with another losing record at 5–7, their third in a row under Walt Kiesling. The Browns bounced back after their loss to Steelers to win four of the next six games, but a loss to the Chicago Cardinals in their last game doomed them to their first losing season, at 5–7, in team history. More significantly, it was also the first time since they began play in the AAFC in 1946 that they had not won a conference championship.

What had fueled the Steelers-Browns rivalry in its early years was Steelers fans' frustration with the lopsided record between the two teams. In their first seven seasons of competition, the Browns had won 12 of the 14 games against the Steelers. After the 1956 season, two decisions made by Walt Kiesling would intensify the rivalry and add a new measure of frustration and anger for Steelers fans, who, more and more, saw Browns fans as spoiled and smug and their team as a bully.

After the 1956 season, Paul Brown, disappointed in the play of his quarterbacks in the first losing season of his 11-year pro coaching career, was determined to find a replacement in the NFL draft for Otto Graham. He had his eye on Purdue's All-American quarterback Len Dawson. The Steelers, however, had their first-round pick just ahead of the Browns, and Kiesling, though he needed a running back, surprisingly selected Dawson. Frustrated and puzzled by the Steelers, Paul Brown had to settle for Syracuse's All-American running back Jim Brown.

Kiesling's second major decision came just before the beginning of the 1957 season. Detroit Lions head coach Buddy Parker, at odds with Lions management and feeling he'd lost control of a team that he regarded as the worst he'd ever seen in training camp, abruptly resigned his position. Kiesling, who wanted to step down as Steelers coach after three losing seasons, urged Art Rooney, who liked Kiesling and didn't want to fire him, to sign Parker. Two weeks later, Rooney hired Parker, who was moody and impulsive but had a reputation for building champions and beating the Browns.

Buddy Parker arrived in Pittsburgh just as the Steelers-Browns rivalry was beginning to boil over, especially for frustrated Steelers fans who traveled to Cleveland for the annual Saturday night brawl. In the late 1950s, Scott Huler's father watched the Browns play the Steelers on a Saturday night from a front-row seat in the upper deck that nearly proved fatal.

He was seated next to a Steelers fan who, fueled by alcohol, grew angrier and angrier as the Browns rallied to take a late lead in the game: "The guy sitting next to me really got pissed and grabbed me by my collar and was ready to throw me over the edge." Fortunately for Huler's father, an usher intervened, but when the Steelers fan "kept screaming and carrying on the usher suggested that since the Browns were obviously going to win, maybe it wasn't a bad idea for us to start walking out." Huler noted that "almost nothing could move my dad from his seat at a Browns game, but the Steelers rivalry was so tough that even my dad left a minute or so before the end of the game to avoid being tossed on his head from the upper deck."

When Parker looked at his 1957 Steelers squad in training camp, he told Art Rooney, "You've got no quarterback, no runners, no line, and no defense, to speak of." Refusing to go with rookies Len Dawson and Jack Kemp at quarterback, Parker traded two first-round draft picks and starting linebacker Marv Matuszak to the 49ers for Earl Morrall. When Morrall led the Steelers to an impressive 28–7 home opener win over the Redskins, Steelers fans began to think that their team was finally on the way to becoming contenders as they headed into their second game of the season against their nemesis, the Cleveland Browns.

While Buddy Parker was performing radical surgery on the Steelers by trading draft picks for veterans, Paul Brown was taking a more conservative approach, even though his team finished with a 5–7 record in 1956. He thought that he could build his offense around rookie running back Jim Brown, who was the sensation of training camp. He was also impressed with quarterback Milt Plum, his second-round draft pick out of Penn State, but he decided to start University of Illinois's Tom O'Connell, who had played well at the end of the 1956 season. With Brown's powerful running, O'Connell's management of the offense, and a strong defense led by Pro Bowlers Walt Michaels and Don Paul, Brown believed he could coach the Browns back into contention.

Paul Brown's conservative approach gave the Browns a narrow 6–3 victory over the New York Giants in their opener in Cleveland and would prove successful in their second game of the season in Pittsburgh against the Steelers. While Jim Brown rushed for only 39 yards on 15 attempts and O'Connell passed for only 122 yards, the Browns, as usual, took advantage of the Steelers' mistakes—including four turnovers and two missed extra points—to defeat the Steelers 23–12.

By the time Cleveland and Pittsburgh met again, the Browns were 5–1 and on their way to the conference championship, while the upstart Steelers, under Parker, were only a game behind the Browns at 4–2 and still in the conference race. While the Steelers passed and ran for more yardage than the Browns, Cleveland once again methodically controlled the game on offense and scored a defensive touchdown on a Steelers fumble on their way to an easy 24–0 victory.

The two losses to the Browns were painful for Steelers fans, who were hoping that Buddy Parker would turn things around in the one-sided rivalry. After the second loss to Cleveland, they watched the Steelers play erratically for the rest of the season and finish at 6–6 after a win over the Cardinals in their last game of the season.

The Browns continued to play well and, led by Rookie of the Year Jim Brown—who topped the NFL in rushing—ended the season with a 9–2–1 record. A late-season loss to the Lions proved a harbinger of things to come, however, when the Lions, led by Tobin Rote after Bobby Layne suffered a broken leg, crushed the Browns 59–14 in the 1957 NFL title game. It was the same Lions team that Buddy Parker called losers at the beginning of the 1957 season.

· · ·

After the Browns' humiliating loss to the Lions in the 1957 NFL title game, Paul Brown decided to promote Milt Plum to starting quarterback. The Browns' offense still featured the power running of Jim Brown, who would go on in 1958 to shatter the Eagles' Steve Van Buren's NFL rushing record, but Paul Brown hoped the talented Plum would add a more effective passing game to Cleveland's offense. Brown also found a great complement to his offense with Bobby Mitchell, a seventh-round draft pick from the University of Illinois.

While Pittsburgh sportswriters and fans thought that the Steelers, at 6–6, had made a good start under Buddy Parker, the Steelers' coach snapped, "I won't be satisfied until this team wins a championship." Parker was particularly dissatisfied with his quarterback Earl Morrall, who, according to his coach, had trouble spotting open receivers. Parker's unhappiness with Morrall increased when the Steelers lost to the 49ers in their first game of the 1958 season and, a week later, suffered an embarrassing 45–12 loss to the Browns in Pittsburgh. While Morrall threw four interceptions, Plum, in the lopsided victory, was nearly perfect, completing 13 of 14 passes for 197 yards and two touchdowns.

The undefeated Browns and the winless Steelers would meet again in two weeks, but by the time the Steelers traveled to Cleveland, they had a new quarterback, who, like Buddy Parker, had been a Browns' nemesis in the past. Desperate for someone to lead his team, when Parker found out that his old Detroit Lions quarterback Bobby Layne was available in a trade, he dispatched Earl Morrall and two high-draft picks to the Lions for the player Parker called "the greatest leader I've ever been associated with. He'll set the pace for the rest of the players."

In his first game with the Steelers, Layne showed fans what Parker admired in him by leading the Steelers on three touchdown drives in an easy 24–3 win over the Philadelphia Eagles. The next week, however, he struggled against the undefeated Browns. With both Jim Brown and Bobby Mitchell running for over 100 yards, the Browns held Layne to only 133 yards passing in a 27–10 victory over the Steelers.

The Steelers lost their next game to the Giants and dropped to 1–4, but Layne declared, "we're just starting to get to know each other. . . . We're going to stir up some hell the rest of the way." Hell is exactly what the Steelers raised, going undefeated, with one tie against the Washington Redskins, in their last seven games, including a win over the New York Giants. In the last game of the season, Layne set a Steelers record that would last until the 1970s when he passed for 409 yards in a 38–21 win over the Chicago Cardinals. With Parker and Layne united and on a winning streak, Steelers fans had reason to hope more than ever that 1959 would finally bring an NFL championship to Pittsburgh.

While the Steelers were streaking, the Browns, after beginning the 1958 season at 5–0, lost three of their last seven games, including a 30–10 defeat to the defending championship Lions and two losses to the New York Giants. With the second loss to the Giants in the last regular game of the season, the Browns fell to 9–3 (the same record as the Giants) and were forced into a playoff for the conference title.

With Bobby Mitchell already out for the playoff game against the Giants with an injury, the Browns soon lost Jim Brown when he suffered a concussion early in the game. The Giants took an early lead, intercepted three Milt Plum passes, and shut out the Browns 10–0. A week later, the Giants lost a thrilling NFL title game—regarded by many as the greatest game in NFL history—when Steelers discard Johnny Unitas led the Baltimore Colts on an 82-yard drive in overtime and to a thrilling 23–17 victory. Also on that Colts team was running back Lenny Moore, who was passed over by the Steelers in the NFL draft.

If the Steelers had won their two games against Cleveland in the 1958 season, they would have finished ahead of the Browns and the Giants and met Unitas and the Colts for the NFL title.

Going into the 1959 season, Bobby Layne and the Steelers looked ready to end the Browns' decadelong domination and finally bring a championship to Pittsburgh. The Steelers didn't have to wait long for their first challenge. They opened the 1959 season at home against Cleveland to a sell-out crowd at Forbes Field. After trailing 7–0 in a disappointing first half, Bobby Layne kicked a field goal and threw two touchdown passes in the second half to give the Steelers a stunning 17–7 victory. Steelers fans were thrilled with the win, which was Buddy Parker's first over the Browns as Pittsburgh's coach and only the third in 19 games since the teams first played in 1950.

The opening game loss to the Steelers was a bitter disappointment to Browns fans, who were hoping their team would rebound in 1959 after the playoff loss to the Giants. After beating the Cardinals to even their record, the Browns let down their fans again by losing to the Giants, but they won their next five games, including a stunning 38–31 victory over the defending championship Colts in which Jim Brown scored five touchdowns. After the game, Jim Brown said, "I guess this is my most satisfying day. There's nothing like beating the champs."

When the Steelers traveled to Cleveland for their ninth game of the season, they had fallen to a disappointing 3–4–1 record after their exciting win over the Browns. At 6–2, the Browns saw the Steelers game as a springboard to another conference championship. After the Steelers went ahead 14–0, the Browns rallied to take a 20–14 lead on three Plum touchdown passes. An earlier missed extra point, however, would cost the Browns the game when Layne threw a touchdown pass late in the fourth quarter. The Browns' missed extra point gave the Steelers a 21–20 victory.

After defeating the Browns twice in one season for the first time in team history, the Steelers won two of their last three games and finished at 6–5–1. It was a disappointing season for a team that had hope to contend for the NFL championship, but it was another winning season under Buddy Parker. Steelers fans, who began the 1950s watching the Same Old Steelers run the single wing, ended the decade watching the swaggering Bobby Layne throw touchdown passes to talented young receivers Jimmy Orr and Gilbert "Buddy" Dial. Their Steelers had yet to win a championship, but they were an exciting team to watch going into the 1960s and definitely not the Same Old Steelers.

After their second defeat against the Steelers, the Browns lost the following week to the 49ers by another 21–20 score, then suffered a humiliating 48–7 defeat by the Giants, who would go on to lose again to the Colts for the NFL championship. After defeating the Eagles in their last game, the Browns finished with a 7–5 record in 1959. It was a winning season, but it was a disappointment for a team that had won seven NFL conference titles and three NFL championships since entering the NFL in 1950. As the Browns headed into the 1960s, their fans had the great Jim Brown to watch on Sundays, but once again there were serious concerns about Paul Brown and whether the great innovator had become a liability after leading the Browns to so many championship seasons.

CHAPTER FOUR

The 1960s

Paul Brown Fired, Chuck Noll Hired

Before there was the Steeler Nation, Cleveland Browns fans had become the most loyal and fierce in pro football. Attendance rose steadily in the 1960s, and by the end of the decade, more than 80,000 fans on average were attending Browns home games.

Browns fans also increasingly made the trip to Pittsburgh to watch their Browns play and usually defeat the Steelers. In a column that appeared in the *Pittsburgh Post-Gazette* the morning after the Browns and the Steelers had played their last game against each other in the 1960s, Phil Musick wrote that 75 chartered buses had brought Cleveland fans to Pitt Stadium for the annual "bloodletting."

Musick watched fans from "the Garfield Heights Eagles and Teddy's Bar, and Tom's Bar and Tillie's Tavern" make their way to their seats where they broke out the six-packs they had hidden under their coats. After a 24–3 Browns victory, "the cheerful lads from Sgro's Bar on the East Side of Cleveland—pelted unmercifully by snowball-smoking Steeler fans when they carried their bed-sheet around the stadium before the game—folded it up and trudged toward the buses." Noting that the Browns were easy victors and all the beer bottles and whiskey flasks were empty, Musick asked, "Can a Cleveland fan ask for more?"

Far fewer Steelers fans made their way to Cleveland in the 1960s, but Akron native Fred Zumpano remembers going with his father in 1968 to a Saturday night home game and the busloads of Pittsburgh fans "who had come to the game after having drunk all the way there and then they'd fight in the stands. . . . It was a circus. . . . Guys were drinking. Smoking cigars." Thanks to the slugfest in the stands and the lopsided Browns victories, those Saturday night Steelers-Browns games, played in Cleveland from 1963 through 1970, became known as "the Saturday night massacres."

The most severe attacks on Steelers fans didn't come from Cleveland. They were criticized by the Pittsburgh media and even the Steelers organization for not supporting the team. Disgusted at the poor attendance at a Steelers home game, *Pittsburgh Press* sportswriter Pat Livingston wrote, "As a sports town, Pittsburgh ought to hang its head in shame." Pittsburgh born and bred, Art Rooney lamented that "there doesn't seem to be any football enthusiasm in Pittsburgh. Something seems to be gone out of the town."

The harshest attack on Pittsburgh fans actually came from the one of the toughest Steelers ever to play football. Defensive tackle and future Hall of Famer Ernie Stautner claimed, after fans booed an injured Bobby Layne, "This is a lousy sports town, and if Art Rooney had any sense he'd get out of it." Noting that Pittsburgh fans had recently booed the Pirates' great relief pitcher, Roy Face, he asked, "What's wrong with these people? Do they have a inferiority complex or what?" A decade later, just before the Steelers would begin their run of Super Bowl victories, Roy Blount Jr. wrote that there are Steelers fans who view "their city with a certain strange pride as a loser's town."

In 1950, a four-year war between the AAFC and the NFL had ended quietly when the AAFC agreed to cease its operations. The NFL, on its part, accepted three AAFC franchises—the Cleveland Browns, the San Francisco 49ers, and the Baltimore Colts—and expanded from ten to twelve teams, after dropping the New York Bulldogs franchise. A decade later, the NFL, with its increased television exposure and growing popularity, faced another war that would have major consequences for pro football history. In 1960, the American Football League challenged the NFL by beginning operations in eight cities, including New York and Los Angeles.

After a bitter and costly war, the two leagues finally agreed in 1966 to a gradual merger that would take full effect in 1970. By the end of the 1969 season, pro football had expanded from 12 to 26 teams since the beginning of the decade and created a championship game. This game, dubbed the Super Bowl, was first played in January 1967 and would become the most spectacular event in American sports.

·   ·   ·

Going into the 1960s, the most successful NFL franchise played its football in Cleveland. After joining the NFL in 1950, the Browns played in six straight title games, winning three and losing three. After a one-year absence, they played for the 1957 NFL championship; although they lost, it marked their seventh title game in the 1950s. The only worry for Browns fans going into the 1960s was that their team had finished second to the New York Giants in 1958 and 1959. They still had the great running back Jim Brown to lead the team into the 1960s, but there was concern among fans and players that coach Paul Brown had become Cleveland's biggest problem.

The Same Old Steelers started the 1950s with their offense still running the outmoded single wing, but they finally switched to the T formation in 1952. While the change made football in Pittsburgh a little more exciting, the team continued to struggle through most of the decade. They didn't have a winning season in the 1950s until 1958, Buddy Parker's second as the Steelers' coach and Bobby Layne's first as Pittsburgh's quarterback. When the Steelers had another winning season in 1959, even the most skeptical and pessimistic of Steelers fans were cautiously hopeful; going into the 1960s, their team was on the verge of that NFL championship promised by Parker when he came to Pittsburgh.

After Bobby Layne threw four touchdown passes in the Steelers' 1960 opening season victory over an expansion Dallas Cowboys team, they headed to Cleveland for an early showdown with the Browns. After watching the Steelers lose 16 of 20 games played against the Browns in the 1950s, Pittsburgh fans, encouraged by Buddy Parker's two wins against Cleveland in 1959, were looking for a reversal of fortune.

Pittsburgh fans were certainly in a frenzy, but it wasn't their football team that was causing the excitement. After 33 years, the Pirates had clinched the National League pennant and soon would be playing the hated New York Yankees in the World Series. Pittsburgh was so caught up in the Pirates' miraculous championship season that when the Steelers were playing an exhibition game against the Lions at Forbes Field, the public address announcer kept giving fans updates on the Pirates game.

The 1960 World Series would also have an impact on the Cleveland Browns—but for an entirely different reason. After their game with the Steelers, the Browns were scheduled to play the defending Eastern Conference championship New York Giants at Yankee Stadium on Sunday, October 9. It was a critical matchup for both teams, but Game Five of the World Series was scheduled to be played at Yankee Stadium on that date. So the Browns-Giants game was canceled and rescheduled for the week after the end of the regular season.

The Browns opened the 1960 season with an impressive 41–24 road win against the Philadelphia Eagles and hoped to continue their early success against the Steelers before their week off. The Browns had a great start against Pittsburgh and held a 21–0 lead at halftime. The Steelers bounced back in the second half with two touchdowns, but a mixed extra point kept them behind at 21–13. After a Jim Brown touchdown run in the fourth quarter gave the Browns a 28–13 lead, Bobby Layne rallied the Steelers, but they fell short in a 28–20 loss.

When the Steelers met the Browns for the second time in the 1960 season, the Steelers, despite the early-season optimism, were struggling at 2–5–1. After opening the season with victories over the Eagles, the Steelers, and the Cowboys, the Browns had suffered close defeats to the Eagles and the Giants in their next three games. At 5–2 after beating the Cardinals, the Browns were still in contention, but they badly needed a win in Pittsburgh over the struggling Steelers.

The game turned into a defensive struggle, with the Steelers scoring the only touchdown in the first half. In the second half, the Browns rallied to take a 10–7 lead, but Bobby Layne put together a late drive to give the Steelers a 14–10 lead that they held for the much-needed victory. Layne's late-game heroics proved once again that he was the most dangerous quarterback in the NFL, especially with the game on the line in the final minutes.

A Cleveland tie the following week with the Cardinals after the Steelers loss put the Browns at 5–3–1. They went on to win their last three contests, including the delayed game with the Giants at Yankee Stadium, to finish at 8–3–1; however, they couldn't catch the Eagles, who won the conference with a 10–2 record and went on to defeat the Green Bay Packers in the NFL title game.

But the Browns' strong finish was not enough to ease the concerns of their fans, who saw their team finish out of the conference championship game for the third straight season, after dominating pro football for more than a decade. The Browns did play and lost 17–16 to the Lions in the inaugural Playoff Bowl, which matched the second place finishers in the conferences, but there was little fan interest, even in Cleveland, for what Vince Lombardi would call the "Shit Bowl."

Buoyed by their victory against the Browns, the Steelers won their next two games, including an upset victory over the Eagles, but fell short of a winning season when they lost to the Cardinals and finished at 5–6–1. While it was the Steelers' first losing season since Buddy Parker took over the team in 1957, Steelers fans, remembering that Parker had promised to bring a championship to Pittsburgh in five years, hoped that the aging and ailing Bobby Layne had one more season in him—and that 1961 would be the Steelers' year.

The big news for the Browns going into the 1961 season and potentially bad news for their coach was the sale of the team to a new owner. A businessman who made his fortune in New York in advertising, public relations, and the production of television shows, Art Modell, used $250,000 of his own money, borrowed $2.7 million, and found investors for the rest of the money needed to purchase the Browns for $4 million. While Paul Brown had run the team without owner interference since its inception in 1946, Modell wanted to take an active role in the team's operation and decision-making. That included addressing player complaints, led by Jim Brown and Milt Plum, that Paul Brown had become too rigid in his discipline and predictable in his play-calling.

In Pittsburgh, Buddy Parker announced that 1961 would be the Steelers' year. He believed that by trading draft choices for veteran players, ranging from Bobby Layne and John Henry Johnson on offense to Gene "Big Daddy" Lipscomb on defense, he had finally put together a team with the savvy and experience needed to overcome the adversity and injuries that had plagued the Steelers since he became coach. Parker, however, was so concerned about his aging quarterback that a year earlier he'd acquired veteran backup quarterback Rudy Bukich from the Chicago Bears. Parker had Bukich ready just in case Layne's body couldn't survive another season.

For the all of the bluster about a championship, the Steelers started the season with four straight losses, and, as Parker dreaded, they lost Bobby Layne to a shoulder injury. Going into their sixth game of the season against the Browns, the Steelers stood at 1–4 after defeating the Washington Redskins with Rudy Bukich filling in at quarterback.

Despite all the internal dissension and losing their season opener in Philadelphia against the defending NFL championship Eagles, the Browns won three in a row, including a victory over a Cardinals team that had moved their franchise to St. Louis. When they suffered their second loss of the season to the Green Bay Packers to stand at 3–2, the worry was that the

Browns were better than the NFL's mediocre teams but not good enough to defeat the NFL's best.

With Len Dawson, reduced to a backup role by Paul Brown after being acquired in a trade from the Steelers, making a rare start, the Browns jumped off to a 10–0 halftime lead against the Steelers. When the Steelers bounced back in the third quarter to take a 14–10 lead, Brown replaced Dawson, who had throw two interceptions, with Milt Plum. With Plum at quarterback, Cleveland surged into the lead and held off another Steelers rally to eke out a 30–28 victory.

When the Steelers and the Browns met two weeks later in Cleveland, the Browns were 5–2 and once again in contention, while the Steelers, at a disappointing 2–5, were hoping to salvage their season. Those Browns fans who traveled to Pittsburgh saw Cleveland take a hard-fought 7–0 lead at halftime on a Jim Brown touchdown run. Trailing 10–0, the Steelers rallied in the third quarter to tie the game at 10–10. With the Browns ahead 13–10 in the fourth quarter, a late Pittsburgh touchdown drive engineered by Bobby Layne gave the Steelers a 17–13 upset victory that sent unhappy Browns fans back to Cleveland.

The Browns won their next two games, but a loss to the conference-leading Giants just about ended their hopes for the 1961 season. After a loss to the Bears and a meaningless tie with the Giants, they finished with an 8–5–1 record, only good enough for a third-place finish behind the Eagles and the conference championship Giants, who would go on to lose the NFL title game to Vince Lombardi's Packers.

After their victory over the Browns, the Steelers won three of their next five games, but a disappointing 20–0 loss to the Cardinals in their last game of the season doomed them to a 6–8 record and last place in the Eastern Conference. It was their second straight losing season under Buddy Parker, who had predicted a Steelers title going into the 1961 season. It also had fans wondering how much longer the impatient and impulsive Parker, who kept threatening to resign, would stay as Steelers coach.

Coming off their fourth straight season out of the playoffs and their worst finish in their conference since entering the NFL in 1950, the Cleveland Browns went through a major shake-up during the off-season. In the NFL draft, Paul Brown made a highly controversial move when, without Art Modell's knowledge, he traded All-Pro Bobby Mitchell to the Washington Redskins for the rights to Heisman Trophy–winning running back Ernie Davis. Brown's rationale was that the tandem of Brown and Davis, both All-Americans at Syracuse, would give the Browns two powerful running backs in 1962 to match up against the Packers' Paul Hornung and Jim Taylor.

Brown made his second controversial move when he traded All-Pro quarterback Milt Plum to the Lions after the disgruntled Plum claimed that the Browns' offense was "stereotypical" and that "in five years, I called only two plays of my own." When Plum was quoted as claiming, "if Cleveland had an audible system, we would have won a championship," Brown decided that he'd had enough and traded Plum.

In return, the Lions sent former Browns' backup quarterback Jim Ninowski back to Cleveland along with past Heisman Trophy–winning running back Howard Cassady. Doubtful that Len Dawson could run his offense, Brown also acquired frustrated Rams quarterback Frank Ryan, who demanded that he be traded after he spent 1961 backing up Edmund "Zeke" Bratkowski.

In Pittsburgh, Buddy Parker made it clear that he was not stepping down as Steelers coach even though he had failed to produce a championship in the promised five years. He felt that he had a talented veteran team, led on offense by Bobby Layne and John Henry Johnson and on defense by Big Daddy Lipscomb and Ernie Stautner. He was also happy with his rare No. 1 draft pick, fullback Bob Ferguson out of Ohio State: "He'll fit in with the Steelers tradition of hard-running, hard-nosed fullbacks."

While Parker had Ferguson to step in if the aging 34-year-old Johnson faltered, he still had a major concern at quarterback, where a 35-year-old Layne had played brilliantly but sporadically because of injuries. In case Layne couldn't survive another season, Parker traded a future first-round draft to the Chicago Bears for seven-year veteran Ed Brown. With talent and experience on both sides of the ball, Parker told Layne as they headed to Detroit for their 1962 opener, "This is the year. I think we can win it."

Paul Brown's determination to return to the top of the NFL received a devastating blow even before the 1962 season began when Ernie Davis was diagnosed with acute leukemia just before the start of training camp. He was allowed to dress for exhibition games but never played a down in a Cleveland Browns uniform, despite Modell urging Brown to use Davis regardless of his illness. The compromise, according to Cleveland sportswriter Hal Lebovitz, was, "Putting the poor kid in a uniform, introducing him before an exhibition game and having him run across the field in a spotlight."

Scott Huler's father remembers attending the first exhibition game of the 1962 season, at which Ernie Davis was introduced to the fans in his street clothes: "And the place just stood and cheered, just roared. You got chills, just knowing he was never going to play, but was a part of the Browns." Davis died less than a year later, on May 18, 1963.

Without the stricken Davis or the traded Bobby Mitchell, the Browns' running game became so one-dimensional in 1962 that, for the first time in his career, Jim Brown failed to win the NFL rushing title. As for replacing Plum, Paul Brown decided to go with Jim Ninowski as his starting quarterback, with a frustrated Frank Ryan once again waiting in reserve. Brown believed that Ninowski, while not as talented as Ryan, fit the Browns' system and was better prepared to managed the offense.

The Browns started the season with a disappointing 2–3–1 record, before they headed to Pittsburgh for the first meeting of the year with the Steelers. After being trounced 45–7 in their opener against the Lions, the Steelers were also off to a mediocre start and stood with a 3–3 record near the midpoint of the season.

With Bobby Layne playing with injuries and the Browns running their conservative offense, the only score in the first half was a Cleveland defensive touchdown on a Steelers fumble. To make matters worse for the Browns, Ninowski broke his collarbone in the first half when he was sacked by Big Daddy Lipscomb. However, with Frank Ryan coming off the bench and finally getting his chance, the Browns scored 34 points and easily defeated the Steelers 41–14.

The Steelers, as if stung by the lopsided loss to the Browns, battled back to win six of their next seven games and finish with a regular-season 9–5 record, good for second place in the Eastern Conference and a spot in the Playoff Bowl against the Western Division runner-up Lions. While the unpopular Playoff Bowl wasn't much of a consolation prize, the Steelers had finished the regular season with their best record under Buddy Parker, the last three wins coming after Ed Brown replaced Bobby Layne, who was struggling with injuries and playing in his last season.

After their impressive win against the Steelers, the Browns lost their next two games to the Eagles and the Redskins and dropped to 3–5–1 on the season. They bounced back with a win against the Cardinals and, for the second time, easily defeated the Steelers 35–14. In that victory, Frank Ryan gave an indication of things to come when he threw three touchdown passes. The Browns split their next two games, and only a 13–10 win over the 49ers in their last game prevented them from having a losing season. It didn't, however, prevent the impossible from happening in Cleveland.

. . .

The 1963 NFL season opened with two icons missing from the game. In a late-season game in 1962 against the Redskins, Buddy Parker watched Bobby Layne, who was playing on painkillers, crumple to the ground after taking a jarring hit to his side. After watching Layne's teammates help him off the field, Parker decided that the quarterback, who led the Lions to two NFL championships and broke every Steelers passing record when he came to Pittsburgh, needed to retire from the game.

Layne initially resisted Parker's decision and, after making the last appearance of his career in the Steelers' 17–10 loss to the Lions in the Playoff Bowl, told reporters, "What do you want me to say? I know what the ball club thinks but I don't necessarily think the same way." After thinking it over during the winter, Layne announced in the spring that he was not returning to the Steelers and would go back to Texas to pursue his business interests.

Layne's forced retirement wasn't the only loss facing the Steelers going into the 1963 season. During the off-season, Big Daddy Lipscomb was found dead in his Baltimore apartment, the apparent victim of a heroin overdose. When the Steelers gathered at training camp and Parker was asked about Layne and Lipscomb, he admitted, "No, we don't have anybody like those two guys, but who does? You miss leaders like that, no doubt. Lipscomb was a tremendous ball player, and Layne, hell, he was Layne." But Parker was still optimistic about the Steelers' chances after their strong finish in 1962. He was impressed by Ed Brown's performance at quarterback after Layne was injured and believed that his defense, even without Lipscomb, was the team's strength.

While Layne's retirement and Lipscomb's death reverberated around the NFL, the Browns provided the greatest shock in the off-season when owner Art Modell announced on January 9, 1963, that he was relieving Paul Brown of his duties as coach and general manager. A week earlier at the NFL's winter meeting, Modell had tipped his hand at the reason for firing Brown, who still had six years remaining on his contract, when he told NFL commissioner Alvin "Pete" Rozelle, "It's either him or me." When he met with Brown, Modell allegedly said, "The team can never be fully mine as long as you are here because when anyone thinks of the Browns, they think of you."

A clash of egos wasn't the only reason for Modell firing Brown. Modell had been listening to complaints from a number of veteran players, led by Jim Brown, that Paul Brown had become too rigid and out of touch with the modern game. All-Pro defensive back Bernie Parrish admitted, "We hated his guts." Instead of the welfare of his players, all that that Brown worried about, according to Parrish, was protecting "his reputation."

Modell's daunting task after firing Brown was naming a coach to replace a legend. Brown had coached the team named after him since its beginnings in 1946. He had a remarkable 158–48–8 record in his 17 seasons with the Browns and led his team to numerous playoff appearances and seven championships. To fill the void left by Brown, Modell made a conservative choice and selected Blanton Collier, the Browns' offensive backfield coach.

Unlike Paul Brown, Collier was popular with the players, especially Jim Brown. He had a reputation for being a good listener, even though he had a hearing problem, which his players thought was more a convenience than an affliction. He had also been a part of Paul Brown's dynasty, joining the team as an assistant in 1946, and, after a stint as head coach at Kentucky, he had rejoined Brown's coaching staff in 1962. He had replaced the legendary Paul "Bear" Bryant at Kentucky and was replacing another legend with the Browns.

Under Collier, the Browns got off to a great start, winning their first three games of the season before meeting the Steelers on a Saturday night in Cleveland. The Steelers were also off to a good start and had won two games after tying the Eagles in their season opener. The bad news for the Steelers as they headed for Cleveland was that John Henry Johnson, who always seemed to have great games against the Browns, was out with an ankle injury.

That evening, more than 83,000 fans witnessed a seesaw affair in which the lead changed seven times before Cleveland, trailing 20–14 at halftime, came back to defeat the Steelers 35–23 and remain undefeated. Jim Brown, who was having the best year in his career under new coach Collier, rushed for 178 yards and scored a touchdown. The loss dropped the Steelers to 2–1–1 on the season, but the usually pessimistic Parker was impressed by Ed Brown's performance at quarterback and predicted, "We'll win it all if we can get our injured boys back."

The next time the Steelers and the Browns met, Cleveland was at 6–1— their only loss to the Giants—and was in first place in the Eastern Conference, while the Steelers were struggling but still in contention at 4–3–1. Dozens of buses brought fans down the Ohio Turnpike as Cleveland fans helped fill Pitt Stadium to near capacity. One sign proclaimed, "Cleveland Browns Boosters," though someone had crossed out "Boosters" and written "Boozers." One exuberant Browns fan played taps when the Steelers ran onto the field.

Those Cleveland fans who didn't make the trip could watch the game on television, but unless they were outside the 100-mile blackout imposed by the NFL, Steelers fans had to listen to the game on the radio. At Edinboro State College, located 105 miles from Pittsburgh, students from western Pennsylvania areas like Ambridge, Alliquippa, and Coraopolis who were die-hard Steelers fans gathered in the dormitory lounge at Centennial Hall to watch the Steelers-Browns game on an Erie, Pennsylvania, television station. They turned the sound down on the black-and-white set, so they wouldn't have to listen to Cleveland broadcasters, and watched what turned out to be one of the most controversial games in the Steelers-Browns rivalry.

The game began as a defensive struggle with the only score in the first half coming on a Frank Ryan touchdown pass. The turning point in the game came late in the third quarter when Cleveland was on its own 2-yard line and decided to run a sweep with Jim Brown. Steelers linebacker Bob Schmitz, an obscure 14th-round draft pick out of Montana State, shot the gap and tackled Brown in the end zone, but he couldn't bring him to the ground. As defensive back Clendon Thomas closed in to help the clinging Schmitz, Brown threw the ball out of the end zone to avoid a safety, but the referees claimed that the play had been blown dead and awarded the Steelers a 2-point safety.

Trailing 7–2, the Steelers drove down the field late in the fourth quarter and scored on an Ed Brown touchdown pass, then managed to hold on for a 9–7 victory. The controversial safety became one of the most memorable and disputed plays in the history of the Browns-Steelers rivalry. It also moved the Steelers into serious contention in the conference. The following week, they closed the gap even more when they defeated the Redskins, while the Browns lost to the Cardinals.

On Friday, November 23, while the Steelers and the Browns prepared for their next games, tragedy struck America when President John F. Kennedy was assassinated in Dallas. NFL commissioner Pete Rozelle, in what he later admitted was the worst mistake of his career, decided not to cancel Sunday's games.

On Sunday, the day before millions of Americans watched President Kennedy's funeral on television, 34,465 fans showed up at Pitt Stadium to watch the Steelers and the Bears play to a brutally fought 14–14 tie. In Cleveland, fans watched the Browns defeat the Dallas Cowboys, even though owner Art Modell, fearing repercussions because Kennedy was assassinated in Dallas, told Rozelle, "Don't play those damn games." The Browns' public address announcer was instructed to use "Cowboys" instead of "Dallas" when the players were introduced. In his Monday column in the *New York Herald Tri-*

bune, Red Smith wrote, "In the civilized world, it was a day of mourning. In the National Football League, it was the 11th Sunday of the business year."

When the Browns lost their next to last game of the season, it was their fourth defeat and eliminated them from contention, though they did go on to play against the Packers in the Playoff Bowl. Their elimination set up a showdown between the Giants, at 10–3, and the Steelers, at 7–3–3, for the Eastern Conference title. On a cold, wind-swept Sunday in New York, Ed Brown played a terrible game, Frank Gifford made a miraculous game-changing catch, and the Steelers loss 33–17 to the Giants. Steelers writers blamed the loss on Ed Brown's decision to stay sober and not drink with his teammates, dubbed pro football's "Gashouse Gang" for their off-the-field antics during the week. A sober Brown was a bundle of nerves by game time and continually overthrew receivers at key moments.

Buddy Parker would later admit that forcing Bobby Layne to retire was the biggest mistake of his career: "I have no doubt that we would have beaten the Giants with Layne at quarterback that day. Ed Brown was never the leader Layne was, and that's what we needed that day—a leader." Art Rooney, who was confident that his Steelers would beat the Giants and go on to give Pittsburgh its first NFL championship, was disconsolate as he headed back from New York to his hometown. The banner headline in the *Pittsburgh Post-Gazette* the next morning declared, "GIANTS END STEELER HOPES."

The Steelers faced the 1964 season with a bitter, frustrated coach and a demoralized team of aging veterans who believed that they may have lost their best chance at bringing a championship to Pittsburgh and Steelers owner Art Rooney. To make matters worse, a week after the end of the season, Parker traded All-Pro receiver and fan favorite Buddy Dial to New York for the rights to the Giants' No. 1 draft pick, All-American defensive tackle Gordon Scott Appleton from the University of Texas. Parker made the move to replace Big Daddy Lipscomb, but the move backfired when Appleton signed with the Houston Oilers in the AFL.

Even though the Browns didn't make the playoffs for the sixth straight year, they'd finished their first year under Blanton Collier in second place in 1963 at 10–4, just a game behind the Giants. It was a season that, according to Terry Pluto in *Browns Town 1964,* "saved Art Modell's football career." With Jim Brown no longer playing under the shadow of Paul Brown, he had a record-shattering season. With Paul Brown no longer sending in plays, Frank Ryan matured in his game management and play-calling. To make the offense even more potent, Browns drafted and signed All-American receiver Paul Warfield out of Ohio State with their first-round pick.

Despite their unsettled situation going into the 1964 season, the Steelers managed to split their first four games in 1964, including a win over the Giants, before they headed to Cleveland for their first game against the Browns. As expected, the Browns were off to a great start on offense, averaging more than 30 points a game, and had only a tie against the Cardinals to blemish their record in their first four games.

In perhaps their best game of the 1964 season, the Steelers' defense held Jim Brown to just 59 yards rushing and gave up only one touchdown on a Ryan first-half touchdown pass. They took a 16–7 halftime lead on two long touchdown runs by John Henry Johnson and coasted in the second half to a 23–7 victory. On that day, the aging Johnson had the best game of his career, rushing for 200 yards and scoring three touchdowns. It was a particularly galling loss for Jim Brown, who claimed, "There are too many people in this league who would like to see Johnson carried off the field on a stretcher. That uncharitable attitude stems from hard-blocking John Henry's tendency to break things. Like jaws and cheekbones, noses and teeth."

The Steelers' win over the Browns was surprisingly easy and convincing, but it didn't spark a resurgence. When they played the Browns in Pittsburgh three weeks later, losses to the Minnesota Vikings and the Philadelphia Eagles had dropped their record to 3–4. Stung by their loss to the Steelers, the Browns bounced back with wins over the Cowboys and the struggling Giants to improve their record to 5–1–1. In a pregame interview, Parker told Bill School of the *Cleveland Press* that Steelers fans were giving him a rough time: "In fact he had been the target of some hard thrown missiles the previous week." When asked about his preparations for the Browns, he quipped, "I spent most of my time plotting how to escape from the field with my life after the game is over today."

Buddy Parker's teams usually played well against the Browns, and the second meeting in 1964 was no exception. Despite a poor performance by Ed Brown, the Steelers rallied from a 10–0 deficit to tie the Browns at halftime. In the second half, however, the Steelers' offense continue to struggle, and touchdown runs by Ernie Green and Jim Brown, who rushed for 149 yards in the game, gave the Browns a 30–17 victory. School wrote that, after the Steelers' "good fight," Parker "was able to walk off the field with head held high, although still ready to duck"

While the Steelers continued to struggle in 1964 and finished with a 5–9 record, the worst in Parker's eight years, the Browns continued to play well under second-year coach Blanton Collier. They did lose crucial games to the Eagles and the Cardinals near the end of the season, but they were able to clinch the Eastern Conference title with a lopsided win over the Giants in their final game and finish with a record of 10–3–1. Greeted by more than 5,000 fans at the Cleveland airport, Collier's Browns would have two weeks to get ready for their first NFL championship game since their crushing 59–14 loss, under Paul Brown, to Buddy Parker's Detroit Lions in 1957.

To win their fourth NFL championship and their first since 1955, the Browns had to defeat a powerful Baltimore Colts who coasted to the Western Conference title with a 12–2 record. Their offense had scored 428 points, the third highest in NFL history, while their stingy defense led the NFL by allowing only 16 points per game. Sportswriters gave the Browns, a 7-point underdog, little chance of defeating the Colts , even with game being played in Cleveland. Writing in *Sports Illustrated,* Ed Scrake declared that "Cleveland will be playing merely for the dubious pleasure of being thrashed by Baltimore."

While Cleveland fans were upset with sportswriters who belittled their Browns, their greatest animosity was directed against owner Art Modell, who refused to lift the 100-mile television blackout even though the game was a certain sellout. Despite pleas from city officials, Modell remained adamant. Unhappy Browns fans had to travel to cities like Toledo and Erie to see the game. And, of course, there was always Pittsburgh.

Those more than 79,000 fans at the game watched the teams struggle in biting cold weather, with winds gusting off Lake Erie in a first half that ended in a scoreless tie. In the second half, with the wind at his back, the ageless Lou Groza kicked a 42-yard field goal to give the Browns a 3–0 lead. From that point on, the Browns harassed Johnny Unitas and dominated the Colts. With Frank Ryan throwing three touchdown passes to Gary Collins, who was named the game's MVP, and the Browns' defense intercepting two Unitas passes, the Browns shut out the Colts 27–0. While Cleveland fans mobbed Frank Ryan, tore down both goalposts, and celebrated the Browns' victory into the night, they didn't know, as Roger Gordon noted in his *Cleveland Browns: A– Z,* that "it would be the last party of its kind in Cleveland for generations to come."

As the Steelers gathered at their training camp for the 1965 season, Buddy Parker was in a dark and surly mood. After watching his team finish the 1964 season at 5–9, he saw little reason for optimism. Finally, after watching his team play poorly in a 23–9 loss to the 49ers in an exhibition game, he decided that, after eight years, he had enough. Declaring, "I can't win with this bunch of stiffs," he resigned as Steelers head coach. With the regular season just weeks away, Art Rooney replaced Parker with assistant coach Mike Nixon. As for the coach who promised him a championship, Rooney told the press, "I think he wanted to make this team a champion just as bad as I did. Nobody worked at it any harder."

The harmonious and optimistic mood at the Cleveland Browns training camp was in sharp contrast to the Steelers camp. The defense had All-Pro linemen, linebackers, and defensive backs and was coming off a stellar performance, shutting out the powerful Colts in the NFL title game. Their offense, once again, was loaded with talent. They lost Paul Warfield when he broke his collarbone in the College All-Star Game, but they still had the Frank Ryan–Gary Collins passing combination to take the pressure off Jim Brown. They also had an outstanding kick returner in Leroy Kelly, who had the potential of becoming an all-around threat.

The Steelers and the Browns met for the first time in 1965 in Cleveland on a Saturday night. Since Art Modell moved the game with the Steelers to Saturday night in 1963, attendance had leaped in the rivalry games from under 50,000 to over 80,000 on average. The move to Saturday night—which certainly made it easier for Pittsburgh fans to travel to Cleveland, stay overnight, and return to Pittsburgh with little more than a hangover and the fuzzy memory of a Steelers loss—would continue for the rest of the decade.

The Steelers, struggling on offense, had dropped their first three games as they headed to Cleveland, while the Browns, after an early stumble against the Eagles, stood at 2–1. With third-year quarterback Bill Nelsen at quarterback in place of Ed Brown, the Steelers took a surprising 12–10 lead in the rain and mud at Cleveland Municipal Stadium and, after a Jim Brown touchdown, took the lead again 19–17. With time running out and Cleveland on the brink of an upset loss to the Steelers, Frank Ryan hit Gary Collins with a 14-yard touchdown pass to give the Browns a narrow 24–19 victory.

After their scare against the Steelers, the Browns went on to win five of their next six games before they met the Steelers in Pittsburgh at Pitt Stadium. At that point, they had just about clinched the Eastern Conference title with a 8–2 record. The Steelers had gone 0–5 before winning their first game of the season, but, after winning two in a row, they lost their last three games and sunk to 2–8. The game turned into a defensive struggle until Jim Brown broke the game open with his running in the second half, even though the Steelers' Bill Nelsen, having played his finest game of the season despite the chronic pain in his knees, managed to keep the game respectable with three touchdown passes in a 42–21 loss. The win clinched the Eastern Division title for the Browns for the second consecutive year.

With a gimpy Bill Nelsen and an aging Richard "Dick" Hoak replacing an inconsistent Ed Brown and a banged-up John Henry Johnson—and a receiver corps so thin that defensive back Clendon Thomas was switched to wide receiver—the Steelers lost their last three games of the season and finished with a 2–12 record, their worst since the World War II Chi-Pitts went 0–10. At the end of the season, Art Rooney, frustrated with a team that Parker had described as a bunch of stiffs, decided he needed to hire a new coach.

The Browns coasted to the Eastern Division title with a 12–2 record and faced Vince Lombardi's Green Bay Packers, who had dethroned the Western Division Colts on a controversial last-second field goal by Don Chandler in a 13–10 playoff victory. The defending NFL championship Browns thought they matched up well with the Packers. Both teams relied on strong running attacks to control the ball, but while the Packers had the tandem of Jim Taylor and Paul Hornung, the Browns had Jim Brown, who once again dominated the NFL with his running.

What the Browns hadn't counted was a snow- and sleet-soaked Lambeau Field that favored straight-ahead running more than power sweeps. Frank Ryan and Bart Starr traded touchdown passes in the first quarter, but the Browns trailed 7–6 when they botched the extra point. After matching field goals, Cleveland trailed only 13–12 at halftime, but in the third quarter, Taylor and Hornung took control. They rushed for more than 200 yards for the game, while the Packers' defense held Jim Brown to 50 yards and intercepted two Ryan passes. While the losing Browns complained that the field conditions—Ernie Green called it a "slush Bowl"—had distracted them, the Packers went on to defeat the Browns 23–12 and earn their third NFL title in the last four years.

After the Steelers played so poorly in 1965, Art Rooney decided to find a replacement for Mike Nixon. Rooney's son, Dan, who was becoming more involved with the operations of the team, pleaded with his father to go outside his circle of friends: "This business of hiring all friends of the family hasn't gotten us anywhere." In response, Art Rooney contacted Packers coach Vince

Lombardi about hiring Bill Austin, Lombardi's offensive line coach. When Lombardi gave Austin a glowing recommendation, Rooney signed him to a three-year contract.

The challenge ahead for Austin was inheriting a team devoid of young talent. Parker, who hated rookies and claimed that for every rookie on his team he could count on a loss, had traded away draft choices like they were candy. In his eight seasons with the Steelers, from 1957 to 1964, he traded his No. 1 and No. 2 draft picks four times, his No. 3 pick six times, and his No. 4 pick seven times.

Bill Austin was a disciple of the tough-minded Lombardi and tried to copy his methods, but, as Rooney was to find out, Austin was no Vince Lombardi. The team started well enough in 1966 with a tie and a win, but before playing the Browns for the first time, the Steelers lost back-to-back games against the Redskins. Austin's biggest problem going into the Browns game was the loss of quarterback Bill Nelsen, one of the team's few young talents, in their win against the Lions. With Nelsen out with a bad knee, Austin had to turn to Ron Smith, who had played in only nine games with the Los Angeles Rams before the Steelers acquired him in a trade.

If Steelers fans were looking for sympathy, they would not get it from Cleveland fans. They had hoped that their Browns would win their third consecutive Eastern Conference title, then revenge themselves against the Packers on their way to the championship game matching the NFL and the AFL champions in what would become the first Super Bowl.

But going into the 1966 season, Jim Brown stunned Cleveland fans by announcing that he was retiring from football to pursue an acting career in Hollywood after a petulant Art Modell refused to allow Brown to miss training camp until he was finished filming *The Dirty Dozen*. Losing Jim Brown, who in 1965 had led the NFL in rushing for the eighth time in nine years, infuriated Cleveland fans and devastated Brown's teammates. The Browns still had the rest of their championship team in place and hoped that Leroy Kelly could fill the gaping hole left by Brown's departure.

That hope seemed realistic in the first Browns-Steelers game, when Cleveland fans cheered on Kelly as he ran for 113 yards and two touchdowns in a 41–10 romp over the Steelers. The Browns had come into the game with a disappointing 2–2 record but now seemed poised to make a run at another conference championship. The Steelers came out reeling from the Browns game and lost their next two before playing the Browns in Pittsburgh. In their first seven games under coach Bill Austin, the Steelers, after a tie and a win, had lost five straight games. After their easy win over the Steelers, the Browns had moved into contention by winning their next two games and saw their game in Pittsburgh as a springboard to a championship

After their offensive explosion in their first game against the Steelers, the Browns struggled to score in their rematch, managing only a 6–3 lead at halftime. The second half proved a disaster for the Browns and their fans, who had traveled from Cleveland to Pittsburgh and anticipated another easy win over the fading Steelers. With Ryan throwing five interceptions and having his worst game of the season, the Browns failed to score in the second half and suffered a stunning 16–6 upset loss.

The Browns won four of their last six games but finished in second place at 9–5, behind the Cowboys. Disappointed Cleveland fans could take heart from Leroy Kelly's outstanding season, finishing second to Gale Sayers for the rushing title, and Frank Ryan's league-leading 29 touchdown passes; however, when Green Bay defeated the Cowboys and went on to win the first Super Bowl game against the Kansas City Chiefs, they could only hope that next year they'd see their Browns play for the NFL championship.

Long-suffering Steelers fans had no such title aspirations after watching their team finish at 5–9–1 for the season. But their team did win three of their last six games after their upset of the Browns, including impressive wins over the New York Giants and the Atlanta Falcons when Bill Nelsen returned from his knee injury. They could only hope Nelsen would completely recover from his injury and lead the team back to respectability.

The biggest NFL news going into the 1967 season was the league's decision, after adding a team in New Orleans, to split its two conferences into four divisions, thereby adding playoff games between the division winners to its postseason. The Browns and the Steelers were now in the Century Division with the Giants and the Cardinals, while the Cowboys, the Eagles, and the Redskins would join the Saints in the Capitol Division.

The Browns looked to benefit from being in the weaker of the two divisions in the Eastern Conference, but they had some concerns going into the 1967 season. Leroy Kelly had an outstanding year replacing Jim Brown, but Frank Ryan had experienced some discomfort in his throwing arm. They were also worried about their aging veterans, including Lou Groza, who had been inconsistent in his placekicking after so many nearly flawless seasons.

The Steelers' major concern going into the 1967 season was Bill Nelsen's bad knees. To back up Nelsen, Bill Austin decided to sign Alvin Kent Nix, who had been on the Packers' taxi squad (practice squad) in 1966. Unfortunately for the Steelers, Bill Nelsen's knees were still bad, and Nix was not the answer at quarterback. By the time they played their fourth game of the season in Cleveland against the Browns, they had lost their last two games after Bill Nelsen's knees acted up in an opening day win against the Bears.

The Browns were off to their own rocky start, losing their first two games to the Cowboys and the Lions. They were fortunate to play the expansion Saints in their third game and easily won 42–7. The expected win against the Steelers, with Nelsen out, would put the Browns at 2–2 and, they anticipated, serve as a springboard to the division title. Though he threw three interceptions that day, Ryan connected on three touchdown passes to give the Browns a badly needed 21–10 victory.

By the time the Browns and the Steelers met for the second time in 1967, their seasons had moved in predictable directions. The Browns won two of their next three games after beating the Steelers in Cleveland and, at 4–3, were in contention in the Century Division. The Steelers lost their next two games, extending their losing streak to five before beating the Saints, and, at 2–5, were on the verge of their second losing season under Bill Austin. With Bill Nelsen back, the Steelers hoped for a better result from their offense, but once again the Browns controlled the tempo of the game and coasted to a 34–14 victory.

After their loss to the Browns, the Steelers struggled to a disappointing 4–9–1 record, one game worse than Bill Austin's first season as head coach, and had Pittsburgh fans wondering if they were rooting for a team that had become the latest version of the Same Old Steelers. The Browns won four of their last six games and, finishing at 9–5—the same record as last season—captured the weak Century Division title. They met the Cowboys in the conference playoffs, but with Frank Ryan playing with a bad arm, were routed 52–14. At halftime and after the game, Collier told his players that he was "tired of this kind of performance. I don't know the answer but we're going to find out."

Despite their opposite records, the Steelers and the Browns shared similar concerns about their coach and their quarterback going into the off-season. Coach Blanton Collier had led the Browns to an NFL championship in 1964, but their embarrassing playoff loss to the Cowboys had fans, accustomed to dominating teams, worried that the Browns were slipping into mediocrity. Steelers fans would have welcomed mediocrity after two losing seasons under coach Bill Austin, but Austin had one more year on his contract and Pittsburgh fans feared the worst.

The biggest problem for Collier and Austin going into the 1968 season was their ailing quarterbacks. Frank Ryan had been outstanding since taking over the quarterback duties for the Browns, but he was struggling with a potentially career-ending bad arm. Bill Nelsen, when healthy, was one of the most accurate passers in the NFL, but his bad knees had prevented him from lasting through an entire season.

If Ryan faltered, the Browns had his backup, Richard "Dick" Shiner, who had thrown only nine passes in 1967. They decided they needed a more experienced backup and offered Shiner to the Steelers for Nelsen, despite Nelsen's history of knee problems. On the advice of his backfield coach Don Heinrich, who had quarreled with Nelsen over play-calling, Austin made the trade. After taking a physical beating with the Steelers, Nelsen said he was so happy to leave Pittsburgh that "I think I'm gonna include Austin in my will." His comments infuriated Steelers fans, who would have their measure of revenge—but not for a few more seasons.

When Ryan struggled with his bad arm and the Browns lost two of their first three games in 1968, Collier decided to bench Ryan and play Nelsen in their next game against the Steelers, who were off to a dismal 0–3 start. Shiner managed to hold his own against Nelsen, passing for two touchdowns, but Nelsen led Cleveland to a 31–24 victory.

With Nelsen staying healthy, the Browns' win over the Steelers was the beginning of an eight-game winning streak that included a victory over the Colts that gave Baltimore its only loss of the regular season. After their defeat to the Browns dropped the Steelers to 0–4, Pittsburgh extended its losing record to 0–6 before finally winning their first game of the season 6–3 against the 0–6 Eagles. The Eagles-Steelers game was dubbed the "O. J. Simpson Bowl" because sportswriters believed that the loser would end up with the NFL's top draft pick in 1969 and select USC's great running back, O. J. Simpson. The Steelers, to the mixed feelings of their fans, won the game and by the time they played the Browns in Pittsburgh had improved their record to 2–7–1.

The second meeting in 1968 between the Browns and the Steelers turned into an offensive showcase for Cleveland. By the fourth quarter, Nelsen had thrown three touchdown passes to give the Browns a 31–10 lead, and when Frank Ryan came off the bench, he threw for two more touchdowns to give the Browns five in a 45–24 Cleveland romp.

After the Browns defeated them again, the Steelers lost their last four games and finished the season at 2–9–1, their worst under Bill Austin. In Austin's three years as coach, the Steelers won only 11 games, while losing 28 and tying three. It was clear to the Rooney family that the former Vince Lombardi assistant, who prided himself on bringing toughness and discipline to the Steelers, had lost control of the team. At season's end, they fired Austin and began the search for a new coach who they hoped would lead the team to a championship after decades of futility.

After the Steelers game, the Browns extended their winning streak to eight games and clinched their second Century Division title. They headed into the division playoff against a powerful Cowboys team that had defeated the Browns five straight times, including a one-sided 52–14 victory in last year's playoff. The Cowboys finished the season with the NFL's best offense, but this time the Browns' defense would prevail. They shut down quarterback Don Meredith, allowed Dallas only one offensive touchdown, and handily defeated the Cowboys 31–20.

One step away from the Super Bowl, the Browns faced another powerful opponent in the Baltimore Colts. They had handed the Colts their only defeat in the regular season, but this time Baltimore easily defeated the Browns 34–0. One oddity in the game was that Earl Morrall and Bill Nelsen, both former Steelers players, started in place of injured quarterbacks Johnny Unitas and Frank Ryan. While Nelsen did not play well against the Colts and was taken out of the game by Collier in favor of a sore-armed Ryan, he had a productive, injury-free season and was the heir apparent to Ryan, who was likely to retire because of the chronic pain in his throwing arm. The loss was disappointing, but the Browns had moved one game closer to a trip to the Super Bowl.

After the Baltimore Colts lost to the New York Jets in a stunning Super Bowl upset, the Steelers moved quickly to hire a new head coach just days before the 1969 NFL draft. After Penn State's Joe Paterno, to the disappointment of Steelers fans, turned down the job, the Rooneys made an offer to former Browns messenger guard Chuck Noll, who was a Colts assistant defensive coach under Don Shula. After the Colts defeated the Steelers 41–7, in a game that saw Colts defenders tying an NFL record by returning three interceptions for touchdowns, Noll's wife Marianne had "this sudden thought. My God we're going to be in Pittsburgh next year."

Despite the Steelers' reputation for being one of the worst franchises in the NFL, Noll was eager to become a head coach and accepted the offer. When a reporter asked Noll what it was like coming to a city of losers at his press conference, he responded, "Geography has nothing to do with winning. Winning is a product of work and attitude."

With the NFL draft one day away, Noll had to get to work immediately. With the fourth pick in the draft, the Steelers had no chance to get O. J. Simpson, but they had an opportunity to select one of the nation's best college quarterbacks to fill the team's most glaring need.

After the Buffalo Bills took Simpson with the top pick, the Atlanta Falcons selected Notre Dame offensive tackle George Kunz, and the Philadelphia Eagles drafted Purdue running back Marvin Leroy Keyes. The obvious and popular choice for the Steelers was Notre Dame quarterback Terry Hanratty, who played high school football in western Pennsylvania and led the Fighting Irish to the national championship when he was only a sophomore.

To the dismay of Steelers fans and the puzzlement of sportswriters, Noll passed over Hanratty and selected Charles Edward "Mean Joe" Greene, a raw, relatively unknown defensive tackle with a colorful nickname from North Texas State. Steelers fans were relieved when Noll drafted Hanratty in the second round and encouraged, though still doubtful, when Greene was asked the now infamous "Joe Who?" question and shot back that he was the one who was going to tackle O. J. Simpson.

Though the Browns were aging on defense, going the 1969 draft they felt that they had no immediate needs. So, in what seemed like a luxury pick, they drafted Michigan running back Ron Johnson in the first round as a backup and eventual successor to Leroy Kelly. The Browns had a potent passing attack featuring Bill Nelsen, Gary Collins, and Paul Warfield, but their offensive strength throughout the decade had been a powerful running game. With a depth of offensive talent at key positions and with a veteran offensive line and defensive squad, the Browns entered the 1969 season believing that, after falling just short in 1968, they were poised to play their way into the Super Bowl.

When Chuck Noll began his first training camp, he look on a football team lacking in talent. After watching game film, he told Steelers players: "This isn't a good football team and most of you aren't going to be here when this is a good football team." After a rocky training camp, the Steelers opened with a surprising last-minute 16–13 win over the Lions, but by the time Noll faced the Browns for the first time, they were 1–3 and on the way to proving their coach's analysis.

Looking for their third straight Century Division title and their second trip to the Eastern Conference championship game, the Browns opened the season by winning three of their first four games. Their defense was giving up too many points, but their offense was outscoring teams. The pattern continued against the Steelers on a Saturday night in Cleveland, when Pittsburgh, using three different quarterbacks, managed to score 31 points. However, the Browns broke the game open when their defensive backs returned two interceptions for touchdowns to give the Browns a 42–31 victory.

By the time the Browns and the Steelers met for the second time, the Steelers had lost eight straight games and were 1–8. The Browns had a 5–2–1 record and were well on their way to another title in a division in which they were the only team in 1969 to finish with a winning record. Pittsburgh fans and the busloads of fans from Cleveland, who traveled via the turnpike, watched former Steelers Nelsen throw two touchdowns in an easy Browns win. Pittsburgh fans got their wish in the game when Noll started Terry Hanratty, but the anemic Steelers offense was held to a field goal in a 24–3 loss.

The Browns finished the season with a 10–3–1 record and faced a division title game against the Cowboys for the third straight year. Bill Nelsen had an outstanding game for the Browns, who scored four touchdowns against the celebrated "Doomsday Defense." The Browns' defense dominated the Cowboys and added a touchdown on an interception return to give the Browns a convincing 38–14 victory.

One win away from the Super Bowl, the Browns faltered once again, this time against the Minnesota Vikings and their "Purple People Eater" defense. The best Cleveland's offense could do on a bitterly cold day in Minnesota and on a frozen field was a Nelsen touchdown pass with less than two minutes left in the game. By that time, Canadian football refugee Joe Kapp had led the Vikings to a 27–0 lead in a dominating 27–7 victory. At the end of the decade, the Browns had played in 11 championship games in their 20 seasons in the NFL, but the Super Bowl was becoming more and more elusive as the Browns headed into the 1970s.

While the Browns were chasing and just falling short of the Super Bowl, the Steelers ended up losing an unlucky 13 games in a row after their opening win of the season. The season capped off four decades of misery for Steelers fans, but what made matters worse was their 9–31 record since the rivalry with the Browns began in the 1950s. For Steelers fans, the Browns had clearly bullied the Steelers, and, going onto the 1970s, it was long past time for the Steelers to beat the bully.

Despite their dismal 1–13 record, Noll declared that the Steelers were making progress and insisted that the "ultimate goal was a championship." But Noll's determination and the Steelers' hopes for a championship would likely hinge on a coin flip with the Chicago Bears, who also finished with a 1–13 record, for the rights to the No. 1 draft pick in 1970.

CHAPTER FIVE

The 1970s

The Steelers Finally Grow Up

When the Steelers, after decades of losing, finally started playing championship football, they unleashed a joy and passion that Pittsburgh hadn't experienced since Pirates second baseman Bill Mazeroski's dramatic home run ended the 1960 World Series against the New York Yankees.

On any given Sunday at Three Rivers Stadium in the 1970s, Steelers fans were bedecked in black and gold and gathered in fanatic groups celebrating their favorite football hero. Franco Harris had his helmeted Franco's Italian Army, which counted among its honorary members Brigadier General Frank Sinatra. Kicker Roy Gerela had his Gerela's Gorillas, with its leader dressed in a gorilla suit, while Jack Ham had Polish fans parading around Three Rivers with their "Dobre Shunka" ("good ham") signs.

Steelers fans also had Frenchy's Foreign Legion, Rocky and the Flying Squirrels, Lambert's Lunatics, Shell's Bombers, Russell's Raiders, and Bradshaw's Brigade. But what drove Steelers fans into a frenzy was born out of the desperate idea of a popular Pittsburgh radio personality with a nasal voice and an outrageous Pittsburgh way of twisting the English language.

Just before a 1975 playoff game at Three Rivers against the Baltimore Colts, Myron Cope was told by his bosses at WTAE, the Steelers' flagship radio station, that he needed to come up with a gimmick for the game. Cope didn't like the idea, but he knew his contract was up for renewal at the end of the Steelers' season, so he had to think of something to save his job.

Pittsburgh was in the middle of its Rust Belt depression, so Cope tried to figure out a gimmick that wouldn't cost much for the city's working-class fan base. He figured that everyone owned a towel, so in his best Pittsburghese, he told fans on his radio show that "yunz" need to bring a yellow, gold, or black towel to the "Stillers" game. If they didn't own one, they should dye one. He promised that when fans waved their towels, "terrible" things would happen to the Steelers' opponents.

When Cope arrived at Three Rivers for the game, he saw no sign of towels among the fans, but when the Steelers came running out of the tunnel and onto the field, thousands of fans spontaneously began waving their makeshift towels. The Steelers won the playoff game against the Colts, and the next week, Lynn Swann twirled a "Terrible Towel" and led the Steelers onto the field for the AFC championship game. They defeated the Oakland Raiders and went on to win the Super Bowl against the Dallas Cowboys, with Lynn Swann winning the MVP award. Cope's Terrible Towel was well on its way to becoming one of the most popular and famous icons in American sports.

In 1970, the NFL and the AFL finally completed the merger that they had agreed to in 1966, when the 10 teams in the AFL joined the NFL and became the American Football Conference. To balance the merger, three of the 16 NFL teams had to move into the AFC. The remaining 13 NFL teams became the National Football Conference. Both the AFC and the NFC were then divided into three divisions, the Eastern, the Central, and the Western. The division winners and a wild card team with the best record would then meet in conference playoffs to determine the conference champions and the opponents in what became known as the Super Bowl.

NFL officials initially tried to convince Art Rooney to move his Steelers to the AFC conference, but, a traditionalist, he balked at the idea. When Art Modell, lured by the NFL offer of $3 million, agreed to move the Browns, Rooney, at Modell's urging, decided to join Cleveland in the AFC—as long as they preserved their rivalry by playing in the same division. When the Baltimore Colts agreed to join the Browns and the Steelers in the AFC, though not in the same division, the merger was complete.

One added incentive, possibly for Rooney and certainly for Modell, was the opportunity to play in the same conference and division with the Cincinnati Bengals. In 1967, a group of owners headed by Paul Brown bought an expansion AFL franchise that they located in Cincinnati and called the Bengals in honor of Brown's old high school team, the Massillon Tigers. With Paul Brown in control and coaching the team, the Bengals had struggled and finished under .500 in their first two years.

The Bengals were certainly attractive opponents for Cleveland because of Paul Brown's controversial firing, but they also looked like another easy rival for the Browns in a division that included the Steelers, who had won only nine of 40 games played against the Browns since 1950. When a mediocre Houston Oilers team was added to the Central Division, the Browns were regarded as the dominant team in arguably the weakest division in the NFL.

On January 9, 1970, the Friday before the Super Bowl, the Steelers, after finishing in a tie with the Chicago Bears for the worst record in the NFL at 1–13, faced a coin flip by commissioner Pete Rozelle to decide which team would get the top pick in the NFL draft. At the meeting, held at the Fairmont Hotel in New Orleans, Art Rooney's son, Dan, offered the call of the toss to the Bears. Ed McCaskey, son-in-law of Bears coach George Halas, called heads and the coin, a 1921 silver dollar, landed tails.

There was no doubt about the top college player in the 1970 NFL draft. Louisiana Tech's Terry Bradshaw had the chiseled looks of an All-American quarterback and the size and arm of a future Hall of Famer. Several teams offered the Steelers multiple players for the rights to Bradshaw, but Chuck Noll told the Rooneys, "All these guys are going to do is get us closer to mediocrity. Our objective is to win the championship." On January 27, after botching so many decisions on future quarterback greats, including Johnny Unitas and Len Dawson, the Steelers drafted Terry Bradshaw.

The Steelers weren't the only ones to select an outstanding quarterback in the first round of the 1970 draft. Worried about Bill Nelsen's bad knees. the Browns traded All-Pro wide receiver Paul Warfield to the Miami Dolphins for the third pick in the draft. After the Green Bay Packers acquired the second pick from the Chicago Bears and selected Notre Dame defensive tackle Mike McCoy, the Browns drafted Purdue All-American quarterback Mike Phipps.

Trading away one of the most popular Browns players and one of the team's most dangerous offensive weapons was roundly criticized by the Cleveland press and fans. It was reminiscent of the 1961 trade that sent the highly regarded Bobby Mitchell to the Washington Redskins for the draft rights to Ernie Davis. That earlier trade was the beginning of the end of Paul Brown's coaching career in Cleveland, and many thought that Blanton Collier had made the same fatal mistake.

When the 1970 season began, the plans for Terry Bradshaw and Mike Phipps were in stark contrast. Even though Bradshaw had been wildly erratic in preseason games, the Steelers decided to begin the season with their highly touted rookie at quarterback. The move proved disastrous in their home opener when Bradshaw completed only four of 16 passes and ran out of the end zone for a safety in a 19–7 loss to the Houston Oilers. Things didn't go much better in their second game when Bradshaw was tackled for another safety in a 16–13 loss to the Denver Broncos.

The Browns still had veteran Bill Nelsen at quarterback when they opened the season in the first *Monday Night Football* game in NFL history. A record-setting 85,703 Cleveland fans watched their Browns defeat the New York Jets 31–21, despite a strong performance by Joe Namath. After the thrilling win over the Jets, the Browns lost their second game of the season, 34–31, on the road against the 49ers, and they also lost Nelsen when he reinjured a knee.

When the Steelers traveled to Cleveland for their third game of the season, they were 0–2 with Bradshaw at quarterback and had extended their losing streak to 15 games. While Pittsburgh fans were wondering how long Chuck Noll would go with his unsettled young quarterback, Cleveland fans were wondering who would replace the injured Bill Nelsen. Reluctant to play Mike Phipps, Collier decided to start Don Gault, who had been on the Browns' taxi squad (practice squad) the past two years and had played well in preseason games.

On a Saturday night, Cleveland and the usual mob of Pittsburgh fans watched what had to be one of the most poorly played games in the history of the Browns-Steelers rivalry. Bradshaw started the scoring by achieving the dubious distinction of being tackled in the end zone for a safety in his first three games in the NFL. Though he had yet to throw a touchdown pass, he did redeem himself for the safety by running 35 yards for a touchdown to give the Steelers a 7–2 halftime lead.

While Bradshaw was scrambling around and throwing interceptions, Don Gault was showing Browns fans why he had never started an NFL game. Before he was relieved by Mike Phipps in the second half, Gault completed only one pass out of 16 attempts. Fortunately for the Browns, Phipps threw a 52-yard touchdown pass, his first in the NFL, to give the Browns the lead, and when Erich Barnes intercepted a Bradshaw pass and returned it for a touchdown, the Browns went on to a 15–7 victory. Though they didn't need the encouragement, it was a game that drove both Steelers and Browns fans to drink.

After the Steelers' loss to the Browns, their 16th in a row, Pittsburgh fans were wondering if the team would ever win another game. However, relying on a strong defense led by Mean Joe Greene—and occasional flashes of effectiveness from Terry Bradshaw and Terry Hanratty—the Steelers, to the amazement and delight of their fans, won their next four games in a row and moved into a tie for first place with the Browns at 4–4.

When the Steelers and the Browns met for the second time, the Steelers had dropped to 4–6, while the Browns stood at 5–5. The Browns needed the win to stay ahead of the upstart Steelers, but disappointed Cleveland fans who had traveled to Pittsburgh watched the Browns score only three field goals that day, even with Nelsen again at quarterback. That total was more than matched by touchdown passes from Hanratty, who left the game with a concussion, and Bradshaw, who came off the bench; touchdowns sparked the Steelers to a 28–9 victory and gave Chuck Noll his first win over his former team.

While the Steelers lost their last three games to finish at 5–9, the Browns won two of three to finish at 7–7. But the Browns fell short of winning the division when the Cincinnati Bengals, after losing six of their first seven games (including two defeats against the Browns), went on a surprising five-game winning streak and captured the Central Division title with an 8–6 record. Cleveland fans could take some comfort in the victory over Paul Brown in the historic first meeting between the Browns and the Bengals, but the knowledge that late-season losses to their rival Steelers and Bengals cost them a division crown was a bitter reminder that their Browns were drifting into mediocrity and had fallen well short of dominating their division.

Blanton Collier made it easy for the Browns to shake the franchise and its fans out of their off-season doldrums by announcing his retirement after coaching the team since 1963. Art Modell, in his public statement, claimed he wanted Collier to stay, but Collier said his hearing loss had become too severe. He was having trouble communicating with his players during the game and even hearing the postgame questions asked by the press: "We went to every specialist we could find. No one could help him. He was lip-reading all the time, and with the face masks the players had on their helmets he couldn't read their lips. It was so sad."

When Modell fired Paul Brown, he hired Collier, Brown's longtime offensive coach, to run the team. When Collier retired, Modell once again replaced his head coach from within by hiring Collier's defensive coach Nick Skorich. Upon finishing his college career at the University of Cincinnati, Skorich was selected by the Steelers in the 1943 draft. After serving in the military during World War II, he played three seasons (from 1945 to 1947) with the Steelers at guard and linebacker. He was an assistant coach with the Steelers from 1954 to 1957 and was head coach with the Eagles from 1961 to 1963. He had joined the Browns as a defensive coach in 1964.

The backgrounds of Skorich and Noll, with the exception of Skorich's stint as a head coach, were remarkably similar. They played the same position in college and professional football and made their reputations as defensive coaches once their playing careers were over. Their challenges going into the 1971 season, however, were remarkably dissimilar.

Skorich's task was to take an underachieving veteran team and lead them to the top of the Central Division. He still had talented players on offense and a solid core of veterans on defense. The question for Browns fans was whether Skorich had the leadership skills to overcome the team's complacency.

Noll's task was to keep rebuilding the team through the draft. There were signs that the Steelers, with so many young talented players selected in the draft, were developing one of the best defenses in the NFL. But Noll's biggest concern was the erratic play of the young quarterback he hoped was going to be the leader of the team's offense and carry the team to their first championship in franchise history.

Terry Bradshaw's first season in the NFL was a disaster and had badly shaken his confidence. He completed only 38 percent of his passes with six touchdowns in 1970 as opposed to a stunning 24 interceptions. Noll, whose original three-year contact was extended for another three years, hoped that his awful first year hadn't ruined Bradshaw: "He can still be a great quarterback if he doesn't give up on himself."

Bradshaw's greatest adversary, beside his inexperience, was something he had never encountered before. He said, "It took me one half of my first professional game to get booed." Cleveland fans knew all about the viciousness of Steelers fans, but Bradshaw quickly became one of their favorite targets: "They would boo me on the street, they would boo me when I stopped at traffic lights. Booing Terry Bradshaw became a favorite sport in Pittsburgh. Hey, what do you guys want to do tonight? Let's go boo Terry Bradshaw." While Bradshaw would eventually turn the boos into cheers, the emotional scars would last even beyond his Hall of Fame career.

The Steelers opened the 1971 season with a frustrating 17–15 loss to the Chicago Bears when they gave away the game in the fourth quarter on Bradshaw fumbles, but they bounced back with wins over the Cincinnati Bengals and the San Diego Chargers. When they headed to Cleveland for their fourth game, they were facing a Browns team that had easily won their opener over the Houston Oilers and, after a thrilling victory of the defending Super Bowl championship Colts in Baltimore, lost at home to the Oakland Raiders. With both teams at 2–1, the game shaped up as an early test to see if the Steelers or the Browns were ready to contend for the division title.

After taking a 17–7 lead at halftime, Cleveland went on to a 27–17 win and took the lead in the Central Division. When the two teams met again, the Browns had lost their last two games to stand at 4–3, while the Steelers, at 3–4, were still only a game behind the Browns. With the Oilers and the Bengals fading, the game for Pittsburgh fans and Cleveland fans who had made the turnpike run was a rare event—a meaningful game between the rivals.

To the delight of Pittsburgh fans, the Steelers dominated the first half. Their defense shut down the Browns' offense, while the Steelers took a 16–0 halftime lead. The Browns managed a safety and a touchdown in the second half, but the Steelers went on to an easy 26–9 victory. Going into the last four games of the season, the Browns and the Steelers were both 5–5 and tied for the division lead.

At that point the veteran Browns team won four games in a row, while the young Steelers, not surprisingly, faded and lost three of their final four to finish at a 6–8. Winning their first Central Division title, the Browns met the defending NFL champion Colts, who made the playoffs as a wild card team. With Kent State's Don Nottingham (the last pick in the 1971 draft) scoring two first-half touchdowns, the Colts went on to a surprisingly easy 20–3 victory and ended another season of frustrated hope for Browns fans.

Until the 1972 season, the rivalry between the Steelers and the Browns was more emotional than competitive for their fans. The proximity and the working-class, shot-and-a-beer character of Pittsburgh and Cleveland made the Steelers-Browns games stand out, but the Browns had dominated the Steelers since they first met in 1950.

The Browns were in the class of pro football since they began playing in the AAFC in 1946, while the Steelers were one of pro football's weakest franchises since their entry into the NFL in 1933. In 39 years, the Steelers had only eight winning seasons, and one of those was in 1943 when they were the Steagles. The Browns had only two losing seasons in their 26-year history and had won championships in all four of their seasons in the AAFC and four more championships since they moved into the NFL.

The upcoming games in the 1972 season between the Browns and the Steelers, for the first time in their rivalry, looked to be not only competitive but decisive in determining the winner of the division. The defending

Central Division championship Browns had opened the season by making a successful transition at quarterback from Bill Nelsen, whose bad knees restricted him to a backup role, to Mike Phipps and were 6–3 going into their first meeting against the Steelers in Cleveland.

While they were coming off losing seasons in 1970 and 1971, the Steelers were on the rise thanks to a dominating defense and the improved play of Terry Bradshaw. However, the most important factor in their 7–2 start was the running of Franco Harris, Pittsburgh's No. 1 draft pick out of Penn State, who was drawing comparisons to former Browns running back Jim Brown.

With the Steelers poised to take control of the Central Division with a win over the Browns, more Pittsburgh fans than ever before made the drive to Cleveland to see their team all but clinch their first title. They were part of a crowd of over 83,000 fans that braved a cold, windy day to see one of the most exciting games ever played between the Browns and the Steelers, though it didn't start that way.

After a field goal put the Steelers ahead 3–0, the Browns took a commanding 20–3 lead before Bradshaw capped a long drive with a touchdown pass to cut the lead to 20–10 at halftime. In the second half, a field goal expanded the Browns' lead to 23–10, but a Steelers touchdown cut the lead to 23–17 going into the last quarter.

With time running out, Harris broke loose on a 75-yard touchdown run to give the Steelers a 24–23 lead, but Phipps drove the Browns down the field to set up an easy 27-yard field goal that Don Cockroft, to the groans of Cleveland fans, hooked to the left. After the game, Cockroft claimed, "I pulled up. Looked up too quickly." Fortunately for their fans, the Browns' defense held the Steelers on downs and got the ball back.

After two clutch passes by Phipps and a Steelers offside penalty moving the ball to the Pittsburgh 18-yard line, Browns kicker Don Cockroft, with 13 seconds left, kicked a 26-yard field goal to give the Browns a thrilling 26–24 victory and put them in a tie with the Steelers for the division lead. Cockroft, who kicked four field goals that day, said the kick "was the greatest thrill of my career." A despondent Bradshaw claimed, "We have nobody to blame but ourselves." Chuck Noll called the loss "a disaster."

The Steelers and the Browns won their games the following week and, with the teams tied at 8–3, faced a return match in Pittsburgh that could well decide the winner of the Central Division. After their earlier win against the Steelers, the Browns were confident that history was about to repeat itself. As pro football historian Ray Didinger noted, "The Browns had a history of winning the games they had to win; the Steelers had a history of losing the games they had to win and a few others beside."

In the days leading up to the game, Cleveland newspapers were filled with stories that belittled the Steelers as "overrated," singling out the team's defense. The clippings were placed on the Steelers' clubhouse bulletin board by Noll, who drew a red circle around the most inflammatory remarks and wrote, "READ THIS." He told reporters, "The game on Sunday is our season."

As for the Steelers, perhaps linebacker Charles Andrew "Andy" Russell, who was a rookie in the ill-fated 1963 season, best summed up the team's feelings going into the game: "We're at a point where we can right everything for all the bad years." He knew that "our crowd would be ready. They all know that it's the biggest game of the year. And it is my biggest game as a Steeler."

On the Sunday morning before the game, a column appeared in the *Pittsburgh Press* by longtime sportswriter Phil Musick. A Pittsburgh native, Musick wrote that even though he knew that a sportswriter shouldn't root for the home team, "today I'm going to root for justice. The Cleveland Browns have won 25 assorted championships, the pointed-headed Pittsburgh Steelers have won 25 less. If that blindfolded old broad on the scales is not a phony, the Steelers are going to trim the Browns today."

At Three Rivers Stadium, a record crowd of almost 51,00 began chanting and roaring in the minutes leading up to the game. There were also thousands of Pittsburgh fans who couldn't get tickets to the game and, cursing Browns fans who had tickets, had to drive beyond the 100-mile blackout to watch the game on television. They were so fired up for the game that they turned Ohio bars, like ones in Zanesville and Kent, into what was described as "insane asylums."

After the Browns received the opening kickoff, the Steelers' defense ran onto the field to a deafening chorus of "Dee-fense, Dee-fense." After the game, Jack Ham, in his second year with the Steelers and on his way to a Hall of Fame career, said he had never heard anything like it: "The fans had been wild before, but nothing like this. I said to myself, 'We can't let these people down. We just can't.'"

Once the defense took the field, they didn't let Steelers fans down. On Cleveland's first possession, Robert "Bo" Scott fumbled the ball after a hard hit from Andy Russell. The fumble set up a field goal, and, after the Browns drove down the field and missed a tying field goal, the Steelers' defense took over the game. The Steelers led only 10–0 at halftime on a Franco Harris 1-yard touchdown plunge, but defensive end Dwight White later told reporters, "The way we were playing defense, the Browns could have kept coming at us until next Thursday and they wouldn't have scored ten points."

When the Steelers took a 17–0 lead in the third quarter on another touchdown run by Harris, defensive tackle Mean Joe Greene said, "It wasn't a matter of 'how' but 'how much.'" "How much" quickly turned into a 30–0 rout as the Steelers scored another touchdown in the fourth quarter on an 87-yard touchdown pass from Terry Bradshaw to rookie tight end John McMakin and added two more field goals.

With the score mounting, Steelers fans, remembering Bill Nelsen's delight at being traded to the Browns, started chanting, "Put in Nelsen. Put in Nelsen." Recognizing that Pittsburgh fans had singled him out as the enemy, all that Nelsen could say was that "they wanted my blood." As for the Browns' starting quarterback Mike Phipps, by game's end he had been sacked four times, threw an interception to Jack Ham, and passed for an anemic 59 yards.

As the Steelers' score continue to rise, the *Pittsburgh Post-Gazette*'s Al Abrams observed that Browns fans who had made what Cleveland writer Hal Lebovitz had dubbed a "six-pack drive along the turnpike" look like "they were ready to surrender," but they had to endure one last indignity before heading back to Cleveland. In the final minutes, the Steelers, aware that Franco Harris needed 100 yards to tie Jim Brown's record of six consecutive games with at least 100 rushing yards, kept feeding him the ball. When Harris reached 102 yards, Noll took him out of the game to a standing ovation, led by Franco's Italian Army.

After the game, a jubilant Chuck Noll savored the victory over his former team and told reporters, "it was the biggest win for me and the team." Gracious in defeat, Nick Skorich, perhaps remembering his days with the Steelers, said, "They've always been enthusiastic here, but there was a little more emotion today. This was a fine thing for the city."

Steelers players had fun reminding Cleveland reporters of what they had been writing about the Steelers' defense all week, but center Ray Mansfield, a nine-year veteran, best summed up their feelings toward the Browns: "This is like you were a little kid, and the bigger kid was always beating you up. Then, suddenly, you were grown up and you beat up on him. Well, it looks like the Steelers have finally grown up."

During the Browns' loss in Pittsburgh, Mike Phipps had his poorest game of the season, but he bounced back to lead Cleveland to victories in their last two games against the Cincinnati Bengals and the New York Jets and to a wild card position in the playoffs. The Steelers lost Terry Bradshaw to a dislocated finger against the Houston Oilers in the Astrodome, but they won 9–3 on a dominating defensive performance by Mean Joe Greene. In their final game of the season in San Diego, with Bradshaw back, the Steelers dominated the San Diego Chargers, winning 24–2, and gave Pittsburgh its first football title in the Steelers' 40-year history. When the game ended, Chuck Noll was carried off the field on the shoulders of Jim Clack and Ray Mansfield.

For the conference playoffs, the Browns traveled to Miami to face a Dolphins team that had gone 14–0 that season. Despite giving away a touchdown on a blocked punt and Mike Phipps throwing five interceptions, the Browns took a 14–13 lead in the fourth quarter, but they lost 20–14 on a late touchdown run by Miami's Jim Kiick.

The jubilant Steelers hosted the Oakland Raiders, the team they had defeated in the opening game of the season. They led throughout the game, but a Ken Stabler touchdown scramble gave the Raiders a 7–6 late lead. With 32 seconds left in the game, Bradshaw threw a desperate pass from his own 40-yard line. When the football caromed off a collision between Jack Tatum and John "Frenchy" Fuqua, Franco Harris, who said he "was running downfield to give Bradshaw another receiver," caught the ball at shoe-top level and ran the remaining 50 yards into the end zone to give the Steelers a stunning 13–7 victory. Noll thought "it was a fantastic catch. . . . Good things happen to those who hustle."

The miraculous catch would become known in NFL history as the "Immaculate Reception." In Pittsburgh sports history, only Bill Mazeroski's home run in the 1960 World Series rivaled it. The only sad note was that Art Rooney, who thought the Steelers were going to lose, was headed to the locker room to console his players. When he walked off the elevator, a security guard shook his hand and shouted over the roaring crowd, "You won it! You won it!"

A week later, the Steelers faced the Miami Dolphins but fell short of another miracle finish when, after taking an early 7–0 lead and leading 10–7 in the third quarter, made critical mistakes and lost 21–17 to the still-undefeated Dolphins. After the game, Jack Ham said, "I think . . . we now understand what it was all about to win playoff games and to be in pressure situations and what it takes to be a championship football team." Chuck Noll added, "we simply made too many mistakes."

The loss was devastating for Pittsburgh fans, who, after the Oakland Raiders game, thought their Steelers were destiny's darlings, but they had the memories of a wonderful season to warm them through a cold Pittsburgh winter. After close victories over the Browns and the Steelers, the Dolphins turned out to be the darlings of 1972 when they went on to defeat the Washington Redskins in the Super Bowl to complete their historic season at 17–0. Had the Browns defeated the Dolphins the weekend of the Immaculate Reception, they would have played the Steelers for the right to represent the AFC in the Super Bowl.

Going into the 1973 season, Pittsburgh fans, after watching the best season in Steelers franchise history, had every reason to be hopeful. The young Steelers had talented players at key offensive positions, including a 1,000-yard rusher and a quarterback who, after a erratic start to his career, was beginning to show signs of maturity. They also had a dominant defense, led by Mean Joe Greene and "the Steel Curtain." Preseason predictions had the Steelers challenging the Miami Dolphins for NFL supremacy.

Browns fans also had reasons to feel optimistic. Under coach Nick Skorich, the Browns had made the playoffs the last two seasons as a division champion and a wild card entry and, in the 1972 playoffs, had nearly defeated the Super Bowl championship Dolphins. But that optimism was tempered by the tendency of Mike Phipps to throw interceptions in key games.

Scott Huler, who saw his first Browns games in the 1970s, hoped that Mike Phipps would return the Browns to the glory days of the 1950s and 1960s and save the city as well: "Those were dark days in Cleveland in the earl seventies. The Hough riots were part of our lives then; the Cuyahoga River catching fire was part of our lives then; Mayor Ralph Perk's hair catching fire and the plants closing and the jobs leaving and the city declining and nobody goddamn it doing anything about any of it. . . . and we wanted somebody to do something about it and goddamn it we wanted Phipps."

Both the Steelers and the Browns opened the 1973 season with victories before they met in Pittsburgh for their second game of the season. To the delight of their fans, the Steelers' defense, as it had in their last meeting in 1972, completely dominated the Browns, allowing only two field goals and intercepting three Phipps passes. The Steelers took a 16–3 lead at halftime and coasted to a 33–6 win. The Steelers extended their opening season winning streak to four games before losing to the Cincinnati Bengals on the road. After a win against the New York Jets, they defeated the Bengals in Pittsburgh, but the win was costly when Terry Bradshaw suffered a dislocated shoulder.

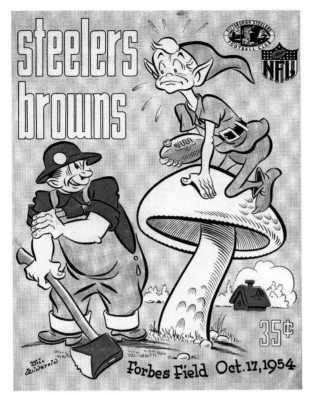

Program cover for the October 17, 1954, game in Pittsburgh won by the Steelers 55–27. It was the first time in eight meetings, since they first played in 1950, that the Steelers defeated the Browns. The "brownie elf" was an early representation of the Browns in advertisements and publicity. (Courtesy Detre Library and Archives, Heinz History Center)

Bill Reynolds, Back, Browns   **Doug Atkins,** End, Browns   **Ray Renfro,** Back, Browns

Left to right: Billy Reynolds, Doug Atkins, and Ray Renfro. Drafted by the Browns in 1953 out of the University of Pittsburgh, Reynolds was used mostly as a kick returner. He played his last season, in 1958, with the Steelers. Atkins played two seasons with the Browns before being traded to the Chicago Bears where he became a Hall of Fame defensive end. A Browns wide receiver from 1952 to 1963, Renfro was one of Otto Graham's favorite targets. (Courtesy Detre Library and Archives, Heinz History Center)

Lou Groza, Tackle, Browns   **Otto Graham,** Back, Browns   **Darrell Brewster,** End, Browns

Left to right: Lou Groza, Otto Graham, and Darrell Brewster. The legendary Groza, dubbed "the Toe," was an offensive tackle and placekicker whose career ranged from 1946 to 1967. Graham was the first and greatest quarterback in Browns history, and he was one of greatest in NFL history, leading the Browns to several championships, including a 1954 NFL title victory over the Detroit Lions. Brewster was a leading wide receiver with the Browns from 1953 to 1958. (Courtesy Detre Library and Archives, Heinz History Center)

Ray Mathews was a versatile Steelers player drafted out of Clemson. In his career from 1951 to 1959, he played halfback and wide receiver and returned kicks. He set a Steelers record by scoring four touchdowns in the Steelers' October 17, 1954, trouncing of the Browns. (Courtesy Detre Library and Archives, Heinz History Center)

PITTSBURGH STEELERS

CLEVELAND BROWNS
OCTOBER 22, 1961 · FORBES FIELD · FIFTY CENTS

Program cover featuring Browns nemesis Bobby Layne for the October 22, 1961, game in Pittsburgh, which was won by the Browns 30–28. The win was sparked by Jim Brown and Bobby Mitchell, who rushed for over 200 yards, and the passing of Milt Plum, who replaced former Steelers quarterback Len Dawson with the Browns trailing late in the game. (Courtesy Detre Library and Archives, Heinz History Center)

Before there was "Mean Joe" Greene, there was Ernie Stautner. Though he weighed only 230 pounds, he was one of the most ferocious defensive tackles in NFL history. Stautner once said that he played mean because, unless he intimidated bigger offensive linemen, he had no chance against them. Number 70 was the only number retired by the Steelers until they retired Greene's 75. (Courtesy Detre Library and Archives, Heinz History Center)

In 1959, after being cut by the New York Giants, Buddy Dial was picked up by the Steelers and soon became Bobby Layne's favorite receiver and a Pro Bowl selection. In the Steelers' 30–28 loss to the Browns on October 22, 1961, he set a Steelers record with 235 yards receiving. (Courtesy Detre Library and Archives, Heinz History Center)

After Buddy Parker brought Bobby Layne to the Steelers in a trade with the Detroit Lions, he also acquired Tom "the Bomb" Tracy (Layne's drinking buddy) from the Lions. Tracy was a versatile halfback, who also kicked extra points and field goals. He led the Steelers in rushing until Buddy Parker brought another former Lions player, John Henry Johnson, to the Steelers in 1960. (Courtesy Detre Library and Archives, Heinz History Center)

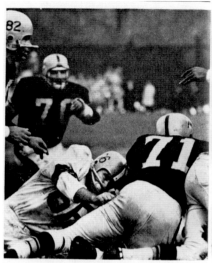

Steeler defense shown in gang tackling to stop the Browns' powerful Jimmy Brown in last year's game at Forbes Field.

After the Steelers drafted Purdue quarterback Len Dawson in 1953, the Browns, who needed a quarterback and wanted Dawson, had to settle for Syracuse running back Jim Brown. Dawson didn't work out for the Steelers and was eventually traded to the Browns. Jim Brown, however, went on to became the greatest running back in NFL history. Known for his strength as well as his speed, Brown often had to be gang-tackled to be stopped by opposing teams. (Courtesy Detre Library and Archives, Heinz History Center)

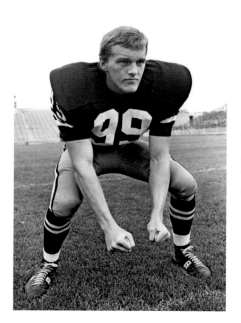

Despite being undersized, the Steelers selected Kent State University linebacker Jack Lambert in the second round of the 1974 NFL draft. He became a starter at middle linebacker in the first Steelers Super Bowl season and was named the 1974 NFL Defensive Rookie of the Year. A ferocious tackler, he became the Darth Vader of the Steelers-Browns rivalry after his late hits on Browns quarterback Brian Sipe. When criticized, he said maybe the NFL should put dresses on quarterbacks. (Courtesy of Kent State Athletics)

Myron Cope created the "Terrible Towel." The color commentator for the Steelers' radio broadcasts, he was told by his bosses to come up with a gimmick for a 1975 playoff game. A desperate Cope appealed to Steelers fans to bring towels to the game, and, if they waved them, terrible things would happen to the Steelers' opponents. This Terrible Towel, autographed by Cope, has the date of the Steelers' fourth Super Bowl victory on it. (Courtesy of the Senator John Heinz History Center, 2001.100.1)

No player stands out more as a representation of the Browns' frustration in recent years with the Steelers than Ben Roethlisberger. An Ohio native who played his college football at Miami of Ohio and was a certain No. 1 draft pick in 2004, he was passed over by the Browns before being selected by the Steelers. Since 2004, "Big Ben" has led the Steelers to three Super Bowls and two victories, while the Browns are still looking for their first Super Bowl and their first NFL title since 1964. (Courtesy of David Finoli)

One of the heroes of the Steelers' sixth Super Bowl victory, James Harrison was born in Akron, Ohio, and grew up a Cleveland Browns fan. Like Jack Lambert, he played his football at Kent State, and, like Lambert, he became one of the most hated players in the Steelers-Browns rivalry. He was a fierce outside linebacker who infuriated Browns fans with his spearing tactics. When several Browns players suffered concussions, Harrison said maybe the Browns should wear better helmets. (Courtesy of David Finoli)

When Pittsburgh fans, frustrated with Terry Bradshaw's uneven play, cheered as Bradshaw left the field holding his shoulder, it also became one of the ugliest moments in Steelers history. After the game, Mean Joe Greene, echoing Ernie Stautner's defense of Bobby Layne, told reporters, "That was vicious. They don't know what it was like to bust your ass out there and take all that, and then hear people cheering when a guy's been hurt."

With Terry Hanratty playing with nagging injuries and an untested Joe Gilliam as the only replacement, the Steelers managed to go 8–2 before heading to Cleveland for a critical game against the Browns. With a win over the Steelers, the Browns could close in on the Steelers' division lead. Complicating matters, however, were the Bengals, who had won their last two games after losing to the Steelers and were closing in on the Steelers and the Browns.

With Gilliam starting at quarterback, the Steelers took an early 7–0 lead, but the Browns bounced back with two touchdowns. Trailing 14–10 at halftime, the Steelers went ahead 16–14 going into the fourth quarter, but Greg Pruitt scored on a late touchdown run to give the Browns a badly needed 21–16 victory. When the game ended, Pruitt had his first encounter of the intensity of the Browns-Steelers rivalry as thousands of jubilant Cleveland fans surrounded him. Worried that he was about to be mobbed, he ran for the tunnel leading to the locker rooms, but in his haste and confusion he entered a hostile Steelers locker room by mistake. Fortunately for Pruitt, he managed to make it back to the Browns' locker room.

Eleven games into the 1973 season, only one game separated the Steelers, the Browns, and the Bengals. The Browns lost two and tied one in their last three games, including a critical loss to the Bengals, to finish out of contention. The Steelers won two of their last three games to finish at 10–4, but they had to settle for a wild card when they lost a tiebreaker to a Bengals team that won its last six games and also finished at 10–4.

In the playoffs, with a shaky Bradshaw back from his injury and throwing three interceptions, the Raiders easily defeated the Steelers 33–17 in Oakland, while the Dolphins, heading for their third Super Bowl in a row, handily won over the Bengals 34–16. The Central Division had placed two teams in the playoffs in each of the last two seasons, but a Central Division team had yet to advance to the Super Bowl.

In the 1974 season, the Steelers and the Browns experienced a complete reversal of fortune. The Browns, after so many winning and championship seasons, finished with their worst record in franchise history. The Steelers, after so many years as the laughingstock of the league and more than 40 years of frustration, finally finished at the top of the NFL.

That reversal, however, came close to never happening when a players strike placed the 1974 season in jeopardy. The National Football League Players Association, after reaching an impasse with team owners over a new contract, declared a strike on July 1, just before the beginning of training camp. Rookies had to cross a picket line to report to training camp on July 15, while veterans, especially those uncertain about their jobs, had to decide whether to honor the strike.

No team benefited more from the strike than the Pittsburgh Steelers. They had an outstanding 1974 draft, with their first four picks—Lynn Swann, Jack Lambert, John Stallworth, and Mike Webster—beginning careers that would take them to the Hall of Fame. They also had the advantage of having one of their quarterbacks in camp. Joe Gilliam, third string behind Bradshaw and Hanratty, decided to cross the picket line and had a clear advantage when the NFLPA ended the strike on August 11 without reaching a contract agreement. Gilliam played so well in training camp and exhibition games that Chuck Noll named him the starting quarterback over an unhappy and brooding Terry Bradshaw.

No team benefited less from the strike than the Cleveland Browns. They had traded away their top pick in the 1974 draft to the San Diego Chargers for linebacker Bob Babich and after selecting Billy Corbett, an offensive tackle from Johnson C. Smith University in the second round, they didn't have another pick until their fifth. They also had serious concerns about Mike Phipps, who had only nine touchdown passes in 1973 while throwing 17 interceptions, but they were reluctant to go into the season with backup Brian Sipe, who had been on the taxi squad the past two seasons. They were also concerned about the condition of their aging veterans, who had so little time to get ready for the season.

As feared, the Browns and Phipps got off to a terrible start. By the time the Browns headed to Pittsburgh for their sixth game of the season, they were 1–4 and had lost their last three games in row. The Steelers were off to a impressive start, with Gilliam making the cover of *Sports Illustrated* after a sensational debut in an opening game victory over the Baltimore Colts. They were 3–1–1 going into their first meeting with the Browns but had begun to have doubts about Gilliam, who was becoming inconsistent after his opening game heroics, and were beginning to turn to Bradshaw and Hanratty.

With Bradshaw and Hanratty struggling with injuries, Gilliam started against the Browns. Even though he played poorly, completing only five out of 13 passes for 81 yards that day, the Steelers, after taking a 14–0 lead, held on for a hard-fought 20–16 win. Phipps did run for a touchdown and threw a touchdown pass to rally the Browns, but the defeat left the Browns with their fourth loss in a row and a 1–5 record.

In their next game, played in Cleveland against the Denver Broncos, Nick Skorich, with his job on the line, pulled Phipps out the game when he threw a fourth-quarter interception and replaced him with Brian Sipe. With the Browns trailing 21–9, Sipes gave Cleveland fans a glimpse of things to come when he ran for two touchdowns to give the Browns a 23–21 upset victory.

After splitting their next two games to go 3–6, the Browns faced a Steelers team that had an impressive 6–2–1 record, even though Noll was still struggling with his quarterback situation. He decided to start Terry Hanratty against the Browns after Bradshaw had played poorly in a loss to the Bengals, while Skorich decided to stay with Sipe.

With Hanratty and Sipe having terrible games, the Steelers and the Browns played one of the sloppiest games in the history of their rivalry. After the game, the *Pittsburgh Press*'s Phil Musick wrote that "it was a game only a mother could've loved. Knute Rockne's mother." Noll described the game as, "Weird. But nice weird."

While Sipe was throwing three interceptions, the Browns also fumbled the ball away four times, including one that was returned by the Steelers for a touchdown. Hanratty did have a touchdown pass, but he also threw an interception that was returned by the Browns for a touchdown. The Steelers managed to eke out a 26–16 win, but even with their 7–2–1 record, they still hadn't found the quarterback capable of leading them to the Super Bowl.

After their dismal loss to the Steelers, the Browns lost three of their next four games. When the Browns lost their last game of the season to the Houston Oilers, they finished at 4–10, the worst record in franchise history. Going into the off-season, they had a serious problem at quarterback after Phipps and Sipe combined for just 10 touchdown passes (nine by Phipps) and 24 interceptions. They also had to find a new coach to replace Nick Skorich, who was fired by Art Modell.

After the shaky win over the Browns, Chuck Noll declared that Bradshaw would be the Steelers' starting quarterback for the rest of the season. He told reporters, "If we're going to the Super Bowl, it's going to be Bradshaw who takes us." The decision was arguably the most important of Noll's career. The

Steelers won three of their last four games and won the Central Division with a 10–3–1 record. With Bradshaw playing well, the Steelers easily defeated Buffalo 32–14 in the first round of the playoffs and traveled to Oakland for the AFC championship and a trip to the Super Bowl.

When Oakland defeated Miami in the first round of the playoffs and Raiders coach John Madden declared in a postgame interview that the two best teams in the NFL had just played, Chuck Noll was infuriated. Rarely given to locker room speeches, he told his team, "The best team in the NFL is sitting right here in this room." With the Steel Curtain, led by Mean Joe Greene, allowing the Raiders only 29 yards rushing, the Steelers, with the help of two interceptions, rallied in the last quarter from a 10–3 deficit to tie the game and defeat Oakland 24–10, on late touchdowns by Lynn Swann and Franco Harris.

In the Super Bowl, the Steel Curtain's defense held the Minnesota Vikings scoreless in the first half and provided the only points in the game with a safety. While Bradshaw was frustrated with the offense's failure to score, center Ray Mansfield told him, with the way the defense was playing, maybe 2 points was "all we'll need." The Vikings did score in the second half, their only points coming on a blocked punt, but the Steelers' offense, behind a record-breaking 158 rushing yards by Franco Harris (who was voted the Super Bowl MVP), controlled the ball on their way to a 16–6 victory over the Vikings. A Bradshaw touchdown pass clinched the victory.

With their disruptive defense and strong running attack, the Steelers, after so many same old years of losing, were NFL Champions. But it was Terry Bradshaw, after so much doubt and ridicule, who threw key touchdown passes against the Raiders and the Vikings to spark the Steelers to victory. As for perennial loser Art Rooney, when handed the Vince Lombardi Trophy by NFL commissioner Pete Rozelle, the Steelers' patriarch modestly said, "Thanks, Pete. They're a great bunch of fellas. I'm not a bit surprised."

A day after the Super Bowl, more than 120,000 delirious Steelers fans celebrated the Super Bowl victory in downtown Pittsburgh in below-freezing weather. Browns fans had little to warm them from another Cleveland winter of cold winds and lake-effect snow, though they did have a new coach with an excellent pedigree. For the third time since firing Paul Brown, Art Modell promoted an assistant coach to take over the head coaching job. This time he selected offensive line coach Alvis Forrest Gregg, one of the pillars of Vince Lombardi's Green Bay Packers offensive line during their championship seasons.

Gregg's major challenge going into the 1975 season was to develop a strong running game to support Mike Phipps, so that the Browns, like Lombardi's Packers, could control the tempo of the game and cut down on turnovers. Gregg's strategy worked out with the running game, but Phipps would continue to throw interceptions, the defense would fall apart, and the 1975 Browns would soon replace the 1974 Browns as the worst team in franchise history.

By the time the Browns faced the Steelers in Cleveland, they were 0–2 and had just been humiliated in a lopsided 42–10 loss to the Vikings. The Steelers, heavily favored to return to the Super Bowl, were coming off a frustrating loss to O. J. Simpson and the Buffalo Bills after winning their opener against archrival Oakland. Any hope by Browns fans that the Steelers were going to suffer a letdown quickly ended when the Steelers rolled to a 28–0 lead in the first half and coasted to a 42–6 win.

The low point of the game came when Mean Joe Greene, frustrated by the Browns holding him, kicked offensive lineman Bob McKay in the groin. The Browns retaliated with punches thrown at Greene, but before the brawl could get completely out of hand, the referees managed to take control. Browns defensive tackle Doug Dieken noted that "Joe Greene was fined $500 [for kicking McKay in the groin]. Deleone got fined like $100 [for punching Greene]. And Bob McKay got fined for getting kicked in the groin."

The easy win over the Browns launched the Steelers into a 10-game winning streak and the division title. The Browns' loss to the Steelers was their third in a row and sent them spinning into a 0–9 start to the season. The losing streak didn't end until they pulled off a shocking upset in Cleveland against Paul Brown's Cincinnati Bengals, who were 8–1 at the time and tied with the Steelers. Going into the game, Phipps had not thrown a touchdown pass in the season, but he threw two in the fourth quarter to lead the Browns to a desperately needed 35–23 win over the Bengals.

When the Steelers and the Browns met in Pittsburgh for their 12th game of the season, the Browns had a modest two-game winning streak after beating the New Orleans Saints, while the Steelers had won their last nine games in a row and would all but clinch the Central Division by beating the Browns. The Browns put a scare into the Steelers by taking a 17–10 halftime lead, but Terry Bradshaw brought the Steelers back with two third-quarter touchdown passes to Lynn Swann. With their defense intercepting three Phipps passes, the Steelers went on to a 31–17 victory.

After their loss to the Steelers, the Browns bounced back to beat the Chiefs but lost their last game to the Oilers to finish the season with a dismal 3–11 record, one game worse than their 4–10 record-breaking 1974 season. With the exception of Greg Pruitt's breakout season, there was little for Browns fans to cheer about, especially with the dismal performance of Mike Phipps, who had only four touchdown passes while throwing 19 interceptions.

After their win over the Browns, the Steelers wrapped up the division title by beating the New England Patriots. After handily defeating the Colts 28–10 in the first round of the playoffs, they faced the Raiders again for the AFC championship, this time at Three Rivers, in a bitterly fought game that was plagued by icy conditions, key player injuries, and 13 turnovers. The Steelers hung on for a 16–10 victory, earning their second consecutive trip to the Super Bowl. After the game, Chuck Noll told reporters, it was "a viciously played game . . . between two great football teams."

In his postgame remarks after the Steelers defeated the Vikings in the Super Bowl, sportscaster Curt Gowdy said that the Steelers "are a very young team. I would say that their best years are still ahead of them. A team that may have not reached its peak, and their future opponents are going to have some trouble." The Steelers had the opportunity to prove Gowdy a prophet when they defended their Super Bowl title against the Dallas Cowboys, regarded by many as "America's Team."

The Steelers struggled against the Cowboys and trailed 10–7 in the fourth quarter. After taking a 15–10 lead, Lynn Swann, who was knocked out of the Raiders game with a concussion, caught a touchdown pass—the last of three of the most remarkable catches in Super Bowl history—to lead the Steelers to a 21–17 Super Bowl victory over the Cowboys in a game that many regarded as the first Super Bowl to live up to its hype. After his brilliant performance, Swann, who had suffered a concussion against the Raiders and was doubtful going into the Cowboys game, became the first wide receiver in Super Bowl history to be named the game's MVP.

After winning two straight Super Bowls, the Steelers were confident that they were on the verge of a dynasty after so many decades as the Same Old Steelers, but injuries would present them with a major challenge. After a disastrous 3–11 season, the Browns brought back Blanton Collier, this time as quarterback coach. They also traded for the return of All-Pro wide receiver Paul Warfield in the hope of steadying the play of Mike Phipps, but it was an injury to Phipps that would change the team's direction.

Both the Steelers and the Browns suffered the loss of a key part of their offense in their first game of the 1976 season. In their opener, the Browns defeated the New York Jets but lost Phipps when he suffered a dislocated shoulder. The Steelers had to open on the road against the hated Raiders. Not only did they lose the game to a bitter rival, they suffered the loss of Lynn Swann to a concussion when George Atkinson delivered a forearm blow to the back of Swann's head. After the game, a furious Chuck Noll said that Atkinson was part of a "criminal element" in the NFL.

The Steelers and the Browns met in Pittsburgh for their second game of the season. With Brian Sipe at quarterback, the Browns took a 14–0 halftime lead, but Terry Bradshaw sparked the Steelers to a 31–14 win, their first on the season. When the Steelers and the Browns met three weeks later in Cleveland, both teams were struggling at 1–3. After two Super Bowl seasons, the Steelers were on the verge of playing themselves out of contention, while the Browns appeared to be spiraling toward another losing season.

Playing on a Cleveland Municipal Stadium field that had turned into a quagmire after overnight rains, the Browns lost Brian Sipe when he suffered a concussion late in the second quarter. Sipe's replacement was 27-year-old free agent rookie Dave Mays, whose only experience had been in the World Football League. After a Steelers mistake early in third quarter set up a Browns touchdown to give Cleveland a 12–10 lead, the game produced one of the most memorable and controversial plays in the history of the rivalry.

Early in the fourth quarter, when Browns defensive end Joe "Turkey" Jones sacked Bradshaw, the fourth in the game for Cleveland, he lifted the Steelers quarterback off his feet and drove him headfirst into the ground. Bradshaw, who suffered a concussion and neck injury on the play, had to be carried off the field on a stretcher to the roaring delight of Cleveland fans. It was the second time Bradshaw was cheered after being injured, though the first time Steelers fans did the cheering. With rookie Mike Kruczek replacing Bradshaw, the Steelers never recovered and lost to the Browns 18–16.

After the game, Noll wouldn't fault Jones, who claimed, "I wasn't trying to do it. I couldn't hear the whistle. I had to get him down and he's strong." Jack Lambert, however, wasn't buying Jones's explanation. He angrily told reporters, "You take somebody and smash them upside down on the ground as hard as you can. That's not trying to hurt somebody?" As far as Lambert was concerned, "It's not football anymore. It's a street fight." Lambert would remember the incident and, in seasons to come, seek out Brian Sipe to exact his measure of revenge. As for the fans' perspective, Scott Huler was at the game and noted, "That was the first game where I noticed the edge of violence in the stands. . . . The fans exuded a hair-trigger fierceness."

The game had a profound impact on both teams for the rest of the 1976 season. Sparked by their first win over the Steelers since 1973, the Browns, with Sipe returning from his concussion, won seven of their next eight games—before losing to the Chiefs in their season finale and finishing with a 9–5 record, a six-game improvement over 1975. With Brian Sipe throwing 17 touchdown passes and Pro Bowl selection Greg Pruitt rushing for 1,000 yards, the Browns finished just one game out of the Central Division title and would have captured the division if they had not lost two games to the 10–4 Bengals.

Upset with the loss of Bradshaw on what they regarded as a dirty play, the Steelers faced moving ahead with rookie Mike Kruczek at quarterback and a dismal a 1–4 start to the season. Noll declared, "We've had our share of good luck over the last few years, and now it's going the other way." His solution was simple: "Terry is hurt. We're putting Kruczek in. We're not throwing the ball. We might have to win 2–0. Whatever it takes."

The plan worked to perfection. By the time Bradshaw returned, the Steelers had won four in a row and three by shutouts. They stretched their winning streak to nine in a row by winning their last four games and finished the regular season at 10–4, good enough for their fifth consecutive trip to the playoffs. They romped over the Baltimore Colts, 40–14, but in a year of injuries, both Franco Harris and Robert "Rocky" Bleier were hurt in the game. Without a running attack, the Steelers struggled offensively in the conference championship game against the Raiders in Oakland. After their 24–7 loss to the Raiders ended their bid to win three consecutive Super Bowls, all Noll could say was, "We played without 50% of our offense. I'm sorry we didn't have more weapons."

The 1977 season was one the most frustrating in the history of the Browns and the Steelers. After nearly making the playoffs in 1976, the Browns— under Forrest Gregg's conservative, disciplined coaching—seemed poised to challenge the Bengals and the Steelers for the Central Division title. With Brian Sipe settling in at quarterback after Mike Phipps (who never lived up to Cleveland fans' great expectations) was traded to the Bears and Greg

Pruitt (with his back-to-back 1,000-yard seasons) established as one of the NFL's premier running backs, Browns fans fully expected the Browns to return to the playoffs after a four-year absence, the longest in team history.

After their injury-plagued season and disappointing loss to the Raiders in the playoffs, the Steelers were a team in turmoil going into training camp. Their defense still had the Steel Curtain intact but lost All-Pro linebacker Andy Russell to retirement. Another All-Pro linebacker, Jack Lambert, was holding out; and their outstanding defensive back, Mel Blount, was refusing to report because of negative comments about him made by Chuck Noll. These comments were made during Noll's appearance in court after George Atkinson filed a law suit against Noll for accusing Atkinson of being a part of a criminal element in the NFL.

When the Steelers and the Browns met in Cleveland for their third game of the season, the Browns were off to an impressive 2–0 start, including a 13–3 opening win against the Bengals, and were in position to take early control of the Central Division. The Steelers were at 1–1 after an easy opening victory against the San Francisco 49ers and a bitter home loss to their nemesis, the Super Bowl championship Oakland Raiders.

Cleveland fans expected their Browns to challenge the Steelers, and they were not disappointed for most of the first half when the Browns scored twice to go ahead, 14–7. The Steelers, however, tied the game before halftime and, in the second half, took the lead on Terry Bradshaw's third touchdown pass. The Steelers' defense, to the disappointment of Cleveland fans, intercepted three Sipe passes and ended up shutting out the Browns in the second half in a 28–14 win.

The Browns lost the following week to the Raiders but won their next three games before losing to the Bengals. With a 5–3 record, they were still very much in contention when they traveled to Pittsburgh for their second meeting with the Steelers. Since their first meeting with the Browns, the Steelers had lost three of their last five games and, at 4–4, trailed the Browns by one game. The game shaped up as one of the most important in the rivalry since 1972 and would determine the Central Division championship.

To the delight of Steelers fans and to the dismay of the Cleveland fans who had traveled to Pittsburgh by car, bus, and train, the Steelers dominated the Browns in the first half. After a field goal gave the Browns an early 3–0 lead, Bradshaw threw touchdown passes to Swann and Stallworth between Bleier and Harris touchdown runs to put the Steelers ahead 28–3 at halftime. Worse yet for the Browns, Sipe suffered a shoulder injury and was knocked out of the game. The Browns thrilled their fans by mounting a frenzied comeback in the second half on three Dave Mays touchdown passes but lost the game 35–31. The biggest loss for the Browns, however, came after the game when Cleveland announced that Brian Sipe was lost for the rest of the season.

The following week, the Browns managed a win over the New York Giants to go 6–4 but lost their next two games, including a 9–0 shutout to the Los Angeles Rams, to drop out of contention. With two games left in the season, Gregg replaced Mays with third-string quarterback Terry Luck, but the Browns lost their third game in a row to the Houston Oilers. When a frustrated Gregg resigned going into the Browns' last game of the season, he was replaced by defensive line coach Richard "Dick" Modzelewski, who watched Luck throw four interceptions against the Seattle Seahawks in the Browns' fourth loss in a row and a season-ending 6–8 record.

The Steelers won their next three games in a row and, after a loss to the Cincinnati Bengals, defeated the San Diego Chargers 10–9. When the Bengals—who were tied with the Steelers at 9–4 and held the tiebreaker—were upset by the Oilers, the Steelers clinched the division title and headed for the playoffs for the sixth straight year. In their playoff game at Denver, they dominated the first half, but turnovers helped the Broncos to a 34–21 victory. For Tony Dungy, a rookie on the Steelers in 1977, the lost was puzzling: "We had all that great talent, but there were lots of problems. Players unhappy over money mostly. Teams we were better than simply beat us."

The first order of business for the Browns in the off-season was the hiring of a new head coach for 1978. Ever since owner Art Modell fired Paul Brown, he had promoted an assistant coach from within the organization to head the Browns. This time he went outside the Browns family and hired Sam Rutigliano, receivers coach for the New Orleans Saints. In response to the "Sam who?" reaction of Cleveland fans and the press, Modell said, "I needed a fresh perspective, a fresh slant, new ideas, not the same assistant coaches, not the same old way of doing business."

Modell may well have had another reason for hiring Rutigliano, who had a reputation as an innovator in the passing game. Going into the 1977 season, the NFL's Competition Committee, under the influence of Dolphins coach Don Shula, made it more difficult for defensive backs to cover receivers by restricting their physical contact to 5 yards past the line of scrimmage. The change was aimed at the Steelers and the physical play of their defensive backs, especially Mel Blount. With the "Blount Rule" in place, Modell wanted a coach who could transform the Browns' offense into a wide-open, dynamic threat.

In Pittsburgh, Steelers fans and the press wondered if age had finally caught up to the Steelers after their run of championship seasons. The defense, led by the Steel Curtain, had given up 324 points, an increase from the 138 points in 1976. Even with Franco Harris and Rocky Bleier combining for over 1,700 yards and Terry Bradshaw throwing 17 touchdown passes, the offense had turned the ball over in key situations. After the Steelers lost to the Broncos in the playoffs, the *Pittsburgh Post-Gazette*'s Vito Stellino wrote, "They rang down the Steel Curtain on the end of an era this weekend."

Ringing down the curtain on the Steelers became premature when Chuck Noll, in a decision similar to that made by the Browns, opened up his offense. Instead of relying on his defense and running game, Noll gambled that Bradshaw was ready, especially under the Blount Rule, to take control of the team. The gamble paid off when Bradshaw threw for two touchdowns in each of the Steelers' first three games and got the Steelers off to a 3–0 start before hosting a Browns team that had also won its first three games under a new head coach, including an overtime win against the Bengals.

While the game was suppose to be a shoot-out between Bradshaw and Sipe, the only points scored in regulation time were field goals. With the score tied at 9–9, a Tony Dungy interception of a last-second Sipe Hail Mary pass sent the game into overtime, the first played between the two teams in the history of the rivalry. In one of the most stunning plays in the rivalry, Bradshaw, on a flea-flicker, threw a 37-yard touchdown pass to wide-open tight end Bennie Cunningham to give the Steelers a 15–9 victory.

Buoyed by the victory, the Steelers won their next two games to go 6–0 as they headed to Cleveland for their second game of the season against the Browns. After their defeat in Pittsburgh, the Browns lost to the Oilers but bounced back to beat Rutigliano's old team, the Saints. A win against the Steelers would give the Browns a 5–2 record and move them only a game behind the streaking Steelers.

As they had in Pittsburgh, the Browns made a game of it, this time with help from "street fighter" Jack Lambert, who delivered a late hit on Sipe near the Cleveland sideline and was ejected—to the roaring delight of Cleveland fans—after arguing with the referees, who had penalized him for a personal foul. The Browns took the lead in the second quarter but trailed 13–7 at halftime. In the third quarter, the Steelers, even without Lambert, took control of the game on their way to an easy 34–14 win. Though he was summoned to Pete Rozelle's office, Lambert, remembering Cleveland's late hits on Bradshaw, remained unrepentant and, a week later, told Howard Cosell on *Monday Night Football* that it might be a good idea to "put dresses on quarterbacks" to protect them.

After the Steelers defeated them, the Browns lost three of their next four games and dropped under .500 at 5–6. However, they rallied and won three of their next four games, including an overtime win against the Jets, their third overtime game of the season, to improve to 8–7. With a chance to finish over .500, the Browns disappointed their fans when they were trounced 48–16 by the Bengals. At 8–8, they finished with the same number of losses as they had in 1977, but they had two more wins (in an expanded 16-game schedule) and avoided a losing season.

After their win over the Browns extended their undefeated record to 7–0, the Steelers lost to the Oilers and their sensational rookie, Earl Campbell, but recovered and went on to win six of their last seven games to end the season at 14–2, their best record in their NFL history. Bradshaw made Noll's decision to turn the offense over to him look great when he passed for 28 touchdowns and was named the NFL's MVP.

With Bradshaw throwing touchdown passes to Swann and Stallworth, they easily defeated the Broncos 33–10 in the first round of the playoffs. A week later, in a remarkable performance on a field coated by freezing rain, Bradshaw threw touchdown passes to Swann and Stallworth in a lopsided 34–5 victory over the Oilers. After the game, Jack Ham said that "weather is a state of mind. . . . Nothing bothers this team." The win set up a Super Bowl rematch of the Steelers and the Cowboys a year after reporters sounded the death knell for the Steelers.

One thing that always bothered Chuck Noll was the claim that the Dallas Cowboys were America's team. Adding to the irritation was Thomas "Hollywood" Henderson's claim that Bradshaw was so dumb, he "couldn't spell cat if you spotted him the C and the A." Noll's response was that "empty barrels make the most noise." After a shaky start, Bradshaw played brilliantly and had the game of his career, capping off his MVP season with four touchdown passes in a thrilling 35–31 win over the Cowboys. The victory gave the Steelers a record-breaking third Super Bowl championship and the claim, with their huge following and their Terrible Towels, of being America's team.

When Art Modell hired Sam Rutigliano, he made it clear that he wanted the Browns to bring more entertainment and excitement to Cleveland fans. While the Browns, at 8–8, finished the 1978 season behind the Steelers and the Oilers in the Central Division, they certainly provided plenty of thrills on offense.

Going into the 1978 season, Rutigliano had named Brian Sipe his starting quarterback and told him, "We are going to throw the ball and throw it on first down and from anywhere on the field." Sipe responded by having the best season of his career with 21 touchdown passes and sparked the offense to a 324-point performance. A pleased Modell extended Rutigliano's contract for three more years.

After all the obituaries declaring the demise of the Steelers' dynasty, they went on to their best season in history, going 14–2, dominating their opponents in the AFC playoff and conference championship games, and becoming the first team to win three Super Bowls. After throwing only five touchdown passes in his 1970 rookie season, Bradshaw threw for 28 touchdowns in his 1978 MVP season and was clearly the team's leader on the field. As for the 1979 season and the possibility of a fourth Super Bowl championship, Chuck Noll told reporters in his Super Bowl postgame interview, "I said one thing to my players after the game, and I sincerely believe it. I don't think we've peaked yet."

While the Steelers fell short of their opening seven-game winning streak in 1978, they began the 1979 season with four straight wins, then lost to the Philadelphia Eagles before playing their first game of the season against the Browns in Cleveland. The Browns also started the 1979 season with a four-game winning streak, including an impressive 26–7 win over the Dallas Cowboys on Monday night before losing the following week to the Houston Oilers. After the Browns defeated the Cowboys, Cleveland sportswriter Hal Lebovitz wrote, "There was some doubt in this corner about whether they could play with the big boys. There is no doubt any longer."

The biggest of the big boys and a source of growing frustration and animosity for Cleveland fans played in Pittsburgh. Jonathan Knight in *Kardiac Kids* noted that several Steelers fans "planning on attending the game stayed at a Sheraton Inn that night. When they woke up that Saturday morning, they discovered all the cars in the parking lot with Pennsylvania license plates had their tires slashed."

With both teams at 4–1, the Browns had an opportunity to prove to their fans that they could play with the big boys, but Pittsburgh quickly proved, to the dismay of Cleveland fans, that the Steelers were still the dominant team by scoring four touchdowns, two on Bradshaw passes to take a 27–0 lead. Sipe rallied the Browns to cut the Steelers' lead at halftime to 30–14, but Pittsburgh scored three more touchdowns in the second half to go on to a 51–35 win despite Sipe's four touchdown passes. The Steelers' rushing offense, with Harris scoring on a 71-yard run and Rocky Bleier on a 70-yard run, completely dominated the Browns' defense. While excited by the Browns' offense, Cleveland fans came out of the game stunned at the poor performance by their defense.

The Browns lost their next game against the Washington Redskins but bounced back to go 8–4 as they headed to Pittsburgh for another showdown with the Steelers, who had won four of their six games since beating the Browns and, at 9–3, had a one-game lead over the Browns. To defeat the Steelers, the Browns would have to win at Three Rivers, something the team hadn't done since the stadium opened in 1970.

The second meeting between the Browns and the Steelers turned into another shoot-out. The Browns jumped out in front, 20–6, on two Sipe touchdown passes and led 20–13 at halftime. A third Sipe touchdown pass gave the Browns a 27–13 lead going into the fourth quarter, but the Steelers, sparked by two Harris touchdown runs, tied the score at 30–30 and sent the game into overtime. As they had in Pittsburgh a year earlier, the Steelers won the game in overtime, 33–30, this time on a Matt Bahr 37-yard field goal with only nine seconds left on the clock.

After seeing their Browns win so many close games since Rutigliano became head coach, Cleveland fans were bitter at yet another lost opportunity to beat the Steelers, especially in Pittsburgh. Their Browns had won every overtime game in team history except for their two overtime losses to Pittsburgh. Cleveland did win the next game against the Oilers, but they lost their last two games to the Raiders and Bengals. The loss to the Bengals cost them any chance to make the playoffs. They finished the season at 9–7, three games behind the Steelers who, at 12–4, finished a game ahead of the Oilers.

As disappointed as Browns fans were at the way the 1979 season ended, they had to be excited by the team's performance on offense. Brian Sipe threw 28 touchdown passes, including eight against the Steelers, and broke the Browns' single-season record with 3,793 passing yardage. Wide receivers Reggie Rucker, Dave Logan, and Ozzie Newsome each had an outstanding year, and Mike Pruitt rushed for 1,294 yards. Topping the season off was the selection of Sam Rutigliano as the NFL's Coach of the Year.

The only team that appeared to be standing in the Browns' way to the Super Bowl played its football in Pittsburgh. After the Browns dominated the Steelers for two decades, they managed only five wins in their twenty meetings in the 1970s. Especially galling for Browns fans, who made the annual trip down the turnpike, was the failure of the Browns to win a single game at Three Rivers Stadium.

The Steelers ended the 1970s by proving their were the team of the decade. Led by Bradshaw's passing and Swann's and Stallworth's touchdown catches, they easily defeated the Miami Dolphins 34–14 in the first round of the playoffs and, in an AFC title rematch, bested the Houston Oilers 27–13. Heavy favorites to win the Super Bowl against the Los Angeles Rams, they struggled and trailed 19–17 in the fourth quarter, but two brilliant pass plays from Bradshaw to Stallworth and a key Jack Lambert interception gave the Steelers a 31–19 win and their fourth Super Bowl win.

When things were going badly for the Steelers, an Irish priest and friend of the family told Art Rooney that when his Steelers finally had the luck of the Irish it would last for seven years. By the end of the 1970s, Rooney's Same Old Steelers were now a dynasty. Heading into the 1980s after his Steelers had made the playoffs eight straight years and had won four Super Bowls, the only question was how much longer Rooney's luck of the Irish would last.

CHAPTER SIX

The 1980s

Heartbreaking Losses and the Death of the Chief

At the Browns' training camp before the start of the 1985 season, All-Pro defensive cornerback Hanford Dixon began barking at his teammates and calling them "dawgs" when they made a great defensive play. He saw the defense's pursuit of the quarterback as a cat-and-dog game. His teammates, including his "corner brother" and All-Pro Frank Minnifield, picked up on the idea, while fans attending the training joined in on the barking.

When the Browns played their first home preseason game, Hanford and Minnifield hung a "Dawg Pound" sign at the bleacher section in the east end zone. In doing so, they were recognizing that bleacher fans, usually working-class folks seated in Cleveland Municipal Stadium's cheapest seats, were the most devoted and by far the loudest followers of the Browns. Eventually wearing "dawg" masks and other costumes, they would also prove to be the most notorious.

The late John "Big Dawg" Thompson, the largest member of the Dawg Pound in girth and reputation, was the first to don a costume. A few years earlier, he'd started wearing a papier-mâché elfish brownie mask, but all that changed when fans began barking. He remembered drinking all day Saturday at a local bar with his buddies before heading to a Browns game. When he left the bar, he spotted a nearby costume shop and went in. Spotting a dusty, ugly dog mask on one of the shelves on sale for $12, Thompson "threw 10 dollars on the counter and said it's mine." Over the objections of his wife and friends, he started wearing the mask at games—and the rest is Browns history.

When opponents drove down the field and threatened to score at the Dawg Pound end of the field, they were pelted with Milk-Bone dog biscuits and sometimes worse. The Dawg Pound even influenced the outcome of a 1989 game against the Denver Broncos when their rowdy behavior forced referees to move the teams to the other end of the field. And their reputation spread. When Cincinnati fans pelted the field with objects after a referee's questionable call, Cincinnati Bengals coach Sam Wyche took a microphone and told them, "You don't live in Cleveland. You live in Cincinnati." The Steelers may have had their fans waving Terrible Towels, but the Browns now had a ferocious Dawg Pound waiting to intimidate teams that dare invade their end of the field.

In the two seasons since Sam Rutigliano became Cleveland's head coach in 1978 and named Brian Sipe his starting quarterback, the Browns won so many close games that they were dubbed the "Kardiac Kids." Going into the 1980s, the Kardiac Kids, with their explosive offense, looked poised to challenge the dominance of the Pittsburgh Steelers. An optimistic Art Modell declared, "the offensive team could be the best we've ever had, better than last year, and even better than the Jim Brown years."

A more cautious Rutigliano expressed concern about his defense, but Cleveland fans shared Modell's excitement. Before the season even started, the October 26 Steelers game at Municipal Stadium, with a little help from Steelers fans, was sold out. Rutigliano was well aware that the road to the Super Bowl went though Pittsburgh and understood the intense rivalry between the two cities: "Pittsburgh and Cleveland are almost clones. From an ethnic, from a historical, and from a traditional standpoint—with the tremendous diversity and the people who followed those teams for years—they're very, very much alike."

After the Steelers made their own history by winning their fourth Super Bowl, a relieved and relaxed Terry Bradshaw faced a flood of reporters. The 1979 season was one of Bradshaw's most difficult physically. He had played through several injuries and, in a game against the St. Louis Cardinals, had been carried off the field on a stretcher, only to return in the second half to lead the Steelers to a critical victory. When asked if the Steelers could win a fifth Super Bowl ring, what Mean Joe Greene would call "one for the thumb," Bradshaw admitted, "I honestly don't know. I'm drained. To repeat next year is going to be very difficult, the most difficult thing we've ever done."

When Chuck Noll was asked by reporters, after the Super Bowl victory, if this was the Steelers' best team, he responded, "I don't think I have to say this is the best team we've ever had. I think the facts speak for themselves." The next morning, before leaving Pasadena, he told his wife, Marianne, "Get ready. We're old and we're tired. The drafts haven't been very good. We've got some tough years ahead."

The problem for the city of Pittsburgh was that it had already faced tough years. The Steelers' dynasty had been a source of pride during a devastating economic decline that became known as the Rust Belt depression. Beginning in the 1970s and extending into the 1980s, as reported in Laurie Graham's acclaimed *Singing the City: The Bonds of Home in an Industrial Landscape,* Pittsburgh's steel industry eliminated 90 percent of its workforce. More than 30,000 workers at U.S. Steel lost their jobs, while other related industries, like Westinghouse Electric, closed down. Fathers who had taken their sons to Steelers games in the 1970s were moving their families to other cities in search of work by the 1980s. An estimated 176,000 people left Pittsburgh, including 14 percent of its young people.

Cleveland had gone through similar problems during the 1970s, but, unfortunately for Browns fans, their football team offered little in the way of pride as the city struggled through its own economic depression and population loss. A 1975 study ranked Cleveland second among American cities with the most serious economic and social problems in the country. So many left Cleveland in the 1970s that it dropped out of the top 15 most populated cities. When the polluted Cuyahoga River caught fire, Cleveland was mockingly referred to as "the Mistake on the Lake."

Steelers fans took heart when Pittsburgh opened the 1980 season with a victory over the Houston Oilers, the team they had defeated in the AFC championship game the last two years, and followed that with a close win over the Baltimore Colts. Fans were shocked when the Steelers' defense gave up 17 points in the fourth quarter in a 30–28 upset loss to the Bengals, but they were relieved when the Steelers rolled over the Chicago Bears 38–3 and defeated the Minnesota Vikings on the road to go 4–1 on the season.

That relief lasted only until the following week when the Bengals won their first game ever at Three Rivers Stadium and swept the Steelers in a 17–16 heartbreaker for Steelers fans. Matters got even worse when the Steelers dropped to 4–3 after their defense was riddled by quarterback Jim

Plunkett in a 45–34 loss to the Oakland Raiders on *Monday Night Football*. As they headed to Cleveland, the Steelers, plagued by injuries and inconsistency, were in a three-way tie with the Browns and the Oilers and only a game ahead of the 3–4 Bengals.

Any hope that the Browns would challenge the Steelers' dominance seemed dashed when Cleveland opened the season with a road loss to the New England Patriots. The mood in Cleveland darkened even more when they lost to the Oilers on *Monday Night Football* in front of more than 80,000 frustrated and unhappy fans. At 0–2, the Browns were already two games behind the undefeated Steelers. The 1980s were beginning to feel a lot like the 1970s.

The Browns, however, finally started to play like contenders in their next two games. They defeated the Kansas City Chiefs for their first win of the season and evened their record at 2–2 with a win over the Tampa Bay Bucs. After a disappointing close loss to the Denver Broncos, the Browns bounced back with a victory over the Seattle Seahawks to even their record at 3–3. A week later, they defeated the Green Bay Packers 26–21 on a Sipe touchdown pass with 13 seconds left in the game. After the game, the Browns' Dave Logan told the press, "If we had lost this one, it would have made it hard to get up for Pittsburgh next week, but that won't be the case now."

An estimated 15,000 Steelers fans headed to Cleveland by bus, train, and automobile. Author Jonathan Knight noted that "about a thousand" would be coming via a "City of Championship" promotional package offered by a Pittsburgh radio station: "For $68.00 Steelers fans got a ticket to the game as well as a round trip seat on a steam train owned by the B&O Historical group."

Those headed to Cleveland were used to cheering on a Steelers victory, but they had good reason for feeling apprehensive on this trip. The Steelers had won their last seven games against the Browns, but Pittsburgh, coming into a contest that would determine the division lead, was decimated by injuries After he bruised his thumb against the Raiders, Terry Bradshaw was out for the Cleveland game along with Franco Harris, Lynn Swann, and John Stallworth. The Steelers were also banged up on defense, where they biggest loss was All-Pro linebacker and Sipe nemesis Jack Lambert.

Pittsburgh fans would find little sympathy in Cleveland, where, after so many losses in the 1970s, Browns fans' hatred of the Steelers had reached a new level of intensity. Browns offensive tackle Cody Risien remembered fans telling him, "'We don't care if you win another game all year.' That was their mentality. They hated the Steelers."

Browns offensive guard Joe DeLamielleure said that "every team has its rival, but the difference here was that there were more fights in the stands than on the field." Defensive back Thom Darden agreed: "When you have people who share similar passions such as drinking beer and being crazy and you put that in a football stadium, it's combustible. I always said that I was glad I was playing because I wouldn't want to be in the stands."

Anticipating the worst, the Cleveland police were on high alert; Lt. William Stilnack claimed, "All the drunks from Cleveland and Pittsburgh are here, but our drunks at least made it off the bus." When the game started and Pittsburgh and Cleveland fans weren't throwing insults and objects at each other, they saw Steelers backup quarterback Cliff Stoudt lead his team to a surprising 13–7 halftime lead. In the third quarter, the Steelers increased their lead to 26–14. Steelers placekicker Matt Bahr's extra-point try had hit the goalpost and gone wide, but it didn't seem to matter going into the fourth quarter.

Stoudt, who had outplayed Browns veteran Brian Sipe to this point in the game, began to struggle and opened the door for the Browns. Sipe, returning to the game after his arm went numb when he was sacked by the Steelers, threw a touchdown pass to cut the Steelers' lead to 26–20, but Don Cockroft matched Bahr's gaffe by missing the extra point. With 5:38 left in the game, Sipe tied the game with another touchdown pass. When Cockroft, who had missed an earlier try, kicked the extra point, the Browns took a 27–26 lead. Stoudt tried to rally the Steelers, but he threw an interception with 2 minutes left that clinched the game for the Browns.

After the game, Browns center Tom Deleone, blissfully ignorant of the Browns' domination of the Steelers in the 1950s and 1960s, declared, "Cleveland fans have been taking it for years. Now they can start giving it back." The loss to the Browns was bitter for Steelers fans, especially those who had traveled to Cleveland for the game, but their larger concern was a defeat that put Pittsburgh at 4–4 halfway through the season and dropped them into third place, a game behind the 5–3 Browns and Oilers.

With Terry Bradshaw, Franco Harris, and Lynn Swann returning from injuries, the Steelers recovered with close wins over the Bucs and the Packers. The victories helped them stay close to the Browns going into their rematch at Three Rivers Stadium. A Steelers win would put the them into a tie with the Browns at 7–4 and no worse than a game behind the Oilers, who stood at 7–3 going into their game with the Bears. A Browns win would be their first ever at Three Rivers and break a 10-year jinx. It would also all but end the Steelers' eight-year streak of postseason appearances, including four Super Bowls.

Those Browns fans making the trip to Pittsburgh by car found a roll of toilet paper attached to a Pennsylvania Turnpike tollbooth with a sign that read. "Cleveland Browns Crying Towels Here." While around 15,000 Steelers fans attended the game in Cleveland's spacious 83,000-seat Municipal Stadium, only several hundred Browns fans could find tickets for Three Rivers, with its 25,000 fewer seats. Those who had a ticket and found their way into Three Rivers, buoyed by the Browns' victory over the Steelers in Cleveland, were confident that they didn't need the crying towels and were about to witness the end of the Three Rivers jinx.

The optimism was also evident in the Browns' head coach and players as they headed to Pittsburgh. Rutigliano told the press, "The interesting thing about this game is we are in a position now where we are going in not with the hope of winning or the hope of playing well, but with the confidence knowing we have beaten them before and that we played against them and can do it again." Echoing his coach, Ozzie Newsome said, "This week, it's what the Steelers have to do to beat the Browns—for the first time since I've been here. We've always tried to find a way offensively to beat them. This week they've got to find a way to beat us."

But the jinx looked like it was still at work when Bradshaw capped a long Steelers drive with a touchdown pass to give the Steelers a 7–0 lead at the beginning of the second quarter. The Browns scored two touchdowns in the first half on Sipe passes, but they held only a 13–7 lead when Cockroft missed an extra point. With both defenses playing well and the offenses committing critical mistakes and turnovers, that lead held up until the closing minutes of the game.

With 1:51 left to play, the Browns, backed up at their own 5-yard line on fourth down, decided to have their punter take a safety rather than risk a blocked kick. The Steelers, taking a page from the Kardiac Kids, took over at their own 46-yard line and drove down the field. With 13 seconds left in the game and the Steelers on the Browns' 3-yard line, Bradshaw rolled left and hit Swann with a touchdown pass to give the Steelers a dramatic 16–13 victory.

After the dramatic win over the Browns, Bradshaw told reporters, "We've got a chance now, but we have to win every game." However, age, injuries, and retirements proved too much to overcome. The Steelers lost three of their last five games, including a dismal 6–0 loss in Houston to the Oilers in which Bradshaw threw three interceptions and Harris fumbled the ball away twice. They finished the season with a 9–7 record and, for the first time since 1972, finished out of the playoffs.

The Browns' loss to the Steelers ended their six-game winning streak and knocked them out of a first-place tie with the Oilers, who defeated the Chicago Bears that Sunday. A week later, the Browns bounced back by easily defeating the Bengals and moved back into a tie for the division lead when the Oilers were upset by the New York Jets. The following Sunday, they took over first place when they defeated the Oilers 17–14 in Houston on a game-saving interception by Clarence Scott. They held on to the division lead with a close victory over the Jets but fell back into a tie with the Oilers when the Vikings, stealing a page from the Kardiac Kids' script, defeated Cleveland 28–23 on a 46-yard Hail Mary pass with seconds left in the game.

Needing a win in their final game of the season against the Bengals in Cincinnati to make the playoffs, the Browns—after trailing the Bengals 10–0 and 17–10—took a 24–17 lead only to see the Bengals tie the game going into the final quarter of the regular season. With only 1:25 left, the Browns took the lead on a 22-yard Cockroft field goal and held off a frantic Bengals drive to win the game 27–24 and clinch their first playoff appearance since 1972. It was a fitting victory for a team that had been dubbed the Kardiac Kids for winning, and sometimes losing, games in the final seconds. As Jim Braham wrote in the *Cleveland Press,* it was a finish "scripted in heaven or Hollywood."

The Browns held the tiebreaker against the Oilers and, as division champions, drew a bye in the first round. When the Raiders upset the Oilers in the wild card game, they became the Browns' opponent. In a bitterly cold Sunday in Cleveland, on a frozen field with wind chills below zero, the Browns met the same team that the Steelers had defeated in 1972 on Franco Harris's Immaculate Reception. After waiting nine years for the Browns to return to the playoffs, Browns fans would witness a play that also became one of the most memorable in NFL history; but for Cleveland, the play would live in infamy.

Trailing the Oilers 14–12, Cleveland's Kardiac Kids were on their own 15-yard line with 2:22 left in the game. They drove down the field and, with 49 seconds left, were on the Raiders' 13-yard line, poised to run down the clock and kick a game-winning field goal. Worried that Cockroft, who had struggled in the bad weather, would miss the kick, Rutigliano called a pass play, "Red Right 88." To the horror of Browns fans, the pass was intercepted in the end zone. Instead of another miracle finish, the Kardiac Kids ended the season with the most infamous call in team history. The headline in the Cleveland *Plain Dealer* blared, "Kardiac Arrest."

After the Raiders made history by becoming the first wild card team to win the Super Bowl, Brian Sipe, who threw the fatal Red Right 88 interception, was named the NFL's MVP and Sam Rutigliano won his second consecutive AFC Coach of the Year award. The honors, however, was small compensation for Browns fans devastated by the playoff loss. Their only hope in the off-season was that the 1980 season wasn't a fluke. They wanted their Browns to recover from the Red Right 88 fiasco and replace the Steelers as the dominant team in the Central Division.

Pittsburgh fans were disappointed by the Steelers' failure to make the playoffs after an eight-year run, but they were not surprised. While a defiant Bradshaw declared, "Next year, everyone will write us off, and we'll come back and blow them out," Rocky Bleier's retirement in the off-season was the latest reminder that the Steelers were a fading dynasty, vulnerable more than ever to age and injury.

As they had in 1980, the Browns started the 1981 season with two losses, but they eased the concerns of Cleveland fans with wins over the Cincinnati Bengals and the Atlanta Falcons before a loss to the Los Angeles Rams dropped their record to 2–3. The Steelers also lost their first two games of the season, but they bounced back with wins over the New York Jets, the New England Patriots, and the New Orleans Saints to move above .500 at 3–2. Going into their first meeting of the year in Pittsburgh, both teams—but especially the Browns—felt a sense of urgency. Another loss would make it difficult to stay in contention for the playoffs.

The Steelers struck first with a Bradshaw touchdown pass and a field goal, but Sipe's touchdown run cut the Steelers' lead to 10–7 by halftime. Neither team scored in the third quarter, but the most important play of the game came in the Browns' last series of the quarter, when Sipe suffered a concussion on another vicious hit from Jack Lambert and had to be replaced by backup quarterback Paul McDonald.

After the Steelers increased their lead late in the fourth quarter to 13–7 on another field goal, the inexperienced McDonald led the Browns on an 83-yard drive, but his pass into the Steelers' end zone was intercepted to end the threat and give the Steelers a 13–7 victory and, to the dismay of Cleveland fans who made the turnpike trip, a continuation of the Three Rivers jinx.

McDonald's intercepted pass wasn't as devastating as Red Right 88, but it dropped the Browns to 2–4 on the season and put their playoff hopes in jeopardy. The Browns bounced back with wins over the New Orleans Saints and the Baltimore Colts, but losses to the Buffalo Bills and the Denver Broncos dropped their record to 4–6. A win over the San Francisco 49ers gave Browns fans some hope; however, to have any chance at making the playoffs, they had to win their last five games, beginning in Cleveland against the Steelers.

After defeating the Browns in Pittsburgh, the Steelers were humiliated by the Bengals, 34–7, in Cincinnati, but they defeated the Oilers the following week to move into a first-place tie at 5–3 with the surprising Bengals. Close losses to the 49ers and the Seahawks dropped them out of first place, but a win over the Atlanta Falcons gave them a chance at the playoffs—as long as they defeated the Browns and won the rest of their games. It was clear that the Steelers-Browns game would all but eliminate the losing team from the playoffs.

In a sloppy game plagued by 12 turnovers, the Steelers scored two touchdowns in the first quarter but led only 12–3 when they failed to convert the extra points. The missed kicks seemed important when the Browns cut the Steelers' lead to 12–10, but the points were Cleveland's last in the game. In the second half, the Steelers scored three touchdowns and held off the Browns with key interceptions. With Sipe having the worst game of his career and throwing six interceptions, the Steelers easily defeated the Browns 32–10.

The Browns never recovered from their defeat to the Steelers. They lost their next two games to division rivals, the Bengals and the Oilers, then finished out the season with losses to the Jets and the Seahawks. The five-game losing streak gave the Browns a dismal 5–11 record in 1981 after their miraculous Kardiac Kids 1980 season. What made the Browns' collapse even more galling for Cleveland fans was the surprising success of Paul Brown's Bengals, who won the division and went on to play in the Super Bowl, something their Browns had yet to accomplish.

After the Steelers' victory over the Browns, they defeated the Rams, but a loss to the Raiders knocked them out of contention. Without Bradshaw, who broke his throwing hand against the Raiders, they were officially eliminated in a loss to the Super Bowl–bound Bengals and finished the season the season at 8–8 after losing to the Oilers. It was their second season out of the playoffs since winning their fourth Super Bowl and further evidence that the Steelers' dynasty years were over.

Going into the 1982 season, the Browns and the Steelers faced major challenges, but an event beyond their control would be a bigger threat to their fortunes than injuries and aging veterans. After a contentious off-season of negotiations between the National Football League Players Association and NFL owners over issues that included revenue sharing, minimum salaries, and retirement benefits, the NFL's 1982 season came to a halt after two games. The strike would last for eight weeks and force the NFL to cancel seven games.

After going 5–11 in 1981, the Browns had gone through a major transformation in the off-season. Key players were gone, including Lyle Alzado and Greg Pruitt, who were traded to the Raiders, and Thom Darden and Reggie Rucker, who retired. The decline in Brian Sipe's performance, after his 1980 MVP season, was also a major concern. They did open the 1982 season with a dominating win over the Seattle Seahawks, but a close loss to the Philadelphia Eagles on the eve of the strike had Cleveland fans wondering if the 1981 season was about to repeat itself.

After finishing at 8–8 in 1981—the first time since 1972 that the Steelers failed to have a winning record—the team suffered its biggest loss one day after the season ended when Mean Joe Greene, after a brilliant 13-year career, walked into Chuck Noll's office and said he was retiring. Greene wasn't the first Steelers player from their dynasty years to retire, but he, more than any other player, represented the dominance of the Steelers in the 1970s. At the press conference announcing Greene's retirement, Noll said, "There will never be another Joe Greene."

Without Greene, the Steelers did open the 1982 season with key wins against the Cowboys and the Bengals before the strike, but Pittsburgh fans still wondered if the loss of Greene marked the end of the team's goal of winning a fifth Super Bowl ring, what the retiring Greene had called "one for the thumb."

After several weeks, with the 1982 season on the verge of cancellation, the NFLPA and NFL owners finally reached agreement on a five-year contract that included a onetime $6 million payment to the union for time lost and an improved system for salaries and benefits. To salvage the season, the NFL cobbled together a nine-game season, with seven remaining games, followed by a postseason tournament in which the top eight teams in each conference would compete for the Super Bowl. Of the remaining games in the season, the Browns and the Steelers would meet twice in their last three games, after the NFL scheduled them to play on what would have been the wild card weekend.

The Browns struggled when they returned to the playing field and, at 2–4, were in jeopardy of missing the playoffs before their first game against the Steelers in Cleveland. The Steelers fared better and were 4–2 going into their first game against Cleveland. A loss to the Browns wouldn't knock them out of contention for one of the eight conference playoff spots, but at the very least, it would hurt their seeding in the tournament.

With Brian Sipe struggling, the Browns started his backup Paul McDonald against the Steelers. With McDonald at quarterback, the Browns managed only a field goal in the first half and trailed the Steelers 7–3 on a Bradshaw touchdown pass. That touchdown was the only offensive score for the Steelers in Bradshaw's worst game of the season. Intercepting four passes and recovering a Bradshaw fumble, the Browns scored a touchdown in the third quarter and held on, after their punter took a safety, for a 10–9 victory.

Before their meeting in Pittsburgh for the add-on game of the shortened season, the Browns defeated the Oilers to climb to 4–4, while the Steelers beat the Patriots to go 5–3. During the rematch in Pittsburgh, it was McDonald who threw four interceptions, while the Browns also gave up a touchdown on a blocked punt. With Bradshaw throwing two touchdown passes, the Steelers took a 13–7 lead at halftime and went on to an easy 37–21 victory as the Three Rivers jinx continued for the Browns.

The loss dropped the Browns to 4–5, but they still made the playoffs as an eighth seed. They also became the only team in NFL history, along with the 4–5 Lions, to make the playoffs with a losing record. They traveled to the Los Angeles Raiders, where they gave up more than 500 yards in a 27–10 lopsided loss to the top-seeded Raiders. It was their fifth consecutive playoff loss since they defeated the Cowboys in 1969.

The Steelers, with a fourth seed in the tournament, faced the San Diego Chargers. Favored to move on, they dominated the game behind the passing of Bradshaw. But, with an 11-point lead in the fourth quarter, Bradshaw threw a costly interception that sparked the Chargers to a come-from-behind 31–28 victory. Like the Browns, the Steelers were eliminated from the tournament in the first round.

While both teams made the playoffs in 1982, the Browns and the Steelers seemed more like teams in flux rather than on the rise. After two losing seasons, the most critical decision for Sam Rutigliano going into the 1983 season was his quarterback. With both the veteran Brian Sipe and the inexperienced Paul McDonald struggling and combining for only nine touchdown passes and 16 interceptions in 1982, Rutigliano, with his own job likely on the line, decided to go with the 34-year-old Sipe, who had only one year remaining on his contract, in the hope that he had the experience as well as the incentive to lead the Browns to a winning season and the playoffs.

The Steelers lost two more future Hall of Famers, Jack Ham and Lynn Swann, from their dynasty years to retirement, but Chuck Noll was excited about Bradshaw's performance in 1982 and was convinced that his 35-year-old veteran was still in his prime going into the 1983 season and capable of leading the Steelers to another Super Bowl. That belief was shattered when Bradshaw, without the team's knowledge, underwent surgery on his right elbow during the off-season and reported to training camp still recuperating. With Bradshaw possibly out for the 1983 season, a furious Noll had to decide between backups Cliff Stoudt and Mark Malone (the Steelers' top pick in the 1980 draft) for his starting quarterback.

Sipe made Rutigliano look good by leading the Browns to a 4–2 record going into their first meeting against the Steelers in Pittsburgh. With the more experienced Cliff Stoudt getting the call from Noll over Mark Malone, the Steelers matched the Browns' 4–2 record in their first six games and looked to use their seemingly invulnerable home-field advantage against the Browns to move into contention for the division lead. With the Browns struggling again at Three Rivers and already trailing 10–0 in the first quarter, Sipe threw an interception that was returned for a touchdown. Leading 34–10 at halftime, the Steelers coasted in the second half to a comfortable 44–17 victory.

After suffering their worst loss of the season, the Browns dropped two of their next three games to go 5–5. They bounced back, however, with wins over the Bucs, the Patriots, and the Colts to move back into contention for a playoff spot at 8–5, before losing games to the Broncos and the Oilers to go 8–7 and closing out the season in Cleveland against the Steelers. After their convincing win over the Browns, Pittsburgh won their next four games to take the division lead but dropped three straight games to the Vikings, the Lions, and the Bengals and, at 9–5, needed a win over the Jets in New York in their next-to-last game of the season to secure a the playoff spot before heading to Cleveland.

With Cliff Stoudt struggling, Terry Bradshaw—still suffering from pain in his right elbow—started the Jets game and threw two touchdown passes before his elbow gave out. The last touchdown pass gave the Steelers a 14–0 lead on their way to a 34–7 victory and the Central Division title. It was also the last touchdown pass of Bradshaw's Hall of Fame career.

The Steelers finished the season with a meaningless 30–17 loss to the Browns, who had dropped out of playoff contention. In the win, Sipe finished the 1983 season and his career with the Browns in grand style with four touchdown passes against the Steelers, while Lambert nearly started a brawl after yet another vicious late hit on Sipe. A week later, Pittsburgh, without Bradshaw, fell behind to the Los Angeles Raiders in the first quarter when a Stoudt pass was returned for a touchdown and suffered a lopsided 38–10 in the first round of the playoffs. After their victory over the Steelers, the Raiders would go on to win the Super Bowl.

After Brian Sipe threw 26 touchdown passes in the 1983 season and led the Browns to a 9–7 record, Cleveland fans had reason to anticipate a winning season in 1984 and a possible playoff appearance, but what they got was one of the most disastrous years in Browns history. The trouble started the day after the 1983 season ended when Brian Sipe told Sam Rutigliano that the New Jersey Generals of the newly formed United States Football League had offered him a $2.3 million three-year contract. When the Browns refused to match the offer because of the cost and the risk of injury, they lost the veteran. They decided to replace him with Paul McDonald in the hope that McDonald was ready to step into the starting role. It was a major miscalculation and would cost Rutigliano his job.

The Steelers also lost a quarterback in the off-season when Cliff Stoudt signed with the Birmingham Stallions of the USFL, but their major concern was the health of Terry Bradshaw. When Bradshaw showed up at preseason minicamp and discovered that he still had pain in his right elbow, he told Chuck Noll, "I can't play anymore. It's over." The forced retirement of Bradshaw wasn't the only major loss for the Steelers. When Franco Harris held out for a pay increase and a contract extension, the Steelers, reluctant to meet Harris's demands, placed him on waivers, where he was claimed by the Seattle Seahawks.

The mistake the Browns made in not signing Sipe and starting McDonald was clear from the very beginning of the 1984 season when Cleveland lost its first three games, including an opening day shutout against the Seahawks. McDonald did throw two touchdown passes in a 20–10 win over the Steelers in Cleveland to give the Browns their first victory of the season, but his interceptions were costly in the next four games and dropped the Browns to 1–7. At that point, owner Art Modell, who had given his coach an earlier vote of confidence, fired Rutigliano and replaced him with Marty Schottenheimer, the team's defensive coordinator.

An All-American linebacker while at the University of Pittsburgh, Schottenheimer spent several seasons in the AFL after being drafted by the Buffalo Bills in 1965. His coaching career in the NFL began with the New York Giants in 1975. He started out as linebackers coach and became the Giants' defensive coordinator in 1977. When Rutigliano signed him in 1980 as defensive coordinator, he was coaching linebackers with the Detroit Lions. After replacing Rutigliano, Schottenheimer led the Browns to a 4–4 finish and an overall 5–11 record and was hired by Modell as Cleveland's permanent coach for the 1985 season.

Without Bradshaw and Harris, the Steelers entered the 1984 season with 1980 No. 1 draft pick Mark Malone at quarterback, backed up by David Woodley, who was acquired in a trade with the Miami Dolphins, who now had Dan Marino. At running back, they went with a tandem of veteran workhorse Frank Pollard and 1980 first-round pick Walter Abercrombie to replace Harris.

Despite all the changes, the Steelers, though they suffered a 20–10 loss in Cleveland, managed a 4–4 record through their first eight games. After a modest two-game winning streak, they lost three of their next four to drop to 7–7 going into their last two games of the season against the Browns and the Raiders. To have any chance of making the playoffs, they would have to win both games, beginning with the Browns in Pittsburgh.

The Steelers took an early 17–6 lead, and, after the Browns fought back to tie the game at 20–20, a field goal late in the fourth quarter gave the Steelers a critical 23–20 victory. The Steelers went on to clinch a playoff spot with a 13–7 win in Los Angeles against the Raiders and, in the first round, met John Elway and the Broncos in Denver. Heavy underdogs, the Steelers, resembling the Steel Curtain on defense, sacked Elway four times, intercepted two of his passes, and defeated the Broncos 24–17.

The following week, they faced the heavily favored Dolphins and Pittsburgh native and former Pitt All-American Dan Marino, who was passed over by the Steelers in the 1983 draft. The Steelers' Mark Malone, playing one of his best games, threw for over 300 yards and three touchdowns, but he couldn't overcome Marino, who threw for over 400 yards and four touchdowns in a 45–28 win over the Steelers. The victory earned the Dolphins their second trip to the Super Bowl in the 1980s, where they lost to the 49ers. It was Marino's first Super Bowl and, as it turned out, his last.

. . .

Unlike the offensive-minded Sam Rutigliano, coach Marty Schottenheimer believed that championships were won by teams with strong defenses; however, going into the 1985 season, the Browns had to address their quarterback situation after Paul McDonald's poor performance in 1984. They made two moves that they hoped would solve their immediate problem and also give them a long-term solution. They gave the Detroit Lions a third-round draft pick for eight-year veteran Gary Danielson and, in a supplement draft, traded two first-round and two third-round draft picks to the Buffalo Bills for the rights to Miami All-American Bernie Kosar, who was a Browns fan while growing up in Ohio. Schottenheimer's plan was to start Danielson at quarterback until Kosar was ready to take over.

The drafting of Kosar was a godsend for Browns fans, who after so many frustrations and disappointments in the 1970s and 1980s, needed a morale boost and a reassuring hug. Mentioning that he grew up a "huge Browns fan" and remembering that his father took him to numerous games, including "those Browns-Steelers games," Kosar said, "I wanted the opportunity not only to play for the Browns but the biggest issue of it was wanting to go back and live in that part of the country. To live in Cleveland. I grew up as a Youngstown guy, a Cleveland guy, and I wanted to live there. I had my family and friends there, and it made a great situation."

After leading the team into the playoffs and the conference championship game, Mark Malone was the clear choice over Dave Woodley as the Steelers' starting quarterback, but Noll and his staff had serious reservations about Malone. He was an impressive athlete, who while playing as a wide receiver once caught an 88-yard touchdown pass from Terry Bradshaw, but he was no Bradshaw when it came to playing quarterback. Assistant coach Dick Hoak said the problem was that Malone didn't have the instincts for the position and simply lacked Bradshaw's powerful arm.

With Malone at quarterback, the Steelers opened the season with an impressive home win over the now Indianapolis Colts before heading to Cleveland to play the Browns, who lost on the road to the St. Louis Cardinals. After scoring 45 points against the Colts, the Steelers were shut down by Cleveland's defense and failed to score until the fourth quarter. The Browns led 10–0 at halftime and went on to a 17–7 victory.

After defeating the Steelers and suffering a loss to the Cowboys, the Browns won their next three games, including a victory over division rival Houston. But they dropped their next two games, including a loss to the Bengals, and were 4–4 on the season. After losing to the Browns, the Steelers lost four of their next six games, including two costly defeats to the Bengals to fall to 3–5. Beating the Browns in Pittsburgh was critical if the Steelers were to remain in contention.

Like the earlier meeting in Cleveland, the game quickly turned into a defensive struggle, with two field goals giving the Browns a 6–0 halftime lead. The Steelers, with Woodley started for a slumping Malone, took a 7–6 lead in the third quarter, but the Browns, with Kosar replacing an injured Danielson at quarterback, went ahead 9–7 in the fourth quarter. With time running out in the game and on the Steelers' season, Pittsburgh drove deep into Browns territory, kicked a 25-yard field goal, and held on for a dramatic 10–9 victory—and an extension of the Three Rivers jinx for 16 years.

The Steelers won their next two games against the Kansas City Chiefs and the Houston Oilers, but they went into a tailspin, losing four of their last five games to end the season with a losing record at 7–9. Their quarterbacks were the biggest problem, throwing a combined 27 interceptions on the season. Fans were so disappointed in the Steelers performance that only 36,953 showed up for the last game of the season against Buffalo. It was the smallest turnout in the history of Three Rivers.

The Browns, relying on a strong running game that produced two 1,000-yard runners in James Kevin Mack and Earnest Byner, won four of their last five games to finish at 8–8, good enough for the Central Division title, while the Steelers and the Oilers finished at 7–9. Heavy underdogs, the Browns played the Dolphins in the division round of the playoffs and, after taking a surprising 21–3 lead, lost to the Dolphins 24–21 on a late rally led by Marino, who passed for 238 yards. While the defense faltered and Kosar was held to only 68 yards, Cleveland fans thought that, despite the disappointing loss, Schottenheimer had the team on the road to its first Super Bowl.

When Gary Danielson broke his ankle in the Browns' last 1986 exhibition game, Bernie Kosar, in only his second year, had to take over the Browns' offense for the regular season. With a strong running attack, led by Kevin Mack and Earnest Byner, and with linebackers William Clay Matthews and William "Chip" Banks leading a veteran defense, all that Marty Schottenheimer asked from his young quarterback was that he manage the game and avoid making mistakes.

The Steelers thought they had finally found their replacement for Terry Bradshaw when they selected quarterback Walter "Bubby" Brister from

Northeast Louisiana in the third round of the 1986 draft. Tall, strong, and possessed with a powerful throwing arm, Brister seemed to be a clone of Bradshaw, but that was the problem going into the 1986 season. Like Bradshaw, Brister was at best a raw talent, clearly not ready to run the Steelers' offense. That meant that, by default, Mark Malone would start the season at quarterback.

The season opened with predictable results for the Steelers. Outscored 82–17, they lost their first three games to the Seattle Seahawks, the Denver Broncos, and the Minnesota Vikings. They did, however, bounce back to defeat the Oilers for their first win of the season before facing the Browns in Pittsburgh. After losing their opener to the Chicago Bears, the Browns won two of their next three games to go 2–2. Their offense had played well under Kosar, but their defense was a disappointment, allowing 112 points in their first four games.

The problem for the Browns going into their game with the Steelers was what Cleveland fans had dubbed the Three Rivers jinx. Since the Steelers began playing at Three Rivers in 1970, the Browns had never defeated the Steelers in Pittsburgh, a streak that had now reached 16 games. Cleveland fans who traveled the turnpike to Pittsburgh did everything they could think of to break the jinx, including sprinkling dirt from Cleveland Municipal Stadium on Three Rivers' artificial turf, but nothing had worked. Going into the 1986 season, the Browns were a talented team on the rise, while the Steelers were struggling to win games. If ever the Browns were to break the jinx, this would be the year.

The Browns started well by taking a 10–0 lead in the first quarter, but the Steelers capitalized on two Cleveland turnovers to take a 14–10 lead with just under two minutes left in the first half. On the ensuing kickoff, Gerald McNeil thrilled Browns fans who had traveled to Pittsburgh when he took the ball at the goal line and raced 100 yards for a touchdown to give Cleveland a 17–14 halftime lead.

The Steelers came back to take the lead on a Malone touchdown pass and were ahead 24–20 going into the fourth quarter. Midway through the fourth quarter, the Steelers gave the Browns a chance to take the lead when they committed a roughing the kicker penalty on a missed field goal. A few plays later, the Browns went ahead, 27–24, on a Byner 4-yard touchdown run. With time running out, the Steelers drove to the Browns' 35-yard line but fumbled the ball away with less than two minutes left in the game. When the Browns ran out the clock, Cleveland had done what Browns historian and author Jonathan Knight described as "the impossible." They had finally won a game at Three Rivers.

Browns tight end Ozzie Newsome, after playing in his ninth game at Three Rivers, declared, "Now I can retire. The frustration is over." Other Browns players were in a state of disbelief. Linebacker Clay Matthews said that he didn't realize they had won until "the gun sounded." Bernie Kosar admitted he didn't know they won, "Not until I stole the ball and ran off the field." For Marty Schottenheimer, it was "only when I shook Chuck Noll's hand." As for long-suffering Browns fans, the victory had turned a Three Rivers hell into heaven.

When the Steelers lost their next two games, including a 34–0 drubbing by the New England Patriots, to drop to 1–6, the headline in the *Pittsburgh Post-Gazette* read, "The Steelers—Can It Get Any Worse?" They did win three of their next four games, but, at 4–7, they were playing mostly for pride when they traveled to Cleveland to face the Browns, who had won three of five games after their historic win in Pittsburgh and were in contention for the division title at 7–4.

After defeating the Steelers for the first time at Three Rivers, the Browns made history again in a wild, seesaw game that had the Browns and the Steelers exchanging touchdowns until a Kosar touchdown pass gave Cleveland a 21–14 halftime lead. In the second half, the teams exchanged touchdowns and field goals; at the end regulation play, they were tied 24–24. When Kosar won the game with a 36-yard touchdown pass to Webster Slaughter, the Browns, after losing two overtime games to Pittsburgh in past seasons, defeated the Steelers in overtime for the first time in team history. Their sweep of the Steelers was the Browns' first since the 1969 season and sent their fans into a frenzy.

After their second loss of the season to the Browns, the Steelers split their last four games and finished at 6–10, their worst season under Noll since the dynasty years of the 1970s. Particularly distressing for Pittsburgh fans was the team's inconsistency on offense, where Steelers quarterbacks threw only 15 touchdown passes and were intercepted 27 times. After sweeping the Steelers, the Browns won their last four games of the season, including a one-sided 34–3 win over the Bengals in Cincinnati that clinched the Central Division. They finished at 12–4, their best season since the 1980 Kardiac Kids thrilled Cleveland fans.

In the division round of the playoffs, the Browns did their best interpretation of the Kardiac Kids with a dramatic 23–20 double overtime win against the Jets. Trailing 20–10 late in the fourth quarter, Kosar, overcoming two costly interceptions, led the Browns to a touchdown and a tying field goal with 7 seconds left in regulation to send the game into overtime. The game went into double overtime before the Browns' Mark Moseley kicked a game-winning 27-yard field goal. For the game, Kosar completed 33 of 64 passes for 489 yards, an NFL playoff record, and had Cleveland fans dreaming of their first Super Bowl after the win. All that remained for the Browns was to defeat the Denver Broncos and their young quarterback, John Elway. in Cleveland and in front of their rabid hometown fans.

Unfortunately, the 1986 postseason turned out to be 1980 all over again. In front of a roaring Cleveland crowd, the Browns broke a 13–13 tie late in the fourth quarter on a Kosar touchdown pass. With just 5:34 seconds left in the game, Cleveland had the Broncos pinned down on their own 2-yard line, but Elway brought Denver back in what would go down in Browns history as "the Drive." With just 37 seconds left, Elway had the Broncos at the Browns' 5-yard line, where he hit Mark Jackson with a touchdown pass to tie the game. In overtime, the Broncos went on to win the game on a 35-yard field goal and shatter the Browns' dream of their first Super Bowl. Elway's drive had joined Red Right 88 in infamy for Cleveland Browns fans.

As painful as the loss to the Broncos was for Browns fans, they had every reason to believe that 1987 would be the year that Cleveland would finally go to the Super Bowl. Their team had a young, talented quarterback, outstanding running backs, and a solid defense. It was a team that appeared to be just reaching its prime. Pittsburgh fans had every reason to be demoralized after the Steelers went 6–10 in 1986. The team still had not found an answer at quarterback since Bradshaw's retirement, and they seemed to be floundering on offense and defense.

The only problem for Browns and Steelers fans going into the 1987 season was another threatened strike after the five-year labor agreement signed in 1982 had expired. Locked in another impasse with the owners, the players' union had planned a walkout if no agreement was reached after the second game of the season. It was the same strategy that cost the NFL seven games in its shortened 1982 season. This time the owners vowed that if there were a walkout, they would continue the season with replacement players.

With a labor dispute hanging over the 1987 season, the Steelers opened with a surprising win over the San Francisco 49ers, while the Browns were upset by the New Orleans Saints. When the Steelers met the Browns in Cleveland for the second game of the season, the teams lived up to their fans' expectations. The Browns took a 10–3 lead at halftime and, behind two Kosar touchdown passes and six interceptions by the Cleveland defense, breezed to 34–10 victory.

After the second game of the season and with no labor settlement in sight, the players' union went through with the threatened walkout. The owners responded by continuing the season with replacement players after canceling the third week of the season to allow for the transition. One of the games canceled that week was a *Monday Night Football* Browns-Broncos rematch.

With player defections weakening the effectiveness of the walkout, the strike ended in four weeks. In the three games in which teams used replacement players, the Browns and the Steelers went 2–1 to go 3–2 on the season. After the strike, the Browns split their first two games back against the Rams and the Chargers, then won their next three games before losing two in a row. At 7–5 and needing wins in their last three games, the Browns defeated the Bengals and the Raiders going into their last game of the season in Pittsburgh.

The Steelers lost their first game back against the Dolphins, and, after splitting their next four, Pittsburgh, like Cleveland, had to win their final three games to clinch a playoff spot. They defeated the Chargers, but they lost to the Oilers to go 8–6 on the season before going into their final game against the Browns. They still had a mathematical chance to make the playoffs but needed a strong performance from Mark Malone, who had played poorly.

What the Steelers got was another awful performance from Malone, who had two interceptions after throwing three against the Oilers. The Browns, on a touchdown pass from Kosar, took a 9–3 lead at halftime and held on for a 19–16 win. The victory—their second in a row in Pittsburgh after a long drought—gave Cleveland the Central Division title for the third straight season and yet another chance to earn a trip to the Super Bowl. The Steelers, with Malone throwing five interceptions and no touchdowns in his last two games, finished the season in third place at 8–7 and knew they had to address their quarterback problem in the off-season.

The Browns easily won their division round playoff game against the Colts, 38–21, and faced a return match against the Broncos, but this time in Denver. Any hope for revenge seemed fleeting when the Broncos took advantage of two Browns turnovers to take an early 14–0 lead. By halftime they had expanded the lead to 21–3 and seemed well on their way to another Super Bowl at the expense of the Browns. However, with Kosar throwing three touchdown passes, the Browns rallied to tie the game at 31–31.

An Elway touchdown pass put the Broncos ahead 38–31, but the Browns, with time running out, drove down the field and had the ball on the Denver 8-yard line with a minute left on the clock. Poised to duplicate Elway's drive and send the game into overtime, Kosar handed the ball to Earnest Byner, who momentarily broke free but was hit inside the 5-yard line and fumbled the ball. When Denver recovered the fumble, it ended the Browns' season for the second time in a row when they seemed on the verge of a trip to the Super Bowl. Cleveland wide receiver Brian Brennan described Elway's drive as a "slow death," but "the Fumble" was more like a sudden and fatal heart attack for Cleveland fans.

With the Fumble added to the Drive and Red Right 88, Cleveland fans faced another off-season of bitterness and frustration. While the hated Steelers had won four Super Bowls in the 1970s, their Browns had fallen short of the Super Bowl in the 1980s in devastating losses. That frustration had also strained the relationship between owner Art Modell and coach Marty Schottenheimer. Modell wondered why a veteran team with so much talent had fallen short of the Super Bowl. Going into the 1988 season, he was concerned his Browns were becoming too conservative on offense and not aggressive enough on defense.

The Steelers had bounced back with a winning season in 1987, but they had missed the playoffs for three straight years. A major part of the problem was the loss of every player from the Steelers' dynasty except center Mike Webster, but the immediate concern was the poor play at quarterback. In the off-season, they traded Mark Malone to the Chargers and signed free agent Todd Blackledge, a former No. 1 draft pick of the Kansas City Chiefs. They also had Bubby Brister, who begged Chuck Noll for a chance to win the starting job.

The Steelers also had to face the 1988 season without their patriarch Art Rooney, who died of a stroke on August 25 at the age of 87. Rooney had turned the ownership of the Steelers over to his son Dan in 1975, but he was a constant and beloved presence in Pittsburgh until his death. Praise for Rooney came from all over the NFL and from former Steelers players, including Supreme Court Justice Byron "Whizzer" White, a star tailback for the Steelers in the late 1930s, who said that Rooney "was the finest person

I've ever met." Pittsburgh sportswriter Roy McHugh wrote that Rooney was "a genuinely unpretentious, honest, admirable person. You couldn't help, but like him."

The Steelers defeated the Cowboys in their opening game of the season, but they quickly fell into their worst losing streak since Chuck Noll's first season in 1969. They lost six games in a row, including a 26–9 loss to the Browns in Pittsburgh. Then after a win over the Broncos, they lost four more games, topped off by a 27–7 defeat in Cleveland to the Browns to fall to a dismal 2–10 record. With Brister starting after Blackledge struggled at quarterback, the Steelers managed to salvage part of the season by winning three of their last four games, but they finished at 5–11.

In 1988, the Browns faced their greatest challenge since Marty Schottenheimer became head coach. They split their first two games, but lost both Bernie Kosar and Gary Danielson to injury. With only third-string Mike Pagel healthy, the Browns signed Don Strock, who had retired after spending over a decade as a backup in Miami to Bob Griese and Dan Marino. When Pagel suffered a separated shoulder in a loss to the Seahawks that dropped the Browns to 3–3 on the season, the 38-year-old Strock stepped in at quarterback and led the Browns to a critical win over the Eagles.

With Kosar back from injury, the Browns won five of their next seven games to go 9–5, but Kosar was injured again in a loss to the Dolphins. Facing elimination from the playoffs with a loss to the Oilers in their final game, the Browns, after Strock threw three interceptions in the first half, battled back from a 23–7 deficit; with Strock throwing a game-winning touchdown pass, they defeated the Oilers 28–23 to qualify for a wild card berth and a match against the Oilers.

Unfortunately for Browns fans, Strock never had a chance to repeat his impression of Brian Sipe and the Kardiac Kids when he hurt his wrist early in the wild card game. With Pagel at quarterback, the Browns managed to stay in the game and, trailing 24–16, rallied to get within 1 point of the Oilers before time ran out. It was their fourth straight postseason setback and had their fans wondering if the Browns, plagued by injuries and jinxes, would ever make it to the Super Bowl.

During the off-season, the Browns and the Steelers made major decisions about their head coaches—but not those expected by their fans. There were grumblings in Pittsburgh about Chuck Noll after the Steelers finished with their worse record since Noll's first season in 1969. Pittsburgh fans were openly wondering if it was time for Noll to step down after 20 years. The Steelers did fire several assistant coaches in the off-season, but Dan Rooney squashed rumors about Noll by having the Steelers sign a contract that would run until Noll decided to retire and would guarantee him $100,000 a year for a decade after his retirement.

In Cleveland, fans were frustrated with the Browns' failure to reach the Super Bowl under Marty Schottenheimer, but the Browns had won three division championships and a wild card playoff spot in Scottenheimer's four years as head coach. The team was aging but appeared to still have the talent to make another run at the Super Bowl. The problem in Cleveland was the growing strain between Art Modell and Schottenheimer that reached a breaking point in the off-season. A frustrated Schottenheimer finally agreed to step down as Browns coach and headed to Kansas City to become head coach of the Chiefs. Looking for a more innovative and aggressive coach, Modell decided to hire Leon "Bud" Carson, a longtime assistant defensive coach currently with the Jets and best known as the architect of the famous Steel Curtain of the Steelers' dynasty years.

Cleveland and Pittsburgh fans had an early opportunity to judge the coaching decisions when the Browns opened the 1989 season against the Steelers in Pittsburgh. Cleveland fans who made the trip to Pittsburgh were apprehensive but left Three Rivers Stadium in a state of euphoria. In a rare moment at Three Rivers, Steelers fans, stunned by the team's poor play, began to leave early in what must have felt like a death march.

In the first half, the Browns scored two touchdowns on fumbles by running back Tim Worley, the Steelers' No. 1 draft pick, on their way to a 30–0 halftime lead. The rout continued in the second half when Bubby Brister, who threw three interceptions on the day, had one of his interceptions returned for a Cleveland touchdown. When the game mercifully ended, the Steelers had suffered a humiliating 51–0 loss, the most lopsided in their 79-game history with the Browns. For Carson, in his first game as a head coach, he couldn't help but take the victory of his old team personally: "it was a great day for me. Whatever else has happened in my life, I feel thankful I was around long enough to enjoy this."

The humiliation continued for Steelers fans when Pittsburgh lost 41–10 to the Bengals the following week. With two losses against division rivals by a total score of 92–10, the Steelers looked like they were ready to send Noll into forced retirement, but Pittsburgh miraculously bounced back with solid wins over the Minnesota Vikings and the Detroit Lions. They lost for the second time in the season to the Bengals to drop to 2–3 before heading to Cleveland for a rematch after their brutal opening loss to the Browns in Pittsburgh.

After humiliating the Steelers in Bud Carson's head coaching debut, the Browns defeated the Jets before losing their first game of the season to the Bengals. They followed that loss by getting a bit of revenge in a win against the Broncos, but they lost to the Dolphins to drop on the season to 3–2. After the debacle in the first game between the Steelers and the Browns, a Pittsburgh victory, to the amazement of Steelers and Browns fans, would give the teams the same 3–3 record.

After scoring 51 points in their first meeting, the Browns' offense failed to score in the first half and trailed 3–0 at halftime. The Steelers increased their lead to 10–0 at the end of the third quarter, and, helped by Cleveland turnovers, held on for a stunning 17–7 victory—and sweet revenge for the devastating 51–0 loss to the Browns that opened the season.

The Steelers lost three of their next four games, but, with Brister back at quarterback, they went on to win five of their last six. They finished at 9–7 and qualified for a wild card spot in the playoffs. Shaken by their loss to Steelers, the Browns won their next four games but, after a tie with the Kansas City Chiefs, they lost three games in a row to put their playoff chances in jeopardy. After defeating the Indianapolis Colts, they played their final game against the Houston Oilers and, in a must-win situation, defeated the Oilers to clinch the Central Division title with a 9–6–1 record.

After their disastrous start, the Steelers, in what many regarded as Chuck Noll's greatest coaching job, had come back to play their way into a playoff spot. The miraculous season continued when the Steelers traveled to Houston for the wild card game and defeated the Oilers 23–20 in overtime. The win put the Steelers into a division playoff game at Denver against the Broncos. If the Steelers defeated the heavily favored Broncos and the Browns won their division playoff game against the Buffalo Bills, Cleveland and Pittsburgh would play, in a dream matchup for their fans, for the AFC title, with the winner going to the Super Bowl. It was the first such opportunity since the 1972 season.

Both games turned into shoot-outs, but only Cleveland came out a winner. With Kosar throwing for three touchdowns, the Browns overcame Jim Kelly's four touchdown passes and advanced with a 34–30 win over the Buffalo Bills. In Denver, with an outstanding performance by Brister, the Steelers led throughout the game, but a long Elway touchdown drive late in the fourth quarter gave the Broncos a 24–23 win. Instead of hosting the Steelers, the

Browns traveled to Denver, where the Broncos and Elway denied the Browns a trip to the Super Bowl for the third time in four years—but in less dramatic fashion with a 37–21 win.

As the 1980s came to an end, the Browns, to the dismay of their fans, once again fell one game short of going to their first Super Bowl. They also had the nightmarish memories of Red Right 88, the Drive, and the Fumble to haunt them going into the 1990s. They could look back on a decade that saw the Browns win 12 of 20 games against their archrivals, the Steelers, including a jinx-ending win at Three Rivers, but it was small compensation after high hopes and certainly in no way could prepare them for the 1990s. The worst for frustrated Browns fans was yet to come.

CHAPTER SEVEN

The 1990s

Noll Retires, the Browns Expire

In *On Being Brown,* Scott Huler wrote: "To Browns fans it's like the moment you heard about the space shuttle or John Lennon or John Kennedy. All Browns fans remember the moment in 1995 when they first heard that the team was leaving town." No single loss of a game in Browns history, no drive or fumble, no Red Right 88, was as devastating as the day that Browns fans heard owner Art Modell announce that he was moving the Browns to Baltimore.

Huler remembered going to the last home game in Cleveland against the Steelers, walking past protesting fans and scalpers who were all but giving away tickets. Inside the stadium, he talked with fans about who was there "when Bradshaw was hurt. . . . when Greene kicked McKay" and wondered if Baltimore fans would remember Browns history or even care. More than anything, Huler realized that Cleveland Municipal Stadium was the place where he grew up and that the Browns were taking with them the best moments of his childhood.

When Modell made his announcement, there were four home games left in the 1995 season. John "Big Dawg" Thompson, leader of the Dawg Pound said, "It was like finding out that your best friend had a terminal illness . . . and you could see him only four more times." At the last home game, fittingly against the Cincinnati Bengals, Cleveland lineman Tony Jones, after the Browns' stunning upset of the Bengals, ran to the Dawg Pound with a game ball and tossed it to Thompson, who could only take off his mask and weep at the loss of his best friend. When Jones autographed the ball for Thompson, he wrote, "Keep up the fight, Big Dawg."

Pittsburgh was also in danger of losing a team to another city, but it was the Pirates, not the Steelers, that were on life support. Going into the 1994 season, the Pirates' ownership had decided to sell the team after years of financial problems. If they had no local option, they were willing to sell the baseball franchise to an outside bidder.

Early rumors had the Rooney family buying the Pirates. There was also a potential group of investors that included Dan Marino, who played high school and college football in Pittsburgh. But by the 1995 season, there was no buyer willing to step forward and keep the franchise in Pittsburgh until Sacramento-based Kevin McClatchy, who played prep school football with Dan Rooney Jr., stepped in and saved the franchise. McClatchy not only worked out a deal to purchase the Pirates, he led the effort to build a new ballpark for the Pirates, an effort that would also include the money for a new home for the Pittsburgh Steelers.

Going into the 1990s, the Browns' continuing failure to reach the Super Bowl haunted Cleveland fans, but they still hoped, after another near miss in 1989, that Bud Carson could give them, at the beginning of the 1990s, what had eluded Sam Rutigliano and Marty Schottenheimer in the 1980s. Expecting the worst in 1989 after devastating losses to the Browns and the Bengals, Steelers fans were happy with the Steelers' comeback and playoff run, but there were still nagging doubts about Chuck Noll as he entered the third decade of coaching the Steelers. Noll had become distracted and even more distant from his players. Steelers broadcaster Myron Cope had affectionately dubbed Noll "the Emperor Chaz" because of his dominating presence, but that title now seemed to fit Noll's growing detachment.

The 1990 season started well for the Browns when they defeated the Steelers in their opener in Cleveland. In a defensive struggle, the Steelers led 3–0 at halftime, but the Browns, sparked by a 30-yard touchdown return of a fumble, took a 7–3 third quarter lead on their way to a 13–3 victory. In a game where neither offense rushed for 100 yards or scored a touchdown, the difference was the Browns' ability to take advantage of Steelers turnovers, including two Bubby Brister interceptions.

It was hardly a thrilling start to the 1990 season, but the performance of the Browns' defense against the Steelers was encouraging for Super Bowl–starved Cleveland fans. That same defense, however, gave up 92 points in the next three games in losses to the New York Jets, the San Diego Chargers, and the Kansas City Chiefs. The Browns bounced back with a thrilling 30–29 win over the Denver Broncos but went into another tailspin and lost their next four games, including a lopsided 42–0 defeat by the Buffalo Bills, and stood at 2–7 going into their bye week.

An angry and embarrassed Art Modell decided that he had seen enough and fired Bud Carson in the middle of Carson's second season as head coach. After firing Carson, he named former Browns defensive back and current assistant Jim Shofner as interim head coach. The change made little difference. When they returned after the bye week, the Browns extended their losing streak to eight by losing their next four games, before defeating the Atlanta Falcons. Going into their game in Pittsburgh with the Steelers, they stood at a dismal 3–11.

After their disappointing defeat in their opener with the Browns, the Steelers managed to win five of their next eight games to climb to 5–4 going into their bye week. When they returned, they dropped back to 5–5 in a loss to the Bengals; however, with Brister playing well, they won three of their next four games and, with victories in their last two games, were still, at 8–6, in a position to make the playoffs.

In the game in Pittsburgh, Brister threw four touchdown passes in the first half against the lifeless Browns to give the Steelers a 35–0 halftime lead. The Browns committed eight turnovers in the game, but, mercifully, there was no more scoring in the second half. With a chance to make the playoffs as a wild card, the Steelers traveled to Houston the following week but lost 34–14 to the Houston Oilers. After the game, a distant Chuck Noll simply told his players, "It's over." When the Browns lost their last game of the season and finished at 3–13, Cleveland fans were glad the season was over.

New York Giants tight end Mark Bavaro once described Bill Belichick as "the biggest football geek or nerd that ever stepped foot in the NFL." On February 5, 1991, Art Modell signed the NFL's biggest geek to a five-year contract to coach the Cleveland Browns. At the time, the 36-year-old Belichick was the defensive coordinator for Duane "Bill" Parcells's New York Giants, winners of two Super Bowls, but his football roots went back to the days when his father, then head coach at Hiram College in Ohio, took his son to watch the Browns at their training camp. At the news conference, a jubilant Modell compared Belichick to Don Shula and proclaimed that "maybe I've struck gold on this one."

In Pittsburgh in 1991, 59-year-old Chuck Noll was going into his 23rd season as head coach of the Steelers. His players and assistant coaches had noticed that Noll, a perfectionist in preparing his team for the season, was becoming less and less involved and more and more alienated from his players. Looking back, Dick Hoak, one of Noll's assistant coaches, said that "he wasn't paying attention. He wasn't getting upset over things he used to get upset over."

There was plenty for Chuck Noll to get upset about in the Steelers' 1991 season. Even before the season started, guard Terry Long tested positive for steroids and running back Tim Worley was suspended after testing positive for cocaine. When the season started, the Steelers struggled with distractions and injuries. They managed to split their first four games before the bye week, but they lost two of their next three. They stood at 3–4 going into their first game of the season with the Browns in Cleveland.

The Browns faced their own problems going into the 1991 season. Players complained about the rigorous training camp under Belichick, while reporters found the Browns' new head coach uncooperative. Belichick seemed to have the most serious problems with his offensive players, particularly quarterback Bernie Kosar, who thought Belichick put too much stress on defense and was too conservative in his game plans for the offense.

Like the Steelers, the Browns, despite the dissension, split their first four games before the bye week but lost two of the next three games. The game in Cleveland was an early critical moment in the season for both teams, who were at 3–4. The Browns jumped off to a 10–0 lead, but second-year quarterback Neil O'Donnell, playing for an injured Brister, scored on a quarterback sneak to cut the Browns lead to 10–7 at halftime. Playing cautiously, the Browns took a 17–7 lead in the third quarter and, intercepting two O'Donnell passes, held on after a Steelers late touchdown for a 17–14 victory.

Any hope by Cleveland fans that the win over the rival Steelers would give the Browns momentum evaporated when the Browns lost their next three games. They split their next two contests, and, when they headed to Pittsburgh for the last game of the season, they were a disappointing 6–9 on the season. With rumors swirling that Chuck Noll was retiring at the end of the season, the Steelers continued to struggle after the loss to the Browns. They never reached .500 and matched the Browns' 6–9 record going into what did become the final game of Noll's career.

The only scoring in the first half came on field goals. Tied at 3–3, the Steelers went ahead in the third quarter, then increased their lead to 17–3 in the fourth quarter. A late Browns touchdown cut into the lead, but the Steelers held on for a 17–10 victory. Noll's players didn't carry him off the field, but after the game they presented him with the game ball.

The day after Christmas, Noll walked into owner Dan Rooney's office and told him, "I think it's time for me to get on with my life's work." At a news conference, Noll told reporters, "Probably the thing I appreciate most about football is that it teaches humility, because as soon as you start thinking you're pretty good things can get tough." When a reporter asked Noll if he had any regrets, he quoted Ralph Waldo Emerson, "Your actions speak so loudly that I cannot hear what you say. I'd like to keep it that way." After 39 seasons as a player and coach, Noll, a man a few words, walked away from the game and never looked back.

The fan favorite to replace Chuck Noll was Mean Joe Greene, who had been the defensive line coach under Noll since 1987. The Steelers, however, thought Greene wasn't ready to became a head coach and signed 34-year-old Pittsburgh native Bill Cowher, the defensive coordinator with the Kansas City Chiefs, to a four-year contract. At his news conference, Cowher told reporters, "Chuck Noll was a legend and it would be a mistake to ignore that success. It's something we won't try to put behind us, but will try to build on."

On first glance, Cowher seemed a mirror image of Noll. Both had played with the Cleveland Browns and developed their reputations as defensive coaches. However, Cowher was just the opposite of Noll when it came to relating to players. While Noll often seemed distant and cold, Cowher was so passionate that, when he was special teams coach with the Browns, he was warned by the referees to stop running down the field on kickoffs with his players. He was so excitable that spit would often fly out of his mouth when he congratulated or criticized a player.

Growing up in Pittsburgh's Crafton neighborhood, Cowher, thanks to his father, saw numerous Steelers games, including their annual bloodletting with the Browns at Three Rivers Stadium. But he was also well aware of the passion that Cleveland fans brought to the rivalry: "I first started playing and coaching there. It's a city a lot like Pittsburgh. This is a rivalry that has stood the test of time."

While the Steelers were introducing their new head coach, Cleveland fans were expressing their disappointment in the Browns' 6–10 record during their first season under Bill Belichick. The real struggle for the Browns, however, was not their performance on the playing field. Belicheck's determination to take complete control of the Browns had alienated many of the Browns' veterans, especially those on offense, who believed that it was Bernie Kosar's team. Tight end Alan Scott Galbraith reflected the growing resentment when he said that "we thought that Belichick was short-lived, another Modell quick fix, a flash in the pan. We had no respect for Belichick at all."

The Steelers got off to a great start under Cowher. They won their first three games, including their opener against division rival Houston, before losing to the Green Bay Packers going into their bye week. In their second season under Belichick, the Browns got off to a poor start, dropping three of their first four games, including a 12–0 loss to the Broncos, going into the bye week.

When the Steelers traveled to Cleveland after a week off, they faced former Ohio State quarterback Mike Tomczak, a free agent acquisition during the off-season after Kosar had suffered the first of two severe ankle injuries. With Brister also struggling with injuries, the Steelers starter at quarterback was Neil O'Donnell, in his third year with Pittsburgh. With Kosar and Brister out, both teams failed to score a touchdown in the first half, but in the second half, with the Steelers ahead 6–3, the Browns rallied with two touchdowns for a 17–9 victory.

After beating the Steelers, the Browns won three of their next four games to go 5–4 on the season, but losses to the San Diego Chargers and the Minnesota Vikings dropped their record under .500. They did bounce back with wins against the Chicago Bears and the Cincinnati Bengals, but losses to the Detroit Lions and the Houston Oilers put them at 7–8 and out of contention. Their only incentive going into their last game of the season against the Steelers in Pittsburgh was avoiding a second losing record under Belichick.

After their loss to the Browns, the Steelers, mostly with O'Donnell at quarterback, won seven of their next eight games to go 10–3 on the season and surged into the division lead. Losses to the Bears and the Vikings placed that lead in jeopardy, but a win over the Browns in their last game of the season would give Cowher a division title in his first season as Steelers coach.

In front of a roaring Terrible Towel–waving crowd, the Steelers took an early 7–0 lead. In the second quarter, Brister, playing in place of an injured O'Donnell, threw a touchdown pass to give the Steelers a 17–3 that they took into halftime. Tomczak, playing for an injured Kosar, brought the Browns back with a touchdown pass, but the Steelers held on for a 23–13 victory and the division championship.

As jubilant Steelers fans left Three Rivers, those Browns fans who made the trip to Pittsburgh had to deal with the bitter disappointment that Cowher, a former Browns player and coach, had led their bitter rival to a division championship, while the Browns had suffered their second losing season under Belichick. They could take some comfort when the Steelers, playing at home, lost in the playoffs to the Buffalo Bills after O'Donnell threw two interceptions and was sacked seven times. But they faced another long off-season with that first trip to the Super Bowl more elusive than ever.

While Pittsburgh fans were disappointed in the loss to the Buffalo Bills, Bill Cowher reaped the rewards of taking the Steelers to the playoffs in his first season when he was named the AFC Coach of the Year by the Associated Press and *The Sporting News*. Cleveland fans, however, were beginning to have doubts about Bill Belichick. Not only had the Browns had two losing seasons under Belichick, they were also a team in turmoil.

The focal point for the dissension was the growing animosity between the unpopular Belichick and the popular Kosar, who thought his coach's offensive strategy was prehistoric. Unhappy with Kosar ignoring his play-calling, in the off-season Belichick signed past Heisman Trophy–winning Vinny Testaverde, who, like Kosar, had played college football at Miami. Teestaverde had become a free agent after several seasons with Tampa Bay.

Even though the Browns got off to a 3–0 start, Belichick, looking for an opportunity to play Testaverde, had pulled Kosar with Cleveland trailing the Los Angeles Raiders in their come-from-behind victory in game three. He also benched Kosar at halftime of their fourth game and Cleveland's first loss of the season against the Indianapolis Colts and again in their loss the following week against the Miami Dolphins. By the time the Browns faced the Steelers, Testaverde had led the Browns to a win over the Bengals and, while Kosar fumed on the bench, was the starting quarterback when at 4–2 Cleveland played its first game against their chief rival.

Rarely in the Steelers-Browns rivalry had the two teams been tied for first place when they played each other, but the Steelers had matched the Browns' 4–2 record by winning four games in a row after two opening losses. With both teams tied at 4–2, the winner would take the division lead going into their second bye week of the season. Browns fans and Steelers fans who made the trip to Cleveland expected a great game, and they were not disappointed.

The Browns jumped off to a 14–0 lead on a Testaverde touchdown pass and a spectacular 91-yard punt return by Eric Metcalf, but the Steelers tied the game at 14–14 going into halftime. A second Testaverde touchdown pass gave the Browns a 21–17 lead, but two field goals put the Steelers in front 23–21. With time running out and Kosar in the game after Testaverde suffered a concussion when he was sacked by the Steelers' Kevin Greene, the Steelers punted the ball to Metcalf, who took off on another electric touchdown run, this time for 75 yards to give the Browns a 28–23 lead.

After the Browns held on for a dramatic victory, Belichick said that when he came to Cleveland he was told "the Pittsburgh game was a matter of life and death," but after watching the fan frenzy he now believed "it's more than that." However, that joy was short lived for Browns fans when Belichick, after a disappointing loss to the Broncos, decided to cut Bernie Kosar. Art Modell supported his coach by extending Belichick's contract by two years, but the reaction of Cleveland fans was hostile. While the headline in the Cleveland *Plain Dealer* blared, "Fans in a Frenzy," Kosar supporters wore "Bill Sucks" buttons. In the Browns' first home game after Belichick cut Kosar, a banner hung from the Dawg Pound declaring, "Will Rogers Never Met Bill Belichick."

Belichick might have hoped his decision to get rid of Kosar would put an end to the divisiveness and bring the team's focus back to the playing field, but that didn't happen. They lost their next three games to drop under .500 at 5–6 and, going into their final game of the season against the Steelers in Pittsburgh, were 7–8 and out of the playoffs. A loss to the Steelers would give the Browns their third losing season under Belichick.

The loss to the Browns had dropped the Steelers to 4–3 and in jeopardy of not making the playoffs. While they split their next eight games, they still had a chance to make the playoffs with a win over the Browns. With both offenses struggling, the Browns led the Steelers 9–3 at halftime, but an O'Donnell fourth-quarter touchdown pass gave the Steelers the lead on their way to a 16–9 victory. The Steelers went on to play at Kansas City in the playoffs but suffered a tough 27–24 defeat when an aging Joe Montana, after taking off the glove on his throwing hand that was protecting him from the bitter cold, rallied the Chiefs to victory.

The contrast between the coaching situations in Pittsburgh and Cleveland was remarkable going into the 1994 season. Steelers fans were disappointed in their team's failure in the playoffs, but they had a coach in Bill Cowher, who in his first two years had given them playoff football and raised hopes that they would soon see the Steelers in another Super Bowl.

Browns fans had watched their team suffer through three losing seasons under a head coach who had become one of the most controversial and disliked sports figures in Cleveland sports history. Ignoring growing criticism, Bill Belichick felt that through the draft and free agent signings he finally had a team that would give Cleveland its first Super Bowl; however, as offensive tackle Tony Jones put it, "People just can't forget the Bernie thing."

With a healthy Testaverde at quarterback, the Browns opened the season with a 28–20 victory in Cincinnati over the Bengals before playing at home against the Steelers, who had lost their home opener 26–9 to the Cowboys. The Browns excited their fans by jumping off to a 10–0 lead, but the Steelers went ahead, 14–10, by halftime. The second half was a defensive struggle in which the only scoring was a Steelers field goal. Intercepting four Testaverde passes, the Steelers won a hard-fought 17–10 victory.

While the four interceptions stirred up the Bernie thing, with Testaverde playing better the Browns recovered and went on a six-game winning streak. After a loss to the Denver Broncos, they defeated the Philadelphia Eagles and were atop the Central Division with an 8–2 record. In that span, the Browns' defense allowed 10 or fewer points in five wins, while Testaverde ran the offense dictated to him by Belichick. The success, however, didn't end the dissension, especially after the Browns lost their next two games. Defensive tackle Michael Dean Perry, one of Belichick's most vocal critics, claimed that "the guys were no happier with him. You just don't feel comfortable with him."

After their win over the Browns, the Steelers split their next four games before going on a tear that began with a three-game winning streak. After a loss to the Arizona Cardinals dropped their record to 5–3, they won their next six games and surged into the division lead at 11–3 before playing their next-to-the-last game of the season against Cleveland. Going into the game, the Browns were at 10–4, after a thrilling win against the playoff-bound Cowboys in Dallas. The Browns-Steelers matchup was a dream game in the rivalry. Both teams were headed for the playoffs, but the game, played in Pittsburgh, would determine which team won the division and which team would make the playoffs as a wild card.

Those rabid Cleveland fans who traveled to Pittsburgh for the game and expected the Browns to repeat their performance against Dallas were disappointed when the Steelers took a 14–0 lead in the first quarter, though a Testaverde touchdown pass cut the lead to 14–7 at halftime. The Steelers controlled the ball in the second half, their defense shutting down Testaverde and sacking him five times and intercepting two of his passes on the day. A Steelers field goal in the fourth quarter gave them a 17–7 lead and put the game out of reach for the Browns.

The Browns and the Steelers headed into the playoffs by winning their last game of the season. While the Steelers had a first-round bye, the Browns faced a New England Patriots team coached by Bill Parcells, who had just been voted Associated Press AFC Coach of the Year. It was a matchup of Little Bill and Big Bill. Belichick had been defensive coordinator with Parcells's two-time Super Bowl championship New York Giants just before becoming the Browns' head coach. Belichick rarely showed his emotions, but Cleveland players sensed how much beating his close personal friend meant to him.

Cleveland fans, despite their growing dislike of Belichick, were excited that their Browns were back in the playoffs, but they saw the game against the Patriots as a stepping-stone to a dream game in the next round against the Steelers. The Browns didn't disappoint their coach or their rabid fans. With Testaverde playing a flawless game and Belichick's No. 1 draft pick Eric Turner making a game-saving interception, the Browns defeated the Patriots 20–13. There would be plenty of traffic and hostility between Cleveland and Pittsburgh the following weekend.

That hostility was fueled by disparaging comments made by Browns players during the week that enraged Pittsburgh fans and inflamed the rivalry. When Browns fans, many of them wearing their Dawg Pound masks, arrived at Three Rivers, they were taunted and threatened by Steelers tailgaters. When a limousine filled with Browns fans arrived at the stadium, it was pelted with raw eggs.

The antagonism between the players was on full display even before the game began when Earnest Byner spotted a Terrible Towel that had been dropped by Steelers defensive end Brentson Buckner and stomped on it. Buckner warned Byner, "You're not going to play against the towel, you're going to play against me. It's going to be a long day."

The Browns and the Steelers were meeting in the playoffs for the first time in the history of the rivalry, but the game, as it turned out, was hardly the stuff of legendary encounters. After the taking a 3–0 lead, the Steelers scored three touchdowns, two on Neil O'Donnell passes, to take a commanding 24–3 lead at halftime on their way to an easy 29–9 victory. Browns fans were spotted leaving the game as early as the third quarter. The final indignity for those Cleveland fans who stayed to the bitter end came when the Steelers scored their last 2 points of the game when Testaverde was tackled in the end zone for a safety.

After the game, Steelers linebacker Chad Brown, remembering the Browns' pregame chirping, declared, "The only talking these guys are going to do now is to their travel agents. . . . They're all about talking tough. We're all about being tough." In the Browns' locker room, linebacker Thomas "Pepper" Johnson admitted, "they spanked us like children and sent us home.

The following week, Browns fans gained some measure of satisfaction when Pittsburgh suffered a heartbreaking 17–13 loss to the San Diego Chargers that denied the Steelers a trip to the Super Bowl. Once again, they would have to wait until next year to see their Browns contend for that increasingly elusive championship season.

During the off-season, there was Super Bowl talk in both Cleveland and Pittsburgh. After finally coaching the Browns into the playoffs, Belichick felt that, after four years, he finally had the talent to win a championship. He was also aware that his Browns had lost three games to the Steelers in 1994, including a playoff defeat, and that the road to a Cleveland Super Bowl clearly went through Pittsburgh.

In 1994, the Steelers were one play and 2 yards away from a trip to the Super Bowl, but an O'Donnell pass fell incomplete and ended their season in a painful loss to the Chargers. After three trips to the playoffs under Cowher, the Steelers, despite another defeat, looked poised for a return to the Super Bowl after a 15-year absence. Adding to their excitement, Steelers fans felt that their games with the hated Browns would likely be the key challenge in their trip to the Super Bowl.

The only problem for Browns and Steelers fans going into the 1995 season was the growing frustration of Cleveland owner Art Modell in getting financial help from city officials for a decaying Municipal Stadium. He felt that the stadium, which he described as an "old barn," had become a money pit since he took over its operation in 1975. To make matters worse, after the Indians moved into Jacobs Field in 1994, he had suffered a major drop in revenue, losing $21 million over the past two years. He claimed that the only way he could keep the franchise in Cleveland was for the city to pass a $175 million referendum to provide the funds for badly needed improvements or to support the building of a new stadium.

While waiting for the referendum, Modell saw an opening in Baltimore. It was a city without an NFL team since the Colts, after the 1983 season, had fled to Indianapolis in the middle of the night. On November 6, just before Cleveland would vote on and pass the referendum, Modell—who had opposed the Colts' move to Indianapolis—announced that he had signed a 30-year lease with Baltimore officials, who had agreed to construct a new stadium, and was moving the franchise out of Cleveland at the end of the 1995 season. Fans who were hoping that 1995 would produced a Super Bowl champion out of the Browns-Steelers rivalry were furious and devastated. At the height of its intensity, a rivalry that had begun in 1950 when the Browns entered the NFL and had meant so much to Cleveland and Pittsburgh would soon be gone for good.

A week after Modell made his announcement, the Browns played the Steelers in Pittsburgh on *Monday Night Football.* With the Browns at 4–5 and the Steelers at 5–4, the game should have had major consequences for the playoffs, but Modell's betrayal had turned the contest into a major protest against the Browns' move to Baltimore. Sympathetic Steelers fans wore brown-and-orange armbands in support of Browns fans, and many wore buttons declaring, "Muck Fodell." With lawsuits being filed to prevent the move and sportscasters around the country condemning the move as an act of treachery, the game seemed anticlimactic.

The game, however, did actually have major implications—at least for the Steelers. After the Browns lost 20–3 in a lifeless performance against the Steelers, they went into free fall, losing their next four games, including a 20–17 defeat to the Steelers in Cleveland. The Steelers, with the help of the listless Browns, put together an eight-game winning streak and surged to the division championship. After defeating the Bills and the Colts in the playoffs, the Steelers went on to play in the Super Bowl after a 16-year absence, only to lose 27–17. Their first Super Bowl loss in team history was to a powerful Cowboys team led by Troy Aikman and Emmitt Smith. The Super Bowl ring for the thumb would have to wait for another season.

Before the Browns headed to Baltimore, they gave their fans one last thrill. With the memories of Paul Brown's great teams in the air and former Cleveland players, including Jim Brown, in attendance, the Browns faced the Cincinnati Bengals in their last home game of the 1995 season and what could well be the last NFL game ever played in Cleveland. Absent from the game was Art Modell, who had been receiving death threats ever since he made the announcement that he was moving the franchise to Baltimore. Signs ranging from the heartbreaking to the obscene derided Modell as a base betrayer. Others sent Modell a simple message: "Go to hell, Art Modell."

More than 55,000 fans, including those who traveled from Pittsburgh to watch the historic game, saw a brilliant performance by the Browns. Before the game, Vinny Testaverde said that he hoped "each of us can do something special for the fans to remember. . . . it would be nice for the players to thank the fans in their own way." With Testaverde leading the way, the Browns took a commanding 17–3 lead at halftime and went on to a 26–10 victory.

In the closing seconds, fans chanted, "Modell sucks," while others tore up seats either to throw in anger or keep as souvenirs. At game's end, several Browns players headed to the Dawg Pound to say farewell to Cleveland's most ardent fans. Earnest Byner hugged and shook hands with fans who didn't want to let go of the Browns. Defensive tackle Tony Jones knelt at midfield because he "didn't want the day to be over." But it did end—and so did the existence in Cleveland of one of the most fabled franchises in NFL history.

The attempts to prevent the Browns from leaving Cleveland failed, but lawsuits, protests, and public condemnations had an immediate impact. On June 12, 1996, the NFL reached an agreement with Cleveland officials that in effect protected the Browns' brand and legacy and guaranteed the return of the team once a new stadium was constructed. Modell's Baltimore franchise was declared an expansion team with no claims on the Browns, including the team name.

There was another impact once Modell moved his franchise to Baltimore. On Valentine's Day, Modell, declaring that his team needed a "fresh start," fired Bill Belichick, even though Belichick still had two years remaining on his contract, and replaced him with Ted Marchibroda, who had had been head coach of the Colts for the past nine years. When Modell hired Belichick, he hoped that it was the last time he would hire someone to coach the Browns. In one of the great ironies in NFL history, Bellichick did turn out to be Modell's last head coaching hire—in Cleveland. A disappointed Belichick, instead of packing his bags for Baltimore, headed to the New England Patriots to become Bill Parcells' defensive coordinator once again.

Going into the 1996 season, the Browns-Steelers rivalry was gone, but there was no sense, as yet, that the games between Pittsburgh and Baltimore would spawn a new rivalry. The newly christened Baltimore Ravens split their games with the Steelers in 1996 but struggled to a 4–12 record and a fifth-place division finish. With former Browns quarterback Mike Tomczak and Jerome Bettis (acquired from the Los Angeles Rams), rushing for more than 1,000 yards, the Steelers won the division and defeated the Colts in the playoffs before losing to the Patriots. In their loss to the Patriots, the Steelers failed to score a touchdown against Bill Belichick's defense.

With Kordell Stewart at quarterback, the Steelers returned to the playoffs in 1997 after winning the division with an 11–5 record, including two wins against the Ravens. Baltimore, once again, finished at the bottom of the Central Division with a 6–9–1 record. The Steelers managed only one touchdown against the Patriots in the first round of the playoffs, but it was enough to give the Steelers a 7–6 victory. However, they fell short of the Super Bowl again, when they lost the conference championship to the Broncos.

The Steelers continued their mastery of the Ravens in 1998, but, with Stewart playing erratically, they had trouble scoring points and finished with a disappointing 7–9 record, despite two wins over Baltimore. The Ravens managed to finish in fourth place, ahead of the Bengals, but their 6–10 record was worse than the previous season. Their challenge going into the 1999 season was to find a way to beat the Steelers while they got ready to face a new division challenge.

On March 23, 1998, the NFL announced that the Cleveland Browns would return to the NFL for the 1999 season as an expansion team. Six months later, they awarded majority ownership of the franchise to Al Lerner, who made his fortune in real estate and credit card distribution. Lerner had owned 5 percent of the old Browns and was a controversial figure in Cleveland because he had Baltimore ties and helped Modell with his deal to leave the city. But his bid of $530 million was by far the highest the NFL received for the expansion Browns.

Once again, the Browns turned to a Bill Parcells protégé for their new head coach, but it was not Bill Belichick, who was serving as Parcells's assistant head coach with the New York Jets. After Vikings offensive coordinator Brian Billick turned down the Browns and took the head coaching job with the Ravens, Cleveland offered the position to Chris Palmer. At the time of his hiring, Palmer was the offensive coordinator with the Jacksonville Jaguars and, prior to that, had been the receivers and quarterback coach under Parcells at New England and with the Jets.

One of the reasons the Browns wanted Palmer was his reputation for developing young quarterbacks, including Drew Bledsoe, who led the Patriots to the Super Bowl in the 1996 season. The Browns would have to put together a team from a list of unprotected players and free agents, but they also had the first pick in the NFL's 1999 draft. With that pick, the Browns selected quarterback Tim Couch out of the University of Kentucky. It would be Palmer's task to develop Couch into a franchise quarterback capable of leading the Browns to the Super Bowl that eluded the old Browns.

During the off-season, the Browns acquired veteran quarterback and past Heisman Trophy–winning Ty Detmer in a trade. The plan was to start the 1999 season with Detmer at quarterback while he helped Palmer's staff with the development of Tim Couch. While Detmer had been used mostly as a backup during his career, he had played behind Brett Favre and Steve Young. The Browns hoped that Detmer would soon be backing up another future Hall of Fame quarterback.

That plan went into effect much sooner than the Browns had anticipated. The NFL decided to launch the expansion Browns 1999 season by having them open at home in their new stadium against Cleveland's old rivals, the Pittsburgh Steelers. Cleveland fans were in a celebratory mood, but that was quickly dashed by the Browns' inept performance. The Steelers jumped off to a 20–0 lead at halftime and cruised to a 43–0 victory. The Browns' offense was so awful, gaining only 9 yards passing and 52 yards rushing, that they brought Tim Couch into the game late in the fourth quarter. Couch threw three passes, two incompletions and the first interception of his career.

The Browns' embarrassing loss in Pittsburgh was just the beginning of a disastrous start to the 1999 season. With Tim Couch starting most of the games, Cleveland went 0–7 before defeating the New Orleans Saints on a Couch 53-yard Hail Mary touchdown pass as time ran out. They lost to the Ravens for the second time in the season before traveling to Pittsburgh to play the Steelers.

After a disappointing losing season in 1998, the Steelers had struggled after their opening wins against the Browns and the Ravens; however, after losing three games in a row, they went on a three-game winning streak before their second game of the season against Cleveland. The anticipated win against the hapless Browns would improve their record to 6–3 and put them in contention for a trip to the playoffs.

This time it was Pittsburgh fans who experienced a major embarrassment. The Browns took an early 7–0 lead on a Couch touchdown pass and, with Kordell Stewart struggling at quarterback, held a 7–3 lead at halftime. Trailing 7–6 in the third quarter, the Steelers finally scored a touchdown but made a decision that would cost them the game when they failed a 2-point conversion attempt. Another field goal gave the Steelers a 15–7 lead, but

Couch cut the lead to 15–13 with his second touchdown pass of the game. After the Browns tried and failed to tie the game with a 2-point conversion, they got the ball back. With time running out, Couch, having played the best game of his rookie season, drove them down the field to set up a 39-yard field goal to win the game. It was sweet revenge for Browns fans after the opening game debacle in Cleveland.

The Steelers never recovered from their defeat at the hands of the expansion Browns. They lost their next five games and finished the season with a 6–10 record. After leading Pittsburgh to playoff appearances and a trip to the Super Bowl in his first six seasons, Bill Cowher's Steelers had now suffered through two losing seasons. They had a thousand-yard rusher in Jerome Bettis, but Kordell Stewart had played erratically at quarterback and the defense was a disappointment. With the team heading into a new century, their fans could only hope that Cowher could turn things around and return the Steelers to championship form.

Any hope that the Browns would surge after defeating the Steelers at Three Rivers was dashed when Cleveland lost its last six games to finish at 2–14. Couch had played well at quarterback, but, as he remembered, "There were sacks. Lots and lots of sacks." Although Cleveland fans were happy to have an NFL team once again, they had to wonder how long it would take the expansion Browns to develop into a serious contender. They could only hope that a new century would bring championship football back to Cleveland.

CHAPTER EIGHT

The 2000s and Beyond

Through the Looking Glass

By the 2001 season, the Cleveland Browns and the Pittsburgh Steelers were playing in new stadiums. In 1999, the expansion Browns opened their inaugural season at Cleveland Browns Stadium (renamed FirstEnergy Stadium in 2013), built on the site of the old Cleveland Municipal Stadium. Their first home game, against Cleveland's traditional NFL rival, did not go well when they lost to the Pittsburgh Steelers 43–0.

In 2001, construction was completed on PNC Park and Heinz Field. PNC Park, the new home for the Pittsburgh Pirates, saved the franchise from moving to another city. Heinz Field, built on the site of Three Rivers Stadium, guaranteed that the Steelers would remain in Pittsburgh for the next 30 years. The inaugural game at Heinz Field, appropriately, was scheduled against archrival Cleveland.

Browns fans planning to travel to Pittsburgh hoped that their team would gain a measure of revenge for the 1999 debacle in Cleveland, but, after the terror attacks on 9/11, the NFL postponed its scheduled games that Sunday—including the Browns-Steelers matchup. The Steelers opened their 2001 season a few weeks later with a 16–7 victory against the Cincinnati Bengals. The Steelers didn't play the Browns at Heinz Field until the last game of the season and won easily 23–7.

When the Browns opened their new stadium, the organization set aside a special bleacher section in the east end zone to honor the Dawg Pound. Its members had mixed feelings about becoming official members of the Browns family, but it didn't slow down their outrageous behavior or their notoriety.

They were at their worst in a 2001 game against the Jacksonville Jaguars when they bombarded the field with beer bottles in an incident that became known as "Bottlegate." They were at their most inebriated and goofiest when they hung a two-panel sign at Cleveland Browns Stadium that read, "GPODAWUND."

More than anything, Dawg Pound fans hoped that the new stadium would give them the Super Bowls that the first decade at Three Rivers had brought to the Steelers. At the very least, they were glad to see the destruction of Three Rivers, where the Browns had lost 16 in a row before winning a game and 24 of the 28 games played between the two teams. Steelers fans, now celebrated as the Steeler Nation, anticipated that the Steelers' dominance of the Browns would continue at Heinz Field. More than that, that they hoped that the Steelers' new home would match the Super Bowl run that had begun at Three Rivers.

The rivalry between the Browns and the Steelers would face its most severe test as the NFL entered the twenty-first century. After 50 years and nearly 100 games against each other, Cleveland and Pittsburgh would need their football fans more than ever to sustain a rivalry spawned and sustained by their loyalty and passion.

There had been other great rivalries in the history of the Browns and the Steelers. Browns fans had Sam Huff and the New York Giants to hate in the 1950s, Johnny Unitas and the Baltimore Colts in the 1960s, and John Elway and the Denver Broncos in the 1980s; Steelers fans had coach John Madden's Oakland Raiders and Roger Staubach and the Dallas Cowboys in the dynasty years of the 1970s. Those rivalries, however, were forged in championship battles and heart-stopping plays—like the Immaculate Reception, the Drive, and the Fumble—and faded once there was no longer a championship at stake.

For all the intensity and endurance of the Browns-Steelers rivalry, it's remarkable that the teams rarely played each other in a championship-deciding game. When one team was great, the other team was usually awful. While there were games that had an impact on the Browns' and the Steelers' playoff hopes, the teams, by the end of the century, had met only once in the playoffs and that didn't happen until the 1994 postseason. A year later, the Browns left Cleveland and became the Baltimore Ravens. Cleveland and Pittsburgh fans wouldn't see their teams play each other until the 1999 season. At the beginning of a new century, if there was to be a resurrection of the rivalry, a renewal of the turnpike traffic between the two cities during football season and a return of the taunting and abuse in the stands, it would be up to the fans.

In the 2000 season, it became tempting for Pittsburgh and especially Cleveland fans to focus their hatred on the Ravens. Owned by the despised Art Modell, who moved the Browns to Baltimore; coached by Brian Billick, who turned down an offer to coach the expansion Browns before taking the Ravens job; and built by general manager Ozzie Newsome, one of the greatest players in Browns history; the Ravens did something the Cleveland Browns had never accomplished. In 2000, they played their way into the Super Bowl, then easily defeated the Giants for the NFL championship. The expansion Browns played badly, finished with a 3–13, and fired their coach. The Steelers fared better at 9–7 but finished out of the playoffs.

Both the Browns and the Steelers gained a measure of revenge in 2001. With Paul "Butch" Davis, former offensive coordinator with the Cowboys, taking over the head coaching duties with the Browns, Cleveland improved to 7–9, with more wins than they had in the 1999 and 2000 seasons combined. Those seven wins included a stunning 24–14 upset over the Ravens in front of roaring Cleveland fans, who filled Cleveland Browns Stadium to overflowing. The Steelers, after missing the playoffs for the past three seasons, surged to a 13–3 record and a division championship. In the first round of the playoffs, they defeated the Super Bowl champion Ravens before losing to the New England Patriots, who would go on to win their first Super Bowl under former Browns coach Bill Belichick.

In 2002, the Browns improved to 9–7 and, remarkably, in only their fourth season since returning to Cleveland, made it into the playoffs. As a wild card team, they traveled to Pittsburgh to meet the Steelers, who, at 10–5–1, had won the division championship. Only the second playoff game against each other in their long history, their meeting would produce the most dramatic contest since the Browns-Steelers rivalry began in the 1950s.

With snow falling from the sky and covering the field in patches, conditions made it nearly impossible for the teams to run the ball, but the slippery field made the game a nightmare for defensive backs. Cleveland quarterback Bryan Kelly Holcomb, playing in place of an injury-prone Tim Couch who broke his leg in the last game of the season, and Pittsburgh quarterback Tommy Maddox, who had replaced an ineffective Kordell Stewart, would pass for over 800 yards and throw for six touchdowns in a game that would feature the greatest comeback in the Steelers-Browns rivalry and wouldn't be decided until the last minute.

In the first quarter, the Browns stunned the Steelers and silenced the deafening roar of the Pittsburgh home crowd by taking a 14–0 lead in the second quarter. Antwaan Randle El finally put the Steelers on the scoreboard with a 66-yard punt return, but a Cleveland field goal gave the Browns a 17–7 lead at halftime. As the Steelers took the field for the second half, Maddox, who would receive the NFL's Comeback of the Year in 2002, told his teammates, "If you don't think we can win this game, you need to go back to the locker room."

Early in the third quarter, a Holcomb touchdown pass, his second in the game, gave the Browns a 24–7 lead, but a Maddox touchdown pass cut Cleveland's lead to 24–14 going into the fourth quarter. After a Cleveland field goal, Maddox threw a short touchdown pass to narrow Cleveland's lead to 27–21, but a Holcomb third touchdown pass gave the Browns, who failed on a 2-point conversion, what appeared to be an insurmountable 33–21 lead.

With a little more than five minutes left in the game, Maddox drove the Steelers down the field and hit Hines Ward with a short touchdown pass to cut the lead to 33–28. When the Browns' Dennis Northcutt dropped an easy catch that would have given the Browns a likely game-clinching first down, the Steelers got the ball back and, with Maddox completing key passes, drove to the Browns' 5-yard line with only 58 seconds left on the clock. In a game that was dominated by passing, the Steelers took the lead on a draw play that fullback Chris Fuamatu-Ma'afala ran untouched into the end zone. After the Steelers converted a 2-point conversion to take a 36–33 lead, Holcomb drove the Browns into Steelers territory, but time ran out with the Browns on the Steelers' 31-yard line.

After the game, a jubilant Maddox, who led the Steelers to three touchdowns in the last 19 minutes, reminded reporters that, earlier in his career, he "was fortunate to play behind John Elway [in Denver] and to see the things that he could do in games we didn't think we had a chance to win." All Bill Cowher, who had jumped up and down on his way to the locker room and threw his cap to roaring Pittsburgh fans, could say was, "What a game. . . . It was one of those wins you can't see happening, but you just keep hoping it will keep going the way that it's going."

In the gloom of the Browns' locker room, Kelly Holcomb, who had passed for 429 yards and three touchdowns while starting in only the fourth game of his career, told reporters, "I don't think anybody in the building thought we weren't going to win. Everybody thought we were moving on." Browns linebacker Earl Little said, "I can't believe this. I can't believed this happened to us." Cleveland coach Butch Davis admitted, "I don't know that I've been as disappointed in a long time."

As for Browns fans, none were as despondent and heartbroken as those who had watched the game in a section cordoned off by crime scene tape at the Oregon Bar on Pittsburgh's north side. As they left the bar, Steelers took a moment out of their yelling and cheering to boo them and hurl beer cans at them.

The Steelers went on to lose their next playoff game in overtime to the Tennessee Titans, formerly the Houston Oilers. But the drama of the Browns-Steelers playoff game had brought their rivalry with the Browns back to life and stirred the hope for fans of both teams for a trip to the Super Bowl in the 2003 season.

In the off-season, however, Butch Davis would have to decide on his starting quarterback after Holcomb played so well when Couch was out with injuries. And Bill Cowher would have to decide if Maddox, with his early career failure as the heir apparent to John Elway and his reputation for turning the ball over on interceptions and fumbles, was capable of leading the Steelers to the Super Bowl.

Davis decided to go with Kelly Holcomb as his starting quarterback in 2003, but with Holcomb struggling and Couch faring no better, the Browns finished the season with a disappointing 5–11 record. At season's end, Davis released Couch. As Terry Pluto pointed out in *The Browns Blues,* Couch had been worn down by injuries: "He had multiple concussions. He had a broken thumb. A broken leg. Some broken ribs." Cleveland fans, frustrated with a struggling Couch, actually cheered when he suffered a concussion in 2002 and was replaced Holcomb. Couch broke down in tears after the game.

To replaced Couch, the Browns signed free agent Jeff Garcia after he had been released by the San Francisco 49ers, but Garcia, who had been arrested for a DUI just before signing with the Browns, struggled in 2004 to win games. Late in the 2004 season, with the Browns at 3–8, Davis resigned and was replaced by assistant defensive coach Terry Robiskie. The Browns finished the 2004 season at 4–12, one game worse than the previous season.

With Tommy Maddox as Steelers starting quarterback going into the 2003 season and Kordell Stewart becoming a free agent and signing with the Chicago Bears, Cowher installed Pittsburgh native Charlie Batch as Maddox's backup. Having 32-year-old Maddox and 29-year-old Batch running the team, the Steelers entertained the idea of drafting a quarterback with their top draft pick; however, after trading up in the draft, they instead selected USC safety and future Hall of Famer Troy Polamalu.

After Maddox struggled in 2003 and the Steelers ended the season with a disappointing 6–10 record, Pittsburgh decided to select a quarterback in the 2004 draft. With their first-round pick, they drafted Miami (Ohio) University quarterback Ben Roethlisberger after the Browns had passed on him. Roethlisberger was deeply disappointed but realized he was soon to become a part of the Steelers-Browns rivalry: "It is Ohio. It is the Browns. I thought I was going to the Browns. I am kind of over that, but for me this is AFC North football. This is still a huge rivalry for us."

Cowher hoped to ease Roethlisberger into a starting role, but when Maddox was injured in the second game of the 2004 season, Cowher turned to Roethlisberger, who led the Steelers to 13 wins in a row, a 15–1 record (including two wins against the Browns), and a playoff victory against the New York Jets. Roethlisberger's Cinderella season ended, however, when he played poorly in a loss to the defending Super Bowl championship Patriots. Steelers fans were disappointed but were also excited about the prospect of Roethlisberger leading Pittsburgh back to Super Bowl glory.

The Browns' search for a new head coach for the 2005 season led them to Romeo Crennel, another Bill Belichick protégé. Crennel had been the defensive coordinator for the Browns in 2000 before taking a similar position with the New England Patriots. In New England, Crennel had helped Belichick and the Patriots win back-to-back Super Bowl victories. When Crennel signed his contract, he became the first African American head coach in the history of the Cleveland Browns.

The Browns were aware that they had a major problem at quarterback, but selecting ahead of the Steelers in the 2004 draft, they had passed over Ohio native Roethlisberger and selected University of Miami tight end Kellen Winslow with their first-round pick. They did draft an Ohio quarterback, University of Akron's Charlie Frye in the third round. Going into the 2005 season, they hoped that Trent Dilfer, acquired in the off-season from the Seattle Seahawks, would tutor Frye while serving as starting quarterback. An experienced quarterback, Dilfer had led the Baltimore Ravens to the 2001 Super Bowl.

With Dilfer and Frye rotating at quarterback, the Browns struggled in Crennel's first year as the Browns' head coach and finished the 2005 season with a 6–10 record. One of their worst performances in a dismal year came in the next-to-last game against the Steelers in Cleveland when Frye was sacked eight times in a 41–0 loss. The victory was badly needed by the Steelers, who, at 7–5, needed to win their remaining four games to make the playoffs.

When they defeated the Detroit Lions in their last game of the season, the Steelers finished at 11–5 and, as the wild card team, went on an incredible playoff run with road victories over the Cincinnati Bengals, the top-seeded Indianapolis Colts, and the Denver Broncos. In each game, Roethlisberger led the Steelers to victory with his passing, but in the win against the Colts he had to make a game-saving tackle after a Jerome Bettis fumble.

In Cowher's second trip to the Super Bowl and only Roethlisberger's second season in the NFL, the Steelers defeated the Seahawks 21–10 to give Pittsburgh its fifth Super Bowl victory and its first since the 1979 season. Roethlisberger did not play well, but Willie Parker's 75-yard run and a Hines Ward touchdown reception on a trick play gave Pittsburgh the win. The Steelers finally had given their rabid fans the elusive one for the thumb that had haunted the franchise since the 1980 season. That it came after three critical road victories in the playoffs was fitting for fans that had become so well traveled that they were dubbed the Steeler Nation.

In Romeo Crennel's second season, the Browns traded Trent Dilfer to the 49ers for backup Ken Dorsey and inserted Charlie Frye as the starting quarterback; however, with Frye throwing more interceptions than touchdown passes, Cleveland lost five of its first six games on the way to a 4–12 record in 2006. In Pittsburgh, fans may have hoped for back-to-back Super Bowls, but the Steelers suffered a letdown in 2006 and finished out of the playoffs with an 8–8 record. After the season, Bill Cowher announced that, after 15 seasons, he was stepping down as the head coach of the Steelers.

On January 22, 2007, the Steelers held a press conference to introduce a relatively unknown Mike Tomlin as the Steelers' new head coach. Tomlin, like his predecessors Chuck Noll and Bill Cowher, was a defensive-minded coach, though he had been the defensive coordinator for the Minnesota Vikings for only one year. The 36-year-old Tomlin, like Noll, at 38 and Cowher at 34, became one of the youngest head coaches in the NFL when he signed his four-year contract. He also became the first African American coach in the history of the Pittsburgh Steelers. His hiring validated the "Rooney Rule," a policy instituted by Steelers president Dan Rooney to create opportunities for African Americans to become head coaches in the NFL.

In Tomlin's first game as Steelers head coach, he faced Romeo Crennel's Cleveland Browns. His job on the line after two losing seasons, Crennel decided to start the season with Charlie Frye, but Frye was taken out of Cleveland's home opener in the second quarter after he threw an interception and was sacked five times. With Ben Roethlisberger throwing four touchdown passes, the Steelers romped to a 34–7 victory. The win meant that Tomlin accomplished something Noll and Cowher had failed to do—he won the first game he coached against the Browns.

After the loss to the Steelers, a desperate Crennel made NFL history by trading away his starting quarterback after only the first game of the season. After shipping Frye to the Seattle Seahawks for a sixth-round draft pick, he promoted Derek Anderson, who had been Cleveland's backup since being claimed off waivers in 2005. Cleveland fans expected Anderson simply to fill in until Brayden "Brady" Quinn, the Browns first-round pick out of Notre Dame, was ready to take over. However, in his first game as a starter, Anderson threw five touchdown passes in a 51–45 victory over the Bengals.

With Anderson throwing 29 touchdown passes and playing his way into the Pro Bowl, the Browns went on to a 10–6 record and barely missed out on the playoffs when they finished second behind the 10–6 Steelers, who won the division tiebreaker by beating the Browns twice during the season. The Steelers, in Tomlin's first season, had played their way into the postseason but lost it to Jacksonville in the first round of the playoffs.

After Derek Anderson's brilliant performance in 2007, Cleveland fans had high expectations for the 2008 season, but Anderson was in and out with injuries, and Ken Dorsey and Brady Quinn struggled when they replaced him. After going 3–3, the Browns lost nine out of 10 games, including their last six games, and finished at the bottom of the division with a 4–12 record. At the end of the season, the Browns fired Romeo Crennel. In his four years with the Browns, Crennel's teams had only one winning season, went 24–40, and, especially galling to Cleveland fans, went 0–8 against the Steelers.

In Mike Tomlin's second year with the Steelers, Pittsburgh finished with a 12–4 record and won another division title. They defeated the San Diego Chargers and the Baltimore Ravens in the playoffs and, in a spectacular Super Bowl, defeated the Arizona Cardinals 27–23 in a game that featured a James Harrison 100-yard touchdown run with an interception on the last play of the first half and a game-winning Ben Roethlisberger touchdown pass to a tiptoeing Santonio Holmes with 48 seconds left on the clock. With the victory, Tomlin, at 36, became the youngest NFL head coach to win the Super Bowl.

Laing Kennedy, who grew up in Ontario in the 1950s and listened to the radio broadcast of Browns-Steelers games across Lake Erie on WTAH, became the athletic director at Kent State University in the early 1990s. He remembered a game when Kent State's James Harrison sacked Miami's quarterback Ben Roethlisberger five times. Now they were teammates and Super Bowl heroes.

While Pittsburgh fans basked in the glow of two Steelers Super Bowl wins in the last four seasons, Cleveland fans anxiously awaited the hiring of a new head coach who they hoped would reverse the Browns' fortunes. On January 7, 2009, the Browns announced that they had hired yet another Bill Belichick clone in Eric Mangini. After serving as Belichick's defensive coordinator, Mangini had taken the New York Jets' head coaching job but was fired after three seasons. Mangini was a ball boy when Belichick coached the Browns and, like Belichick, had a reputation for demanding discipline from his players and absolute control of the organization.

A *Sports Illustrated* article called Mangini "the worst coaching hire in the past 25 years," and Cleveland fans would soon agree with that criticism. With Derek Anderson and Brady Quinn rotating at quarterback, the 2009 Browns broke an unwanted team record by losing 11 of their first 12 games. They did manage to defeat the Steelers for the first time since 2005, but they finished last in the division again with a 5–11 record. It was the Browns' eighth losing season in the first decade of the twenty-first century.

After their thrilling Super Bowl victory, the Steelers failed to make the playoffs for the first time under Mike Tomlin, but they did finish with a winning record at 9–7. In the first decade of the twenty-first century, Pittsburgh had only one losing season, made the playoffs six times, and won two Super Bowls. In that 10-year span, much to the distress of Cleveland fans, the Steelers had a 17–3 record against the Browns in a rivalry that had only one moment of greatness when the two teams met in the 2002 playoffs and, once again, risked losing its intensity.

The second decade of the twenty-first century would present even more of a challenge for Cleveland and Pittsburgh fans to sustain the passion of the turnpike rivalry. It started out with a bang for the Steelers and a whimper for the Browns. After not making the playoffs in 2009, the Steelers surged to a 12–4 record and a division title. They defeated the Baltimore Ravens in the division round and played their way into the Super Bowl for the second time in three years with a win over the New York Jets. Any hope of another Super Bowl ended, however, when, the Steelers lost to the Green Bay Packers 31–25 in a game where Ben Roethlisberger threw two costly interceptions.

The Browns started the 2010 season at 1–5, but they had one memorable moment in game eight: a 34–14 trouncing of the New England Patriots. The win was especially gratifying for Eric Mangini, who, when he was coaching the Jets, had alienated himself from Belichick by reporting that the Patriots had violated NFL rules by secretly taping the Jets' sideline signals as well as those of other teams. Belichick and the Patriots were fined $500,000 and had to forfeit their first-round draft pick.

The win improved the Browns' record to 3–5, but Cleveland struggled the rest of the way and finished with another 5–11 season under Mangini. The Browns were humiliated in a 41–9 loss in Cleveland to the Steelers in the last game of the season. In the game, the latest Browns heir apparent at quarterback, Daniel "Colt" McCoy, a third-round draft pick out of Texas, threw three interceptions and was sacked four times. It was Mangini's last game as Cleveland's head coach. After only two seasons, he was fired—despite having two years remaining on his contract.

On January 13, 2011, the Browns introduced Pat Shurmur as their new head coach. Shurmur had been the offensive coordinator with the St. Louis Rams and had a reputation for developing young quarterbacks. With Colt McCoy at quarterback, the Browns managed to split their first six games but lost nine of their last 10 games and finished with a 4–12 record, one game worse than last season, and another last-place finish.

The Steelers bounced back in 2011 after their disappointing Super Bowl loss to the Green Bay Packers and duplicated their 12–4 record, including two wins over the hapless Browns. The hope that they would return to the Super Bowl ended abruptly in the division playoff in Denver when Tim Tebow, in the most spectacular play of his short and uneven NFL career, threw a 66-yard touchdown pass in the fourth quarter to give the Broncos a comeback 26–23 victory over the Steelers.

In the off-season, the Browns drafted Oklahoma State quarterback Brandon Weeden with their first-round selection in the 2012 NFL draft in the hope that Weeden, at age 28, could step right in at quarterback and give Colt Mc-Coy time to mature. The biggest news in Cleveland, however, was owner Al Lerner's sale of the Browns to Jimmy Haslam, who made his fortune running the Pilot Flying J truck stop and paid a reported $1 billion for the Browns franchise. Lerner had taken over the Browns ownership in 2002 after the death of his father. Haslam, who had a minority share in the Steelers, had to sell off his share before the NFL approved the sale of the Browns.

A few months after Haslam became owner of the Cleveland Browns, Art Modell, the most controversial and despised owner in Browns history, died on September 6 at the age of 80. There was praise for Modell from players, coaches, and owners, while some lamented that his move to Baltimore had cost him a much-deserved election to the Pro Football Hall of Fame. There were tributes scheduled at NFL games played on September 9, but the Browns canceled theirs at the request of the Modell family in the fear of a negative reaction from unforgiving fans. One Dawg Pound fan declared, "Modell is probably talking to the devil about relocating Hell."

Cleveland fans had to be excited when Haslam announced that he would run the Browns the way the Rooney family operated the Steelers. But the new owner, rather than stabilizing the franchise, soon sent it into another dizzying, dysfunctional cycle marked by frequent and abrupt changes at quarterback and head coach. When Haslam took over operations midway through the 2012 season, he had already shed Browns president Mike Holmgren, the former Packers head coach, and replaced him with former Philadelphia Eagles president Joe Banner. He also brought in a new general manager, Mike Lombardi, a Bill Walsh San Francisco 49ers protégé.

After the Browns finished the season with a disappointing 5–11 record, Haslam fired Shurmur, who was in only his second year as head coach. Shurmur's last game as Browns head coach was against the Pittsburgh Steelers. With quarterbacks Weeden and McCoy out with an injuries, the Browns started Thad Lewis, who began the season on the taxi squad, and lost the game 24–10. The Steelers, after their Super Bowl season in 2011, had gone 7–4 before a four-game losing streak. The win against the Browns gave them an 8–8 record and prevented Mike Tomlin from suffering his first losing season as Steelers head coach.

With Haslam—after overcoming a business scandal—becoming more and more involved in the Browns' personnel decisions, the Browns hired Rob Chudzinski, offensive coordinator with the Carolina Panthers, as their new head coach. With Colt McCoy gone and Brandon Weeden struggling, Chudzinski, with his team at 1–2, decided to start free agent pickup Brian Hoyer at quarterback. Hoyer led the 1–2 Browns to two victories, but when Hoyer was injured and lost for the season, the team collapsed and finished with a 4–12 record.

Cleveland's last game of the season, for the third straight year, was against the Steelers, and, for the third straight year, it became the last game for a Browns head coach. The Steelers, after finishing 8–8 in 2012, got off to a 0–4 start and stood at 7–8 going into the Browns' game. Once again needing a win over the Browns to avoid a losing season, the Steelers defeated the Browns, 20–17, to finish at 8–8 for the second straight season. Pittsburgh's victory completed a trifecta of fired Browns head coaches, which included Mangini, Shumer, and Chudzinski when Haslam fired his latest head coach after only one season.

With Haslam at the controls, the Browns tried to lure Jim Harbaugh away from the San Francisco 49ers and, when that failed, offered the head-coaching position to Denver Broncos offensive coordinator Adam Gase, who also turned down the job. Twice rejected, the Browns turned to Mike Pettine, the defensive coordinator of the Buffalo Bills, who accepted the offer. The Browns had two first-round picks in the 2014 draft and hoped to solve their biggest problem by selecting a quarterback in the first round. After taking cornerback Justin Gilbert with their first pick, they selected, at Haslam's urging, quarterback Johnny Manziel from Texas A&M with their second first-round pick,

A former past Heisman Trophy winner who was dubbed "Johnny Football" in his college days, Manziel generated a great deal of excitement in Cleveland, but scouts had warned that he didn't have the skills to be a topflight quarterback and also had some character issues. The selection of Manziel also upset Brian Hoyer, who thought he had earned the starting job. Determined to keep Manziel on the sidelines, Hoyer played well in training camp and exhibition games and was Pettine's choice as starting quarterback in their opening game against the Steelers.

Hoyer played well in a 30–27 loss to the Steelers and led the Browns to a surprising 7–4 start. When the Browns lost their next game to the Bills, Pettine, yielding to pressure from ownership and fans to play Johnny Football, started Manziel, who had a disastrous game in a 30–0 loss to the Bengals. Rotating Hoyer and Manziel, the Browns struggled the rest of the way and finished with a 7–9 record. The record was an improvement over the 2013 season, but it was a disappointment after Cleveland's impressive start.

After two mediocre seasons, the Steelers, after their opening victory against the Browns, bounced back in the 2014 season. Sparked by the "Killer Bees," Pittsburgh played its way to a division title and playoff appearance, with an 11–5 record. Ben Roethlisberger, running back Le'Veon Bell, and wide receiver Antonio Brown had an All-Pro record-breaking season, but Bell was out with an injury when the Steelers met the Ravens in Pittsburgh in the first round. When Roethlisberger struggled, the Steelers lost 30–17.

If Mike Pettine wanted a forecast of his fate going into the 2015 season, all he had to do was look at Cleveland's 2015 schedule. The last three Browns head coaches had been fired after losing their last game of the year against the Steelers. In 2015, the Browns once again would end the season with Pittsburgh. There were also more immediate signs that 2015 would be Pettine's last in Cleveland. Brian Hoyer had become a free agent and signed with the Houston Texans. The controversial and inconsistent Johnny Manziel was coming out of rehab, so the Browns, for insurance, signed free agent Josh McCown, who had played quarterback with eight different NFL teams in his up-and-down career.

The looming presence of the Steelers, however, and the uncertainty at quarterback were the least of Pettine's problems. Cleveland mercurial owner Jimmy Haslam decided to embark on a four-year plan based on the analytics that had become popular in baseball after the publication of the best seller *Moneyball.* That meant shedding the team of its veteran players and relying on a stockpile of draft choices. To the despair of Cleveland fans, they were being asked to suffer through another stretch of losing after the Browns had given them only two winning seasons in the 16 years since the Browns returned to Cleveland in 1999.

The Browns did manage to go 2–3 in their first five games, but, struggling to score touchdowns, lost 10 of the next 11 games, including their last game against Pittsburgh. True to form and in keeping with the Steelers' last-game jinx, Haslam fired Pettine, victim No. 4, after the Pittsburgh game.

The Steelers had faced their own controversy when they signed quarterback Michael Vick, who had been suspended and eventually spent time in prison for involvement in a dog-fighting ring. While the signing was widely criticized, Vick kept the Steelers in contention when they lost Roethlisberger for several games with a knee injury, When Roethlisberger returned, he helped the Steelers to a 10–6 finish and a wild card win over the division-rival Bengals before the Steelers were eliminated by Peyton Manning and the Broncos in the next round of the playoffs.

If Cleveland fans feared the worst going into the 2016 season, the Browns would not disappoint them. After firing Pettine and ignoring the recommendation of his staff to hire Sean McDermott, the Carolina Panthers defensive coordinator, Haslam hired Hue Jackson, a former Oakland Raiders head coach and the current Bengals offensive coordinator, because he thought Jackson related well to the players. The only problem for Haslam was that Jackson didn't relate well to analytics.

Even with the owner and his new coach at odds over the operation of the team, the Browns were hopeful heading into the new season, but that optimism soon faded. Former Washington Redskins first-round pick, quarterback Robert Griffin III, signed as a free agent in the off-season, suffered a shoulder injury in an opening loss to the Philadelphia Eagles, and was out for several weeks. When Josh McCown was injured in a second game loss, the Browns were down to rookies Cody Kessler, a third-round draft pick out of southern California, and Kevin Hogan, a free agent who started the season on the taxi squad.

In a season that rapidly became a perfect storm, the Browns suffered loss after loss of quarterbacks and games until they fell to 0–14 before, with Griffin back from injury, they won their first game of the season, 20–17 over the San Diego Chargers. In their last game of the season, they faced the playoff-bound Steelers and lost in overtime to end the season with a stunning 1–15 record, the worst in Browns history. The Steelers, with Roethlisberger throwing 29 touchdown passes, including 12 to Antonio Brown, and Bell rushing for over 1,200 yards, finished the season at 11–5 and defeated the Miami Dolphins and the Kansas City Chiefs in the playoffs. Only one game away from another Super Bowl, the Steelers, giving up Tom Brady's three touchdown passes, lost 36–17 to the New England Patriots in the AFC championship game.

Hue Jackson accomplished one thing in his disastrous first year as the Browns' head coach. Unlike the last four Cleveland head coaches, he wasn't fired after his team played and lost to the Steelers in the final game of the season. When the NFL released its 2017 schedule, however, Jackson may well have shuddered when he saw that the Browns would once again be opening and closing the season against the Steelers.

Cleveland fans might have thought they had seen the worst in 2016, but 2017 would turn into a complete disaster. It began for the Browns and their fans in the first quarter of the home opener against Pittsburgh when the Steelers scored a touchdown on a blocked punt. Cleveland second-round draft pick DeShone Kizer, named the starter at quarterback over free agent Brock Osweiler, had a decent game, scoring on a run and passing for a touchdown. But that blocked punt made the difference in a 21–18 loss.

With Kizer, an Ohio native who starred at Notre Dame, playing inconsistently, the Browns began losing game after game. Kizer started 15 games, and the Browns lost all 15, including overtime losses to the Tennessee Titans and the Green Bay Packers. In the last game of the season, Kizer had his most productive game, passing for 314 yards, but the Steelers, with backup quarterback Landry Jones starting in place of a resting Roethlisberger, won 28–17 in a meaningless game for the playoff-bound Steelers.

The loss to the Steelers made Cleveland Browns history. They finished with a 0–16 season record and an overall 1–31 record under Hue Jackson. At the end of the season, Jackson, to the amazement of Browns fans, somehow survived the Steelers' last-game jinx and was brought back by Cleveland ownership for another year.

After their opening game victory over the Browns, the Steelers struggled to a 3–2 record before winning 10 of their last 11 games, including eight in a row. They won the division title with a 13–3 record, but their 2017 success was tinged with sadness. In April, Steelers owner Dan Rooney died at the age of 84. While his father Art Rooney was the Steelers' founder and one of the most popular figures in Pittsburgh sports history, it was Dan Rooney who took control of the Steelers' operations in 1969 and presided over the Steelers' dynasty of the 1970s. He was also responsible for the Rooney Rule that required NFL teams to interview minority candidates for open head-coaching jobs.

Like his father, Dan Rooney, in 2000, was elected to the Pro Football Hall of Fame, thereby becoming only the second father-son inductees after Tim and Wellington Mara of the New York Giants. At the induction ceremony, where he was presented by Mean Joe Greene, the first member of the Steelers' dynasty to enter the Hall of Fame, Rooney told those in attendance: "The game is your legacy. Protect it. Don't let anyone tarnish it."

Pittsburgh's 2017 was also plagued by controversy. Ben Roethlisberger had an excellent season, but he was unhappy with the play-calling of Todd Haley, his offensive coordinator. He was also having trouble getting along with wide receiver Antonio Brown, who complained Roethlisberger wasn't targeting him enough. Another of the Killer Bees, Le'Veon Bell had a great season, but he was playing for the second straight season with a franchise tag after refusing the Steelers' offer of a long-term contract. That disgruntled offense, with Roethlisberger throwing five touchdown passes, scored 42 points in the division round of the playoffs but made key mistakes in a 45–42 loss to Jacksonville. After the loss, the Steelers fired Todd Haley, who was then hired, to the bafflement and dismay of Cleveland fans, as the Browns' offensive coordinator.

The 2018 season would be the 20th since the Browns returned to the NFL, but there was little cause for celebration among even the most die-hard Cleveland fans. Since 1999, the Browns had only two winning seasons, in 2002 and 2007, and, in their only playoff appearance, they lost to the hated Pittsburgh Steelers.

As for the Steelers-Browns rivalry, it had been one-sided in the past but nothing like the last 19 years. The Browns had defeated the Steelers only six times since 1999, and never twice in one season, while the Steelers won 33 times during that span, including a sweep of the series from 2004 to 2008. It also didn't help the morale of Browns fans that, while no Cleveland team had made it to the Super Bowl, the Steelers played in three more since 1999, winning two, while their new nemesis, the Baltimore Ravens, also won two during that span.

Unfortunately for their fans, the Browns did outpace the Steelers in two critical areas since they returned to Cleveland as an expansion team: head coaches and starting quarterbacks. While the Steelers had only two head coaches—Bill Cowher, who retired after the 2006 season, and Mike Tomlin—the Browns, counting interim coaches, had nine and, during the 2018 season, fired their head coach and added another interim on their way to hiring a new head coach for the 2019 season.

As for quarterbacks, going into the 2019 season, the Steelers, since they drafted Ben Roethlisberger with their top draft pick in 2003, had, barring injuries, only one starter since Roethlisberger replaced an injured Tommy Maddox early in the 2004 season. The Browns, since drafting Tim Couch with the NFL's top draft pick in 1999, had so many starting quarterbacks, including Heisman Trophy winners and No. 1 draft picks, that Cleveland fans couldn't be blamed for losing count.

. . .

In the 2018 draft, the Browns, still desperately seeking a franchise quarterback, selected Oklahoma's Baker Mayfield with the first selection in the draft, the fourth time since 1999 that they selected a quarterback with their top pick. With Tyrod Taylor, acquired from the Buffalo Bills for a third-round draft pick, starting at quarterback and Mayfield watching from the sideline, the Browns, who won only one game in the last two years, opened the 2018 season in Cleveland against the Steelers, who had won the division title in 2017 with a 13–3 record.

After struggling in the first half on a rain-soaked field and leading only 7–0, the Steelers scored two touchdowns to go ahead 21–7 going into the fourth quarter, but the Browns brought the Dawg Pound to life by rallying for two touchdowns to tie the score and send the game into overtime. Both teams had chances to win in overtime, but only a blocked field goal in the closing seconds prevented the Browns from pulling off the upset. While the tie broke a 17-game losing streak for the Browns, Hue Jackson said he was "disappointed for the fans. Didn't want them going home without a victory."

After losing their second game of the season, the Browns finally ended their long winless streak with a victory over the New York Jets, but Taylor was injured late in the game and replaced by Mayfield. With the brash and confident Mayfield at quarterback, the Browns lost two of their next three games. However, after losing an overtime game to the Oakland Raiders, they upset the Baltimore Ravens in overtime to go 2–3–1 before heading to Pittsburgh. The Steelers, with Le'Veon Bell sitting out the season, were struggling and, at 3–2–1, were only a game ahead of the Browns.

With Roethlisberger throwing two touchdown passes and James Conner, playing in place of Bell, rushing for 146 yards and scoring twice, the Steelers, despite Mayfield throwing two touchdown passes, easily defeated the Browns 33–18. Hue Jackson, who had twice escaped the fate of his four predecessors by not being fired after losing to the Steelers in the final game of the season, finally fell victim to the Steelers jinx when he was fired after the team's loss in Pittsburgh. He was replaced by defensive coordinator Greg Williams.

With Mayfield, who had been openly critical of Jackson, leading the way, the Browns won five of their next eight games and, after winning only one game in the last 20 seasons, stood at 7–7–1. Going into Baltimore for their final game of the season, they were poised to finish with a winning record, only their third in 20 seasons and a remarkable turnaround after going 1–31 in their past two seasons.

The Browns-Ravens game also had great significance for the Steelers, who were 8–6–1. They needed a win in their last game of the season against the Cincinnati Bengals and a Baltimore Ravens loss to the Browns to make the playoffs. The Steelers defeated the Bengals and watched on Heinz Field's giant screen as Mayfield, who had already thrown three touchdown passes, drove the Browns down the field with seconds left in the game for what would have been a game-winning touchdown. When the Browns failed to score, the Steelers' season was over—so was Cleveland's hope for a winning season.

At a sports bar in the Squirrel Hill section of Pittsburgh, hundreds of Steelers fans gathered to watch the Steelers play the Bengals. They were joined at the bar by dozens of Browns fans who were there to watch the Browns-Ravens game. In one of the most remarkable moments in the long rivalry between Pittsburgh and Cleveland, Steelers fans, after their Steelers defeated the Bengals, joined Browns fans in rooting for a Cleveland victory. It was as if the Steelers fans who entered the bar had walked through a looking glass that had reversed their loyalties and transformed them into Browns boosters.

After the Ravens won and knocked the Steelers out of the playoffs, Steelers fans returned to form and cursed and threatened Browns fans as they left the bar. For Browns fans, it was the moment they'd been waiting for, the moment when a rivalry that seemed on its deathbed had come to life again. Browns fans could only hope that they'd hear more curses and threats in seasons to come. As one Browns fan said as he left the bar, "I can't wait for the hate." The passion, finally, was back.

EPILOGUE

They Started It

In Street and Smith's pro football yearbook for the 2019 season, the editors selected the Pittsburgh Steelers to win the AFC's North Division, followed closely by the Cleveland Browns. It also had a letter from the editor, written by Scott Smith, titled "Brownie Points," that praised the Browns' rapid rise from 0–16 in the 2017 season to 7–8–1 in 2018.

Smith did acknowledge that "Cleveland owns a particularly heinous set of postseason droughts, including 17 seasons since the Browns qualified for the playoffs, 25 years since they won a playoff game, and a full three decades since they last appeared in the AFC championship game." But he praised the Browns' recent draft selections, including All-Pro defensive end Myles Garrett and Heisman Trophy–winning quarterback Baker Mayfield, and their acquisition of "mega-talented" Odell Beckham Jr. from the New York Giants. He predicted that the Browns' 2019 season will be "the culmination of a rebuilding job" and that it should win general manager John Dorsey the "NFL Executive of the Year in a land slide."

The Street and Smith preview of the Steelers' season, written by Gerry Dulac of the *Pittsburgh Post-Gazette,* ran under the title, "Steelers see the departure of stars Brown and Bell as addition by subtraction." Dulac wrote that the Steelers had already found replacements for the disgruntled Le'Veon Bell and Antonio Brown in rising stars James Conner and John 'JuJu" Smith-Schuster, and, as long as they had Ben Roethlisberger, "they are never out of any game, never out of any season. The Steelers still have the makings of a Super Bowl team."

The preview of the Browns' season, written by Steve Doerschuk of the *Canton (Ohio) Repository*. ran under the title, "Feast on this: Browns have the unmistakable look of a playoff team." Doerschuk wrote that "after twenty years in the slow cooker with only tasteless football to flop on the plate, can it be that John Dorsey has microwaved a hearty feast." With their recent outstanding drafts and acquisitions and the promotion of the popular Freddie Kitchens from offensive coordinator to head coach, the Browns had solved the big problems. And if they could solve some smaller "ifs," they were playoff bound.

For all the optimism expressed in the Street and Smith yearbook, the Steelers and the Browns had disappointing 2019 seasons. The disappointment began for the Steelers when they lost the indispensable Ben Roethlisberger to a season-ending elbow injury in the second game of the season and dropped four of their first five games. With second- and third-string quarterbacks, the Steelers—miraculously—won seven of their next eight games, their only loss to the Browns. But they lost their last three games to finish out of the playoffs with an 8–8 record.

The little "ifs" facing the Browns turned into major problems when Baker Mayfield played erratically and their defense became inconsistent. After losing two of their first three games, they beat the eventual division championship Baltimore Ravens but lost their next four games to go 2–6. They bounced back to win four of their next five games, their only defeat to the Steelers, but lost their last three games to finish with a losing record at 6–10. At end of the season, Kitchens and Dorsey were fired.

The 2019 season was deeply disappointing for both Steelers and Browns fans, but the games between Cleveland and Pittsburgh inflamed the rivalry as never before—and all that it took was a helmet and a T-shirt. When the teams met for the first time on Thursday night in Cleveland, the Browns' defense frustrated and harassed Steelers quarterback Mason Rudolph, intercepting four of his passes, and intimated Steelers receivers, knocking two of them out of the game with concussions.

In the waning seconds of the game, with the Browns leading 21–7, Browns defensive end Myles Garrett tackled Rudolph in the Steelers' end zone after Rudolph had thrown a pass. When Garrett was slow to get off him, an upset Rudolph punched and kicked at Garrett and tried to take off Garrett's helmet.

An infuriated Garrett joined the ranks of rivalry villains Joe "Turkey" Jones and Jack Lambert by ripping off Rudolph's helmet and hitting him on the head with it before he was punched and kicked by Steelers center Maurkice Pouncey.

After the game, when asked if the game-ending brawl had revived the Steelers-Browns rivalry, Freddie Kitchens said, "it takes two to be a rivalry, so we've got to have our part. We've got to do our part." When asked the same question about the rivalry, Mike Tomlin responded, "I didn't know it was dead." As for the NFL, it acted quickly, fining Rudolph $50,000, suspending Pouncey for three games (reduced to two on appeal), suspending Browns defensive lineman Larry Ogunjobi for one game for knocking Rudolph to the ground from behind, and suspending Garrett for the rest of the season. It also warned both the Browns and the Steelers against seeking revenge in the upcoming game in two weeks.

In the days leading up to the rematch, Rudolph apologized for his role in the brawl and said he needed to do a better job of keeping his emotions under control. At first Garrett also seemed contrite, apologizing to fans and his teammates, but when he appealed his suspension he claimed that Rudolph had hurled a racial slur at him. Insulted and hurt, Rudolph denied the accusation, and the NFL, finding no evidence to support the claim, upheld Garrett's suspension.

Two days before the game, Freddie Kitchens added more fuel to the already inflamed rivalry when he was photographed in the company of a Browns fan while wearing a "The Steelers Started It" T-Shirt that was making the rounds in Cleveland. While Kitchens claimed that his daughter wanted him to wear it and that he had on a jacket nearly covering the T-shirt, the photograph went viral. Cleveland fans loved the photo; one blogger wrote, "the rivalry is real. Cleveland, let's go." But Pittsburgh players and fans, in the words of offensive lineman David DeCastro, thought it was "pretty stupid."

The Browns had every reason to feel confident going into their second game of the season with the Steelers. Rudolph had struggled after the game in Cleveland and had been benched by Tomlin. With third-string quarterback Devlin "Duck" Hodges starting the game, the Browns took an early 10–0 lead, but with Hodges completing key passes and the Steelers' running game taking control, the Steelers rallied to tie the score and went on to take a 20–10 lead. A Browns field goal cut the Steelers' lead to a touchdown at 20–13. But, with time running out, Mayfield, who had been harassed by the Steelers defense all afternoon, threw a desperation pass that was intercepted, fittingly, by a former Browns player, defensive back Pat Haden.

After the game, a flustered Freddie Kichens claimed that "the T-shirt had nothing to do with the game," but Steelers players had a different view. Offensive lineman Ramon Foster told reporters, "I know our coach would never do a thing like that. Why throw gas? When you do something like that you put your players in harm's way. He's not on the field." When asked about the T-shirt, Tomlin said, "That's how you deal with that stuff. You beat them." In the days after the game, the most popular T-shirt in Pittsburgh read, "Pittsburgh Finished It."

After another loss in Pittsburgh, Cleveland sportswriter Terry Pluto best expressed the despair of long-suffering Browns fans since the expansion franchise began playing 20 years ago when he wrote: "I don't know how you endure this year after year." The irony of his lament was that it could well apply to both Steelers and Browns fans of any decade since the roller-coaster rivalry began in the 1950s.

For 70 years, Steelers and Browns fans have endured a rivalry in which the teams have taken turns intimidating and dominating each other—a rivalry that, over the generations, has been driven by a passion to beat the bully. That rivalry, as the NFL completed its 100th season, remains as intense as ever. Because of the shot-and-a-beer working-class character of Pittsburgh and Cleveland and their proximity, Steelers and Browns games have been dubbed the turnpike rivalry, but, at heart, the rivalry harkens back to those old school-yard fights in which those watching root for the bully finally to get what's coming to him.

APPENDIX

Record of Browns-Steelers Games
by Decades and Attendance

1950s		
Oct. 7, 1950	Browns (3–1) 30	Steelers (1–3) 17 @ Forbes Field 35,900.
Oct. 29, 1950	Browns (5–2) 45	Steelers (2–5) 7 @ Municipal Stadium 40,714
Oct. 21, 1951	Browns (3–1) 17	Steelers 0 (0–3–1) @ Municipal Stadium 32,409
Dec. 9, 1951	Browns (10–1) 28	Steelers 0 (3–7–1) @ Forbes Field 24,229
Oct. 4, 1952	Browns (2–0) 21	Steelers (0–2) 20 @ Forbes Field 27,923
Nov. 16, 1952	Browns (6–2) 29	Steelers (2–6) 28 @ Municipal Stadium 34,973
Nov. 8, 1953	Browns 34 (7–0)	Steelers 16 (3–4) @ Municipal Stadium 35,592
Nov. 20, 1953	Browns 20 (9–0)	Steelers 16 (4–5) @ Forbes Field 32,904
Oct. 17, 1954	Steelers 55 (3–1)	Browns 27 (1–2) @ Forbes Field 31,256
Dec. 12 1954	Browns 42 (9–2)	Steelers 7 (4–5) @ Municipal Stadium 28,064
Nov. 20, 1955	Browns 41 (7–2)	Steelers 7 (5–7) @ Municipal Stadium 53,509
Dec. 4, 1955	Browns 30 (8–2–1)	Steelers 7 (4–7) @ Forbes Field 31,101
Oct. 6, 1956	Browns 14 (1–1)	Steelers 10 (1–1) @ Forbes Field 35,398
Oct. 28, 1956	Steelers 24 (2–3)	Browns 16 (1–4) @ Municipal Stadium 50,358
Oct. 5, 1957	Browns 23 (2–0)	Steelers 13 (1–1) @ Forbes Field 35,570
Nov. 10, 1957	Browns 24 (6–1)	Steelers 0 (4–3) @ Municipal Stadium 53,709
Oct. 4, 1958	Browns 45 (2–0)	Steelers 12 (0–2) @ Pitt Stadium 31,130
Oct. 19 1958	Browns 27 (4–0)	Steelers 10 (1–3) @ Municipal Stadium 66,852
Sept. 26 1959	Steelers 17 (1–0)	Browns 7 (0–1) @ Forbes Field 33,844
Nov. 22, 1959	Steelers 21 (4–4–1)	Browns 20 (6–3) @ Municipal Stadium 68,563
1950s total wins: Browns 16 Steelers 4		

1960s

Oct. 2, 1960	Browns 28 (2–0)	Steelers 20 (1–1) @ Municipal Stadium 67,692
Nov. 20, 1960	Steelers 14 (3–5–1)	Browns 10 (5–3) @ Forbes Field 35,215
Oct. 22, 1961	Browns 30 (4–2)	Steelers 28 (1–5) @ Forbes Field 29,692
Nov. 5, 1961	Steelers 17 (3–5)	Browns 13 (5–3) @ Municipal Stadium 62,723
Oct. 28, 1962	Browns 41 (4–3)	Steelers 14 (3–4) @ Forbes Field 35,417
Nov. 25, 1962	Browns 35 (6–4–1)	Steelers 14 (6–5) @ Municipal Stadium 53,601
Oct. 5, 1963	Browns 35 (4–0)	Steelers 23 (2–1–1) @ Municipal Stadium 84,684
Nov. 10, 1963	Steelers 9 (5–3)	Browns 7 (7–2) @ Forbes Field 36,465
Oct. 10, 1964	Steelers 23 (3–2)	Browns 7 (3–1–1) @ Municipal Stadium 80,530
Nov. 1, 1964	Browns 30 (6–1–1)	Steelers 17 (3–5) @ Pitt Stadium 49,568
Oct. 9, 1965	Browns 24 (3–1)	Steelers 16 (0–4) @ Municipal Stadium 80,187
Nov. 28, 1965	Browns 42 (9–2)	Steelers 21 (2–9) @ Pitt Stadium 42,757
Oct. 8, 1966	Browns 41 (3–2)	Steelers 10 (1–3–1) @ Municipal Stadium 82,607
Nov. 6, 1966	Steelers 16 (2–5–1	Browns 6 (5–3) @ Pitt Stadium 36,690
Oct. 7, 1967	Browns 21 (2–2)	Steelers 10 (1–3) @ Municipal Stadium 82,949
Nov. 5, 1967	Browns 31 (5–3)	Steelers 14 (2–6) @ Pitt Stadium 47,131
Oct. 5, 1968	Browns 31 (2–2)	Steelers 24 (0–4) @ Municipal Stadium 81,865
Nov. 17, 1968	Browns 45 (7–3)	Steelers 24 (2–7–1) @ Pitt Stadium 41,572
Oct. 18, 1969	Browns 42 (4–1)	Steelers 31 (1–4) @ Municipal Stadium 84,078
Nov. 16 1969	Browns 24 (6–2–1)	Steelers 3 (1–8) @ Pitt Stadium 47,670

1960s total wins Browns 15 Steelers 5

1970s

Oct. 3, 1970	Browns 15 (2–1)	Steelers 7 (0–3) @ Municipal Stadium 84,349
Nov. 2, 1970	Steelers 28 (5–6)	Browns 9 (5–6) @ Three Rivers 50,214
Oct. 10, 1971	Browns 27 (3–1)	Steelers 17 (2–2) @ Municipal Stadium 83,391
Nov. 7, 1971	Steelers 26 (4–4)	Browns 9 (4–4) @ Three Rivers 50,202
Nov. 19, 1972	Browns 26 (7–3)	Steelers 24 (7–3) @ Municipal Stadium 83,009
Dec. 30, 1972	Steelers 30 (9–3)	Browns 30 (8–4) @ Three Rivers 50,350
Sept. 23, 1973	Steelers 33 (2–0)	Browns 6 (1–1) @ Three Rivers 49,396
Nov. 25, 1973	Browns 21 (7–3–1)	Steelers 16 (8–3) @ Municipal Stadium 67,773
Oct. 20, 1974	Steelers 20 (4–1–1)	Browns 16 (1–5) @ Three Rivers 48,100
Nov. 17, 1974	Steelers 26 (7–2–1)	Browns 16 (3–7) @ Municipal Stadium 77,739
Oct. 5, 1975	Steelers 42 (2–1)	Browns 6 (0–3) @ Municipal Stadium 73,595
Dec. 7, 1975	Steelers 31 (11–1)	Browns 17 (2–10) @ Three Rivers 47,962

Sept. 19, 1976	Steelers 31 (1–1)	Browns 14 (1–1) @ Three Rivers 49,169
Oct.10, 1976	Browns 18 (2–3)	Steelers 16 (1–4) @ Municipal Stadium 76,411
Oct. 2, 1977	Steelers 28 (2–1)	Browns 14 @ Municipal Stadium 80,588
Nov. 13, 1977	Steelers 35 (5–4)	Browns 31 @ Three Rivers 47,055
Sept. 24, 1978	Steelers 15, (4–0)	Browns (3–1) OT @ Three Rivers 48,573
Oct. 15, 1978	Steelers 34 (7–0)	Browns (4–3) 14 @ Municipal Stadium 81,302
Oct. 7, 1979	Steelers 51 (5–1)	Browns 35 (4–2) @ Municipal Stadium 81,260
Nov. 25, 1979	Steelers 33 (10–3)	Browns 30 (8–5) @ Three Rivers 49,112

1970s Total Wins Steelers 15 Browns 5

1980s

Oct. 22, 1980	Browns 27 (5–3)	Steelers 26 (4–4) @ Municipal Stadium 79,015
Nov. 16, 1980	Steelers 16 (7–4)	Browns 13 (7–4) @ Three Rivers 54,563
Oct. 11, 1981	Steelers 13 (4–2)	Browns 7 (2–4) @ Three Rivers 53,225
Nov. 22, 1981	Steelers 32 (7–5)	Browns 10 (5–7) @ Municipal Stadium 77,958
Dec. 19, 1982	Browns 10 (3–4)	Steelers 9 (4–3) @ Municipal Stadium 67,103
Jan. 2, 1983	Steelers 37 (6–3)	Browns 21 (4–5) @ Three Rivers 52,312
Oct. 16, 1983	Steelers 44 (5–2)	Browns 17 (4–3) @ Three Rivers 59, 263
Dec. 18, 1983	Browns 30 (9–7)	Steelers 17 (10–6) @ Municipal Stadium 72,313
Sept. 23, 1984	Browns 20 (1–3)	Steelers 20)1–3) @ Municipal Stadium 77,312
Dec. 9, 1984	Steelers 23 (8–7)	Browns 20 (4–11) @ Three Rivers 55,825
Sept. 16, 1985	Browns 17 (1–1)	Steelers 7 (1–1) @ Municipal Stadium 79,042
Nov. 3, 1985	Steelers 10 (4–5)	Browns 9 (4–3) @ Three Rivers 51,976
Oct. 5, 1986	Browns 27 (3–2)	Steelers 24 (1–4) @Three Rivers 57,327
Nov. 25, 1986	Browns 37 (8–4)	Steelers 31 (4–8) @ Municipal Stadium 76,452
Sept. 20, 1987	Browns 34 (1–1)	Steelers 10 (1–1) @ Municipal Stadium 79,543
Dec. 26, 1987	Browns 19 (10–5)	Steelers 13 (8–7) @ Three Rivers 56,394
Oct. 2, 1988	Browns 23 (3–2)	Steelers 9 (1–4) @ Three Rivers 56,410
Nov. 20, 1988	Browns 27 (7–5)	Steelers 7 (2–10) @ Municipal Stadium 77,121
Sept. 10, 1989	Browns 51 (1–0)	Steelers 0 (0–1) @ Three Rivers 57,920
Oct. 15, 1989	Steelers 17 (3–3)	Browns 7 (3–3) @ Municipal Stadium 78,840

1980s Total Wins Browns 12 Steelers 8

1990s

| Sept. 9, 1990 | Browns 13 (1–0) | Steelers 3 (0–1) @ Municipal Stadium 78,290 |
| Dec. 23, 1990 | Steelers 35 (9–6) | Browns 0 (3–12) @ Three Rivers 51,665 |

Oct. 27, 1991	Browns 17 (4–4)	Steelers 14 (3–5) @ Municipal Stadium, 78,285
Dec. 22, 1991	Steelers 17 (7–9)	Browns 10 (6–10) @ Three Rivers 47,070
Oct. 11, 1992	Browns 17 (2–3)	Steelers 9 (3–2) @ Municipal Stadium 78,080
Dec. 27 1992	Steelers 23 (11–5)	Browns 13 (7–9) @ Three Rivers 53,776
Oct. 24, 1993	Browns 28 (5–2)	Steelers 23 (4–3) @ Municipal Stadium 78,118
Jan. 2, 1994	Steelers 16 (9–7)	Browns 9 (7–9) @ Three Rivers 49,208
Sept. 11, 1994	Steelers 17 (1–1)	Browns 10 (1–1) Municipal Stadium 77,774
Dec. 18, 1994	Steelers 17 (12–3)	Browns 7 (10–5) Three Rivers 60,808
Jan. 7, 1995 (playoff)	Steelers 29	Browns 9 @ Three Rivers 58,185
Nov. 13, 1995	Steelers 20 (6–4)	Browns 3 (4–6) @ Three Rivers 58,639
Nov. 26, 1995	Steelers 20 (8–4)	Browns 17 (4–8) @ Municipal Stadium 67,269
Sept. 12, 1999	Steelers 43 (1–0)	Browns 0 (0–1) @ Cleveland Browns 73,136
Nov. 14, 1999	Browns 16 (2–8)	Steelers 15 (5–4) @ Three Rivers 58,213

1990s Total Wins Steelers 10 Browns 5

2000s

Sept. 17, 2000	Browns 23 (2–1)	Steelers 20 (0–2) @ Cleveland Browns 73,018
Oct. 22, 2000	Steelers 22 (4–3)	Browns 0 (2–6) @ Three Rivers 57,659
Nov. 11, 2001	Steelers 15 (6–2)	Browns 12 (4–4) OT @ Cleveland Browns 73,218
Jan. 6, 2002	Steelers 28 (13–3)	Browns 7 (7–9) @ Heinz Field 59,189
Sept. 29, 2002	Steelers 16 (1–2)	Browns 13 (2–2) OT @ Heinz Field 62,864
Nov. 3, 2002	Steelers 23 (5–3)	Browns 20 (4–5) @ Cleveland Browns 73,718
Jan. 5, 2003 (playoff)	Steelers 36	Browns 33 @ Heinz Field 62,595
Oct. 5, 2003	Browns 33 (2–3)	Steelers 14 (2–3) @ Heinz Field 64,595
Nov. 23, 2003	Steelers 13 (4–7)	Browns 6 (4–7) @ Cleveland Browns 73,658
Oct. 10, 2004	Steelers 34 (4–1)	Browns 23 (2–3) @ Heinz Field 63,609
Nov. 14, 2004	Steelers 24 (8–1)	Browns 10 (2–6) @ Cleveland Browns 73,703
Nov. 13, 2005	Steelers 34 (7–2)	Browns 21 (3–6) @ Heinz Field 63,491
Dec. 24, 2005	Steelers 41 (10–5)	Browns 0 (5–10) @ Cleveland Browns 73,136
Nov. 19, 2006	Steelers 24 ((4–6)	Browns 20 (3–7) @ Cleveland Browns 73,296
Dec. 7, 2006	Steelers 27 (6–7)	Browns 7 (4–9) @ Heinz Field 55,246
Sept. 9, 2007	Steelers 34 (1–0)	Browns 7 (0–1) @ Cleveland Browns 73,089
Nov. 11, 2007	Steelers 31 (7–2)	Browns 28 (5–4) @ Heinz 64,781
Sept. 14, 2008	Steelers 10 (2–0)	Browns 6 (0–2) @ Cleveland Browns 73,048
Dec. 28, 2008	Steelers 31 (12–4)	Browns 0 (4–12) @ Heinz Field 63,558

Oct. 8, 2009	Steelers 27 (4–2)	Browns 14 (1–5) @ Heinz Field 64,398
Dec. 10, 2009	Browns 13 (2–11)	Steelers 6 (6–7) @ Cleveland Browns 69,009

2000s Total Wins Steelers 18 Browns 3

2010s		
Oct. 17, 2010	Steelers 28 (4–1)	Browns 10 (1–5) @ Heinz Field 65,168
Jan. 2, 2011	Steelers 41 (12–4)	Browns 9 (5–11) @ Cleveland Browns 68,303
Dec. 8, 2011	Steelers 14 (10–3)	Browns 3 (4–9) @ Heinz Field 60,754
Jan. 1, 2012	Steelers 13 (12–4)	Browns 9 (4–12) @ Cleveland Browns 68,266
Nov. 25, 2012	Browns 20 (3–8)	Steelers 14 (6–5) @ Cleveland Browns 69,661
Dec. 30, 2012	Steelers 24 (8–8)	Browns 10 (5–11) @ Heinz Field 52,831
Nov. 24, 2013	Steelers 27 (5–6)	Browns 11 (4–7) @ FirstEnergy 71,513
Dec. 29, 2013	Steelers 20 (8–8)	Browns 7 (4–12) @ Heinz Field 56,361
Sept. 7, 2014	Steelers 30 (1–0)	Browns 27 (0–1) @ Heinz Field 64,958
Oct. 12, 2014	Browns 31 (5–2)	Steelers 10 (3–3) @ FirstEnergy 67,431
Nov. 15, 2015	Steelers 30 (6–4)	Browns 9 (2–8) @ Heinz Field 64,402
Jan. 3, 2016	Steelers 28 (10–6)	Browns 12 (3–13) @ FirstEnergy 66,693
Nov. 20, 2016	Steelers 24 (5–5)	Browns 9 (0–11) @ FirstEnergy 67,431
Jan. 1, 2017	Steelers 27 (11–5)	Browns 24 (1–15) @ OT Heinz Field 55,921
Sept. 10, 2017	Steelers 21 (1–0)	Browns 18 (0=1) @ FirstEnergy 65,971
Dec. 31, 2017	Steelers 28 (13–3)	Browns 24 (0–16) @ Heinz Field 50,704
Sept. 9, 2018	Browns 21 (0–0–1)	Steelers 21 (0–0–1) @ FirstEnergy 67,431
Oct. 28, 2018	Steelers 33 (5–2–1)	Browns 18 (2–5–1) @ Heinz Field 63,780
Nov. 14, 2019	Browns 21 (4–6)	Steelers 7 (5–5) @ FirstEnergy 67,431
Dec. 1, 2019	Steelers 20 (7–5)	Browns 13 (5–7) @ Heinz Field 62,157

2010s Total Wins Steelers 16 Browns 4

SELECTED BIBLIOGRAPHY

Dicks, Rudy. *The '63 Steelers: A Renegade's Team Chase for Glory.* Kent, OH: Kent State Univ. Press, 2012.

Didinger, Ray. *Great Teams' Great Years: Pittsburgh Steelers.* New York: Macmillan, 1974.

Finoli, David. *Classic Steelers: The 50 Greatest Games in Pittsburgh Steelers History.* Kent, OH: Kent State Univ. Press, 2014.

Gentile, Sean. "Steelers Fans and Browns Fans, Drinking (and Cheering) Together. It Happened," *Pittsburgh Post-Gazette,* Dec. 31, 2018.

Gordon, Roger. *Blanton's Browns: The Great 1965–69 Cleveland Browns.* Kent, OH: Kent State Univ. Press, 2019.

———. *Cleveland Browns: A –Z.* New York: Sports Publishing, 2015.

Graham, Laurie: *Singing the City: The Bonds of Home in an Industrial Landscape.* Pittsburgh: Univ. of Pittsburgh Press, 1998.

Huler, Scott. *On Being Brown: What It Means to Be a Cleveland Browns Fan.* Cleveland: Gray & Co., 1999.

Knight, Jonathan. *Classic Browns: The 50 Greatest Games in Cleveland Browns History.* Kent, OH: Kent State University Press, 2015.

———. *Kardiac Kids: The Story of the 1980 Cleveland Browns.* Kent, OH: Kent State Univ. Press, 2003.

Livingston, Pat. *The Pittsburgh Steelers: A Pictorial History.* Virginia Beach, VA: Jordan & Co., 1980.

MacCambridge, Michael. *Chuck Noll: His Life's Work.* Pittsburgh: Univ. of Pittsburgh Press, 2016.

Neft, David S., Roland T. Johnson, Richard M. Cohen, and Jordan A. Deutsch. *The Sports Encyclopedia: Pro Football.* New York: Grosset & Dunlap, 1974.

O'Connor, Ian. *Belichick: The Making of the Greatest Football Coach of All Time.* New York: Houghton Mifflin Harcourt, 2016.

Pluto, Terry. *The Browns Blues: Two Decades of Utter Frustration: Why Everything Kept Going Wrong for the Cleveland Browns.* Cleveland: Gray & Company, 2018.

———. *Browns Town 1964: The Cleveland Browns and the 1964 Championship.* Cleveland: Gray & Company, 2003.

Pomerantz, Gary M. *Their Life's Work: The Brotherhood of the 1970s Pittsburgh Steelers, Then and Now.* New York: Simon & Schuster, 2013.

Pro Football Reference. www.pro-football-reference.com.

Roberts, Randy, and David Welky, eds. *The Steelers Reader.* Pittsburgh: Univ. of Pittsburgh Press, 2001.

Wickersham, Seth. "The Clash of the Cleveland Browns: How Hue Jackson, Jimmy Haslam and Baker Mayfield Collided," www.espn.com, Jan. 24, 2019.

Other sources related to the Browns-Steelers rivalry that were also helpful: media guides, game programs, and websites, ranging from official team to unofficial fan sites.

INDEX